EntreCulturas 1

Communicate, Explore, and Connect Across Cultures

Ann Mar

Robert L. Davis

Maritza Sloan

George Watson-López

Wayside™
PUBLISHING

Printed in the USA

6 7 8 9 10 KP 18

Print date: 1022

Hardcover ISBN 978-1-942400-44-8

Softcover ISBN 978-1-942400-45-5

FlexText® ISBN 978-1-942400-46-2

LOS PAÍSES HISPANOHABLANTES

EntreCulturas 1:
Glosario de instrucciones de clase y actividades

The following expressions will help you understand instructions in class and carry out activities with your classmates.

Mandatos (Commands): singular - plural

actúa - actúen	*dramatize*	**escucha - escuchen**	*listen*
apunta - apunten	*jot down*	**estudia - estudien**	*study*
asigna - asignen	*assign*	**evalúa - evalúen**	*evaluate*
busca - busquen	*look for*	**explica - expliquen**	*explain*
cambia - cambien	*change*	**hazle(s) - háganle(s)**	*ask him/her/*
compara - comparen	*compare*	**preguntas**	*them questions*
comparte - compartan	*share*	**incluye - incluyan**	*include*
comprueba - comprueben	*check/confirm*	**indica - indiquen**	*indicate*
contesta - contesten	*answer*	**investiga - investiguen**	*research*
conversa - conversen	*converse*	**lee - lean**	*read*
convierte - conviertan	*convert*	**mira - miren**	*watch*
crea - creen	*create*	**nombra - nombren**	*name*
decide - decidan	*decide*	**piensa - piensen**	*think*
di - digan	*say*	**pregúntale(s) - pregúntenle(s)**	*ask him/her/them*
empareja - emparejen	*pair*		
encuentra - encuentren	*find*	**pon - pongan**	*put*
entrevista - entrevisten	*interview*	**sé - sean**	*be*
escribe - escriban	*write*	**toma - tomen**	*take*
escoge - escojan	*choose*	**trae - traigan**	*bring*

Sustantivos

el compañero / la compañera	*classmate*
el dato	*fact*
el ejemplo	*example*
la imagen	*image*
el informe	*report*
la oración	*sentence*
la tabla	*table, chart*
el papel	*role*
la respuesta	*answer*

Palabras interrogativas

¿Cómo?	*How?*
¿Cuál? ¿Cuáles?	*Which/What?*
¿Cuándo?	*When?*
¿Cuánto/a?	*How much?*
¿Cuántos/as?	*How many?*
¿Dónde?	*Where?*
¿Por qué?	*Why?*
¿Qué?	*What/Which?*
¿Quién? ¿Quiénes?	*Who?*

Otras palabras y expresiones útiles

a continuación	*which follow, below*
a la derecha	*on the right*
a la izquierda	*on the left*
antes de	*before*
después de	*after*
hay	*there is/there are*
luego	*then/later*
¡ojo!	*attention! /watch out!*
otra vez	*again*
según	*according to*
siguiente	*following*
trabajando	*working*

Expresiones útiles: Decir la hora

¿Qué hora es?	*What time is it?*
Es la 1:00 (una).	*It's one o'clock.*
Son las 2:00 (dos).	*It's two o'clock.*
Son las 5:15 (cinco y cuarto).	*It's five fifteen.*
Son las 3:30 (tres y media).	*It's three thirty.*

For minutes from :31 to :59, there are three ways to tell the time. For example, for 6:40:

Son las seis y cuarenta.

Son las siete menos veinte.

Faltan veinte para las siete.

Sevilla, España

i

Acknowledgements

We extend our sincere gratitude and appreciation to all who accompanied us on our journey from the conception to completion of the *EntreCulturas* program. We had the privilege to work with a committed, talented, and dependable professional team that served as our anchor throughout the development process.

Eliz Tchakarian, Senior Editor, and Janet Parker, Curriculum Development Coordinator, were dedicated partners who coached us every step of the journey and consistently helped us pull the pieces together for production. Megan McDonald, Lourdes Cuellar (editors and behind-the-scenes writers for the programs) and Kelsey Hare (permissions consultant) were instrumental and persistent with acquiring permissions for the authentic materials. We commend our outstanding editors, María Solernou, Ana Martínez Álvarez, and María Matilla whose advice and editing were indispensable to the completion of the series. Our series would not have been as truly authentic nor as interesting without the generous contribution of our international video bloggers, young people from across the Spanish-speaking world; thank you for sharing your lives with our readers!

We thank Anthony Saizon for the thoughtful design. Derrick Alderman and Rivka Levin, our talented and artistic production team, brought the manuscripts to life on the engaging and colorful pages of the final product. We thank Wayside Publishing Assistant Editors Nathan Galvez, Shelby Newsted, Sawyer McCarron, and Rachel Ross, who designed many of the beautiful graphics and graphic organizers used in the series in print and online.

The Wayside Publishing marketing team was led by manager Michelle Sherwood, who was assisted by Nicole Lyons. In collaboration with the Wayside Publishing Sales team, they successfully got the word out to Spanish teachers about *EntreCulturas*, a new instructional tool and innovative approach to developing students' intercultural communicative competence.

This project was possible due to the leadership, vision, and wisdom of Wayside Publishing president, Greg Greuel, who believed in us to get the job done!

Ann Mar, Robert L. Davis, Maritza Sloan, and George Watson-López

Manzanillo, Costa Rica

World-Readiness Standards
For Learning Languages

GOAL AREAS	STANDARDS		
COMMUNICATION Communicate effectively in more than one language in order to function in a variety of situations and for multiple purposes	**Interpersonal Communication:** Learners interact and negotiate meaning in spoken, signed, or written conversations to share information, reactions, feelings, and opinions.	**Interpretive Communication:** Learners understand, interpret, and analyze what is heard, read, or viewed on a variety of topics.	**Presentational Communication:** Learners present information, concepts, and ideas to inform, explain, persuade, and narrate on a variety of topics using appropriate media and adapting to various audiences of listeners, readers, or viewers.
CULTURES Interact with cultural competence and understanding	**Relating Cultural Practices to Perspectives:** Learners use the language to investigate, explain, and reflect on the relationship between the practices and perspectives of the cultures studied.	**Relating Cultural Products to Perspectives:** Learners use the language to investigate, explain, and reflect on the relationship between the products and perspectives of the cultures studied.	
CONNECTIONS Connect with other disciplines and acquire information and diverse perspectives in order to use the language to function in academic and career-related situations	**Making Connections:** Learners build, reinforce, and expand their knowledge of other disciplines while using the language to develop critical thinking and to solve problems creatively.	**Acquiring Information and Diverse Perspectives:** Learners access and evaluate information and diverse perspectives that are available through the language and its cultures.	
COMPARISONS Develop insight into the nature of language and culture in order to interact with cultural competence	**Language Comparisons:** Learners use the language to investigate, explain, and reflect on the nature of language through comparisons of the language studied and their own.	**Cultural Comparisons:** Learners use the language to investigate, explain, and reflect on the concept of culture through comparisons of the cultures studied and their own.	
COMMUNITIES Communicate and interact with cultural competence in order to participate in multilingual communities at home and around the world	**School and Global Communities:** Learners use the language both within and beyond the classroom to interact and collaborate in their community and the globalized world.	**Lifelong Learning:** Learners set goals and reflect on their progress in using languages for enjoyment, enrichment, and advancement.	

Essential Features

Learners maintain an online *Mi portafolio* to self-assess, reflect, and upload evidence for each Can-do statement displayed alongside activities in the Student Edition. Building their collections of artifacts allows learners to form vital habits leading them to efficiently continue learning beyond the classroom.

SELF-ASSESSMENT

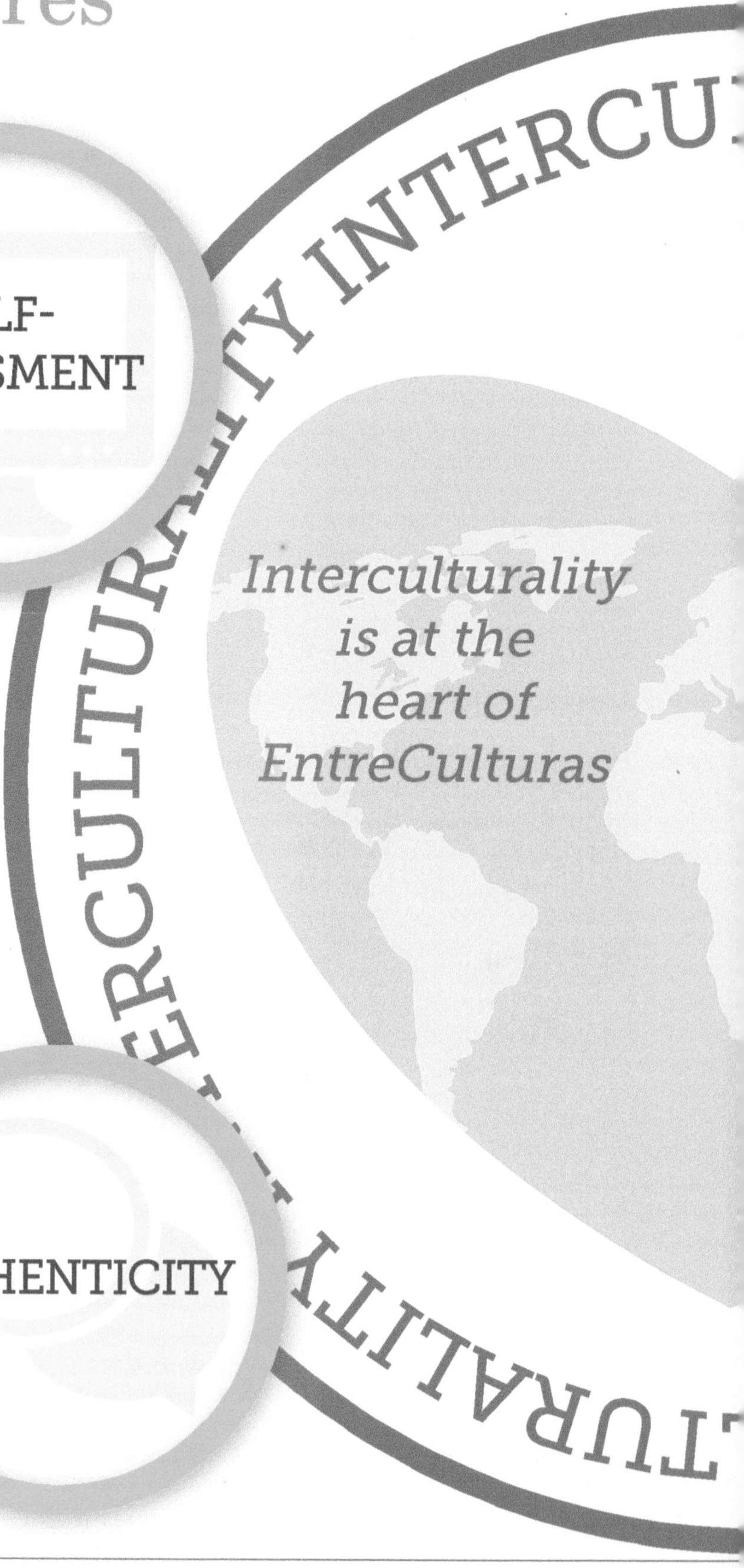

Interculturality is at the heart of EntreCulturas

INTERCULTURALITY

With *EntreCulturas*, learners explore and compare Spanish-speaking communities to their own communities. Authentic video blogs created by native speakers allow learners to compare their lives with those of their peers. Activities and assessments are based on authentic sources and set in theme-related, real-life cultural contexts.

AUTHENTICITY

PERFORMANCE-BASED ASSESSMENT

Units include performance-based formative assessments, *En camino*, which solidify culturally appropriate communication skills relating to learners' communities. *Vive entre culturas*, summative integrated performance assessments, engage learners in global intercultural contexts. Analytic rubrics that include intercultural and communicative learning targets accompany summative assessments.

Our vision is a world where language learning takes place through the lens of interculturality, so learners can discover appropriate ways to interact with others whose perspectives may be different from their own.

RESOURCES FOR TEACHERS AND STUDENTS

The **online Explorer** provides all audio/video resources, scaffolding for Student Edition activities, vocabulary and grammar reinforcement, including flipped classroom videos, additional activities, formative and summative assessments, rubrics and other teacher resources.

APPENDICES

In the Teacher Edition, you are provided audio and audiovisual transcripts, answer keys, instructional strategies, Can-do statements for each unit, and rubrics. **Indices** include a Grammar and Learning Strategies Videos Index as well as a Grammar Index. **Glossaries** are in the Student Edition.

EntreCulturas
Mission and Vision

EntreCulturas is a three-level, standards-based, thematically-organized program consisting of 19 in-depth units that provide learners with opportunities to interact and engage with authentic materials and adolescent speakers of the language. By learning in an intercultural context, students acquire communication skills and content knowledge while exploring the products, practices, and perspectives of Spanish-speaking cultures.

EntreCulturas **Mission**

EntreCulturas aims to prepare learners to communicate, explore, and connect across cultures in order to foster attitudes of mutual understanding and respect.

EntreCulturas **Vision**

Our vision is a world where language learning takes place through the lens of interculturality, so students can discover appropriate ways to interact with others whose perspectives may be different from their own.

Asunción, Paraguay

Dear students,

Welcome to *EntreCulturas*!

In today's world, we all live *entre culturas*: That is, we live around and among people and influences from a variety of cultures. As we live, learn, work, and play in our communities and abroad, we interact in person and online with people whose experiences and perspectives may be different from our own.

The learning materials in the *EntreCulturas* program were designed to help you communicate in Spanish, and to develop the attitudes and habits of mind to interact appropriately with Spanish speakers, respecting differences and recognizing the many things we share as human beings.

Thank you for the commitment you have made to learning another language. The opportunity to experience interactions across cultures and connect with diverse people in our communities and around the world has brought each of us great personal and professional satisfaction. We hope that through this program you too will embrace the opportunities that will come to you as you live *entre culturas*.

Sincerely,

Ann Mar, Robert L. Davis, Maritza Sloan, and George Watson-López

Al empezar

UNIDAD 1

¿Quiénes somos? Identidades

UNIT GOALS
Review learning
targets for
interpretive,
interpersonal, and
presentational
communication as
well as intercultural
learning.

Unit Goals

- Interact to express your identity, ask for and give personal
  information and express preferences about activities.

- Interpret images, video, audio, and print texts in Spanish to gain
  insights into identity.

- Present basic information about yourself.

- Investigate, explain and reflect on the role of language and music
  in shaping identity in Paraguay, in Texas and in your community
  as well.

34

⊕ EXPLORER

EntreCulturas 1 Explorer resources include video blogs, audio/video authentic resources, vocabulary PowerPoints, grammar and learning strategies videos, additional vocabulary practice, discussion forums, and more. You will collect evidence of your growth in Mi Portafolio in Explorer, as well.

⊕ Essential Questions

Who am I? How does what I do define who I am?

How am I similar to and different from young people in the Spanish-speaking world?

How do language and music shape identity?

ESSENTIAL QUESTIONS

Connect day-to-day learning to bigger questions.

There are many sides to our identity. We may be students, athletes, artists and volunteers. In this unit you will learn to talk with Spanish speakers about who you are, and start to develop another aspect of your identity: bilingual communicator connecting across cultures.

MARÍA LAURA RAMÍREZ GONZÁLEZ, NUESTRA VIDEO BLOGUERA DE PARAGUAY

COMUNICA

Integrate language and culture as you communicate around the unit theme.

EXPLORA

Explore cultural products, practices, and perspectives through authentic sources.

VIVE ENTRE CULTURAS

Apply what you have learned in the final assessment.

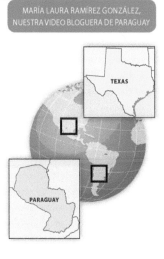

TEXAS

PARAGUAY

35

Compara y comunica

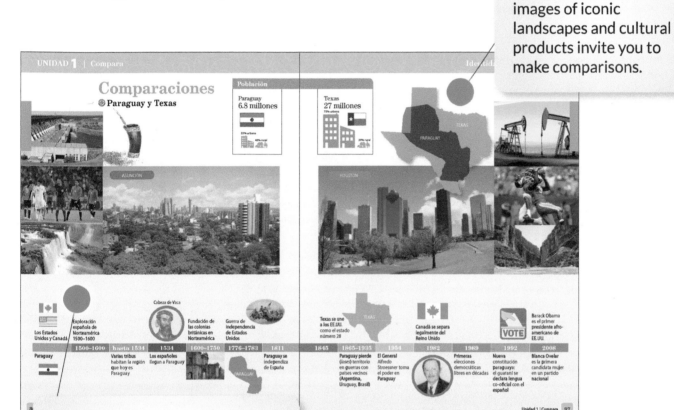

TIMELINE

The timeline highlights the unit's country of focus, encouraging connections with social studies and comparisons with the U.S.

VIDEO BLOG

AVAILABLE IN EXPLORER ONLY, THESE AUTHENTIC VIDEOS FROM SPANISH-SPEAKING TEENS INVITE YOU TO SHARE THEIR WORLD.

ACTIVIDAD

Activities are framed around all types of communication.

THE COMPASS INDICATES ADDITIONAL SUPPORT ONLINE IN EXPLORER.

Vocabulario

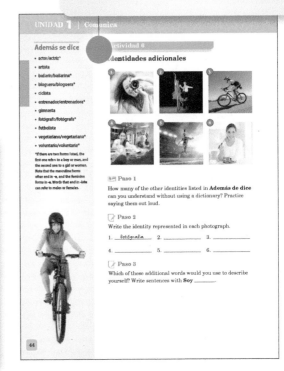

ADEMÁS SE DICE

Additional vocabulary provides personalization, extension, and variation of skills.

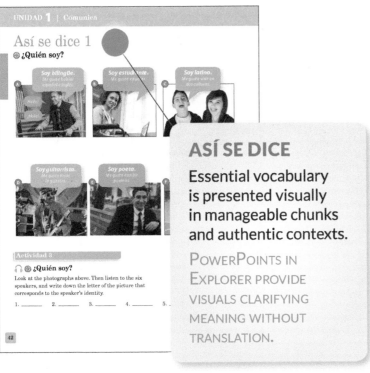

ASÍ SE DICE

Essential vocabulary is presented visually in manageable chunks and authentic contexts.

POWERPOINTS IN EXPLORER PROVIDE VISUALS CLARIFYING MEANING WITHOUT TRANSLATION.

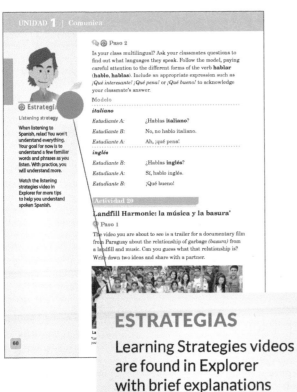

ESTRATEGIAS

Learning Strategies videos are found in Explorer with brief explanations throughout the book.

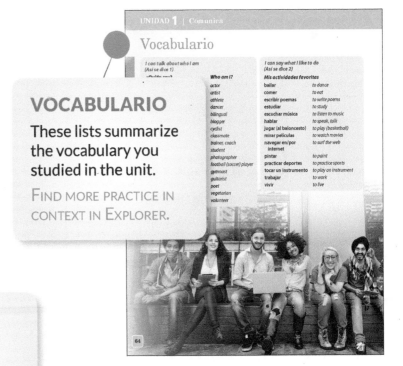

VOCABULARIO

These lists summarize the vocabulary you studied in the unit.

FIND MORE PRACTICE IN CONTEXT IN EXPLORER.

Gramática: Observa y Enfoque en la forma

DETALLE GRAMATICAL

Just-in-time grammar details will help you communicate.

OBSERVA

Examples of new structures in context develop your skill as a "grammar detective."

YOU WILL FIND HELPFUL VIDEOS CALLED OBSERVA AND ENFOQUE EN LA FORMA IN EXPLORER.

SÍNTESIS DE GRAMÁTICA

The summary contains helpful explanations of grammatical structures.

FIND MORE PRACTICE IN CONTEXT IN EXPLORER.

Identidades | UNIDAD **1**

Actividad 8

Veinte preguntas: Mi identidad

Paso 1

Look at these words. Select and write five that describe your identity. Don't let anyone see your words!

actor/actriz	bailarín/bailarina
entrenador/entrenadora	futbolista
pianista	gimnasta
artista	voluntario/voluntaria
estudiante	bloguero/bloguera
poeta	guitarrista
atleta	ciclista
fotógrafo/fotógrafa	latino/latina
profesor/profesora	vegetariano/vegetariana
bilingüe	

Paso 2

Working with a **compañero** or **compañera**, ask questions like the one in the model until you discover a word on your partner's list. Then switch roles and answer your partner's questions. NOTE: Read the **Detalle gramatical** on pronouns, and notice that you don't need them in this interchange!

Modelo

Estudiante A:	¿Eres atleta?
Estudiante B:	Sí, soy atleta./No, no soy atleta.

Detalle gramatical

El verbo ser

The verb **ser** is one way to express identity in Spanish.

(yo) soy	*I am*
(tú) eres	*you (familiar, informal) are*
(ella) es	*she is*
(él) es	*he is*
(—) es	*it is*

The words in parentheses above are subject pronouns, like I, you, he, she in English. But Spanish doesn't use these pronouns the way English does. If you study the examples in this chapter, you'll see that the verb alone tells you who is talking: **soy** = *I am*. Also, there is no subject pronoun for "it." Just use the verb: **Es** = *it is*.

Mi progreso comunicativo

I can ask and answer questions about my identity.

Unidad 1 | Comunica **47**

UNIDAD **1** | Comunica

Observa 1

¿Quién soy?

*Hablo español y guaraní. Y tú, ¿**eres** bilingüe?*

*Sí, ¡**soy** bilingüe también! Hablo español y francés.*

¿Qué observas?

Read the dialogue above and notice the words in bold used to introduce identities (**eres**, **soy**). Can you figure out when to use **eres** and **soy**? Discuss with classmates and teacher, view the Observa 1 resources for this unit in your Explorer course, and check the **Síntesis de gramática** at the end of this section to help you find out.

46

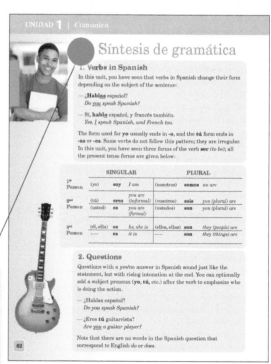

UNIDAD **1** | Comunica

Síntesis de gramática

1. Verbs in Spanish

In this unit, you have seen that verbs in Spanish change their form depending on the subject of the sentence:

— ¿**Hablas** español?
Do you speak Spanish?

— Sí, **hablo** español, y francés también.
Yes, I speak Spanish, and French too.

The form used for **yo** usually ends in -**o**, and the **tú** form ends in -**as** or -**es**. Some verbs do not follow this pattern; they are irregular. In this unit, you have seen three forms of the verb **ser** *(to be)*; all the present tense forms are given below:

		SINGULAR				PLURAL	
1st Person	(yo)	**soy**	*I am*		(nosotros)	**somos**	*we are*
2nd Person	(tú)	**eres**	*you are (informal)*		(vosotros)	**sois**	*you (plural) are*
	(usted)	**es**	*you are (formal)*		(ustedes)	**son**	*you (plural) are*
3rd Person	(él, ella)	**es**	*he, she is*		(ellos, ellas)	**son**	*they (people) are*
	.....	**es**	*it is*		.....	**son**	*they (things) are*

2. Questions

Questions with a yes/no answer in Spanish sound just like the statement, but with rising intonation at the end. You can optionally add a subject pronoun (**yo, tú,** etc.) after the verb to emphasize who is doing the action.

— ¿**Hablas** español?
Do you speak Spanish?

— ¿Eres **tú** guitarrista?
Are you a guitar player?

Note that there are no words in the Spanish question that correspond to English *do* or *does*.

62

Evaluaciones: En camino y Vive entre culturas

EN CAMINO

Formative assessment measures your progress towards unit goals.

FIND SUPPORTING MATERIALS IN EXPLORER.

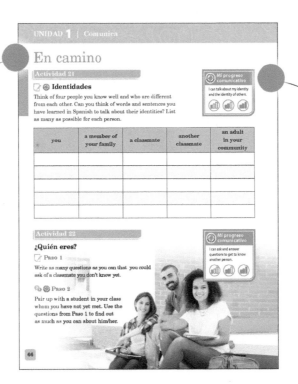

MI PROGRESO COMUNICATIVO

You will provide evidence of growing proficiency in Mi Portafolio in Explorer, which contains all Can-do statements included throughout the unit.

VIVE ENTRE CULTURAS

A final assessment is set in an authentic cultural context.

FIND SUPPORTING MATERIALS IN EXPLORER.

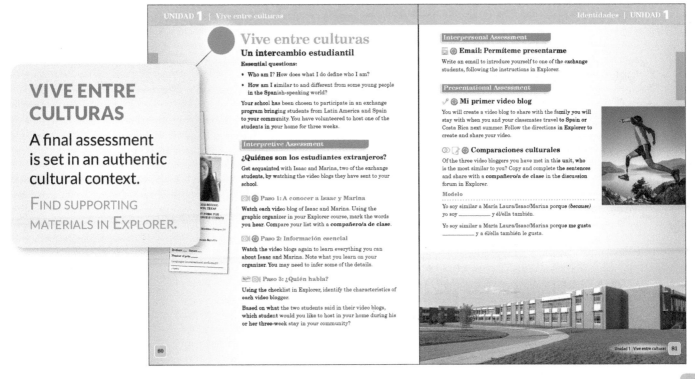

Interculturalidad/Interculturality

UNIDAD **1** | Explora

América

This song was recorded by Los Tigres del Norte.

Actividad 33

Antes de leer y escuchar

Paso 1: Mis experiencias

Working in groups of four, answer the following questions.

1. Do you listen to music with lyrics in Spanish? List several Latino or Spanish-language musical artists popular in your community.

2. What different styles of Latin music are you familiar with? Give specific examples.

Paso 2: Investiga

Read "La música de los Tigres del Norte" in your Explorer course, and research the group using the Internet, your library, and/or other resources. Then share with a partner at least two interesting facts you learned.

Actividad 34

A escuchar y leer

1. Listen to "America" to determine its tone. Which of these adjectives describe the "feeling" of the song? Sad, happy, romantic, angry, lively, depressing?

2. Complete the following phrase, repeated several times in the song:

   _____ *América* _____ _____.

3. Listen again while reading the lyrics, found in Explorer. As you listen and read, underline the cognates you find.

AMERICA, written by Enrique Franco. Published by TN Ediciones Musicales. Copyright Secured. Used by permission, all rights reserved.

©Dwight McCann

Enfoque cultural

Producto cultural: Los mapas expresan la identidad

How many continents did you learn that there are in the world? In many English-speaking countries, students learn that there are seven: Africa, Antarctica, Asia, Australia, Europe, North America and South America. But in Latin American schools, students are taught that there are six: África, América, Antártida, Asia, Europa y Oceanía. In fact, in Latin America to be "americano/americana" means something different from being an "American" in the USA. It means that you are from any one of the countries which make up the Americas: North America, Central America and the Caribbean, or South America.

Conexiones

Go to the appropriate Explorer discussion forum to answer the Reflexión intercultural below.

ENFOQUE CULTURAL
Knowing about cultural products, practices, and perspectives lays a foundation for intercultural reflections.

SHARE YOUR REFLECTIONS IN THE EXPLORER DISCUSSION FORUM.

Actividad 35

América: ¿una o más?

After reading the **Enfoque cultural** above, prepare two versions of the world map. One should show the six continents typically represented in Spanish, each a different color and labeled with Spanish names. The other map should have the seven continents and colors, with labels in English.

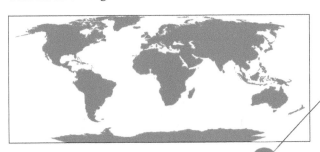

Reflexión intercultural

Why do you think **los latinoamericanos** see two continents as one? What do these continents share? The shape of the map of Texas is very recognizable. Are there maps that express identity where you live?

Share your observations in Explorer.

REFLEXIÓN INTERCULTURAL
After a variety of experiences with cultural products, practices, and perspectives, you will reflect on your growing intercultural awareness.

SHARE REFLECTIONS IN THE EXPLORER DISCUSSION FORUM.

Mi progreso intercultural

I can recognize different perspectives on the meaning of the word *América*.

MI PROGRESO INTERCULTURAL
This unique self-assessment feature clarifies intercultural goals.

Explorer/Guía digital

The online Explorer is the other half of your textbook, connecting you with language learning resources that inspire continued exploration.

Whether learning about Paraguay through Maria Laura's video blogs, studying grammar through flipped classroom videos, or updating language learning portfolios with new achievements, you can practice all modes of communication at your own pace and within your own comfort zone.

VIDEO BLOGS FROM NATIVE SPEAKERS

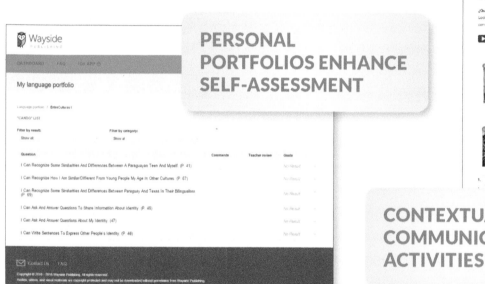

PERSONAL PORTFOLIOS ENHANCE SELF-ASSESSMENT

CONTEXTUALIZED COMMUNICATIVE ACTIVITIES

FlexText®

FlexText is Wayside's unique e-textbook platform. Built in HTML5, our digital textbook technology automatically adjusts the book pages to whatever screen you're using for optimal viewing.

Your FlexText can be accessed across all of your devices. And page by page, just like the printed textbook, FlexText allows students and teachers to use *EntreCulturas* on the go.

Icons Legend

The icons in this program:

- Indicate the mode of communication
- Reference the five goal areas as listed in the *World-Readiness Standards for Learning Languages*
- Provide a signpost where Explorer offers more support
- Prepare teachers and learners for the type of each task/activity

Icon	Description	Icon	Description
	Linguistic or cultural comparisons		Interpretive Visual
	Connections		Interpersonal Speaking
	Communities		Interpersonal Writing
	Cultures		Presentational Speaking
	Explorer		Presentational Writing
	Interpretive Print		External link in Explorer
	Interpretive Audio		Grammar
	Interpretive Print and Audio		Vocabulary
	Interpretive Audiovisual		Journal

Unit Goals

Interact in Spanish, asking and answering some questions to meet and get to know new people.

Interpret ads, charts, graphs, and images to learn about diverse places, people and cultures where Spanish is spoken.

Reflect on how to communicate respectfully when meeting people from other cultures.

Essential Questions

How widely used is Spanish in the world, on the Internet, and in my community?

How do I begin a conversation when meeting a Spanish speaker?

What strategies will help me communicate in Spanish as I begin to learn the language?

Table of Contents

UNIDAD PRELIMINAR: ¡Hola!

Contexto comunicativo e intercultural

UNIDAD 1: Identidades

Contexto comunicativo e intercultural

UNIDAD 1
¿Quiénes somos? Identidades

Unit Goals

Interact in Spanish to express your identity, ask for and give personal information and express preferences about activities.

Interpret images, video, audio and written texts in Spanish to gain insights into identity.

Present basic information about yourself in Spanish.

Investigate, explain, and reflect on the role of language and music in shaping identity in Paraguay, in Texas, and in your community as well.

Essential Questions

Who am I? How does what I do define who I am?

How am I similar to and different from young people in the Spanish-speaking world?

How do language and music shape identity?

Unit Goals

Exchange information about your life at school, including people, places, calendars, schedules, and student activities.

Interpret images, videos, schedules, and calendars to gain insights into what school life is like in Costa Rica.

Present information about your own life at school.

Investigate and reflect on how a country's educational system mirrors cultural values and perspectives.

Essential Questions

What places, people, and activities define student life?

How is student life at my school similar to and/or different from student life at a school in Costa Rica?

How do schools reflect the values of their communities?

UNIDAD 2: La vida en la escuela

Contexto comunicativo e intercultural

SUMMATIVE ASSESSMENT

UNIDAD 3: Mi familia es tu familia

Contexto comunicativo e intercultural

UNIDAD 3
Mi familia es tu familia

Unit Goals

Exchange information in Spanish about home life and family.

Interpret short texts about family structure and activities.

Prepare and present a collection of images and descriptions to share information about your home, family, and friends.

Explore traditions, languages, people, and the geography of Spain and Colorado.

Essential Questions

Who makes up my family?

What places and activities bring us together as a family?

How is my family similar to and different from families in the Spanish-speaking world?

Table of Contents

Unit Goals

Share preferences, opinions, and habits about food choices and food purchases.

Interpret photographs, videos, ads, blogs, and menus to understand food traditions.

Create and present a series of menu items based on your food preferences and food traditions from a Spanish-speaking country.

Recognize how traditions relating to meals and food reflect identity and how sharing in the food of another culture opens doors to intercultural communication.

Essential Questions

What are some iconic foods from the Spanish-speaking world?

How do food products and food practices shape our cultural identity?

How can exploring new foods lead me to new intercultural experiences?

UNIDAD 4: La comida es cultura

Contexto comunicativo e intercultural

UNIDAD 5: La vida es un carnaval

Contexto comunicativo e intercultural

UNIDAD 5
La vida es un carnaval

Unit Goals

Express preferences for leisure activities.

Make simple social plans.

Interpret print and audiovisual material about the Dominican Republic celebration of Carnaval.

Recognize the mutual influences between the Dominican Republic and the U.S., including sports and music.

Essential Questions

What leisure activities help to define my community and me?

How do celebrations reflect the history and culture of a place?

How do leisure activities create bridges between cultures?

Table of Contents

Unit Goals

Share information, opinions, and preferences about weather, clothing, outdoor activities, and the natural surroundings in your community and in the Spanish-speaking world.

Interpret blogs, promotional materials, and reports on climate and weather to plan your day.

Create and present travel information for Spanish-speakers who are planing to visit your community.

Identify some of the unique geographical features that have shaped and defined the culture of a community.

Essential Questions

How do the culture, climate, and the people around us affect how we live, work, and play?

What makes a place unique?

How do my surroundings shape my identity?

UNIDAD 6: El mundo en el que vivo

Contexto comunicativo e intercultural

SUMMATIVE ASSESSMENT

Valencia, España

Bienvenidos a EntreCulturas

In today's world, we all live *entre culturas* (between cultures). Through technology and face-to-face, we can interact with people with different cultural backgrounds every day. As you use *EntreCulturas* you will learn to speak Spanish, and you will explore the cultures of the Spanish-speaking world. Everything you learn will help you interact appropriately and respectfully with people whose experiences and perspectives may differ from your own.

Christian Garita Carvallo es de México.

Marina Ferrara Hernández es de España.

Paola Pablino Hernández es de República Dominicana.

Isaac Morales Rojas es de Costa Rica.

Melissa Montero Vargas es de Colombia.

María Laura Rámirez González es de Paraguay.

Meet six young people from around the Spanish-speaking world who are inviting you to join them in living *EntreCulturas*. Listen to them introduce themselves, then locate their countries on the map.

UNIDAD PRELIMINAR
¡Hola!

Unit Goals

- Interact in Spanish, asking and answering some questions to meet and get to know new people.

- Interpret ads, charts, graphs and images to learn about diverse places, people and cultures where Spanish is spoken.

- Reflect on how to communicate respectfully when meeting people from other cultures.

✦ Essential Questions

How widely used is Spanish in the world, on the Internet, and in my community?

How do I begin a conversation when meeting a Spanish speaker?

What strategies will help me communicate in Spanish as I begin to learn the language?

Compara

El español en el mundo

What can you learn from these charts about Spanish in today's world?

 Paso 1

Scan the chart **"10 idiomas más usados en Internet"** and answer the the following questions.

Which do you think is ranked on this chart: countries or languages? Why?

Is Spanish represented? Which word is the clue?

Read the chart a second time and answer the following questions.

Los diez idiomas más usados en internet

1. What does this infographic show us?
2. Where does Spanish rank in this chart?
3. What do the numbers represent?
4. How are numbers written differently in Spanish?
5. Which four languages on the list are official languages of countries in the Americas?

10 IDIOMAS MÁS USADOS EN INTERNET

Inglés: 536,6

Chino (mandarín): 444,9

Español: 153,3

Japonés: 99,1

Portugués: 82,5

Alemán: 72,5

Árabe: 65,4

Francés: 59,8

Ruso: 59,7

Coreano: 39,4

Millones de usuarios
18/05/2011
Fuente: scribd | internetworldstats

Infografía: @Culturizando
www.culturizando.com

CULTURIZANDO

 **Paso 2**

Scan the chart: "El *ranking* de los países hispanohablantes" *(The ranking of Spanish-speaking countries)* and answer the questions.

El *ranking* de los países hispanohablantes

No.	País	El español = primer idioma	Número de personas que hablan español	% que habla español
1	México	Sí	115.148.235	98,5%
2	**Estados Unidos**	**NO**	**52.588.880**	**16,7%**
3	Colombia	Sí	46.643.840	99,2%
4	España	Sí	46.494.819	98,8%
5	Argentina	Sí	41.410.454	99,4%
6	Venezuela	Sí	29.976.908	98,8%
7	Perú	Sí	26.391.475	86,6%
8	Chile	Sí	17.433.917	99,3%
9	Ecuador	Sí	15.166.260	98,1%
10	Guatemala	Sí	13.338.764	86,4%
11	**Brasil**	**NO**	**12.468.380**	**6,5%**
12	Cuba	Sí	11.176.536	99,4%
13	República Dominicana	Sí	10.267.764	99,6%
14	Bolivia	Sí	9.164.589	87,9%
15	Honduras	Sí	8.133.160	99,0%
16	**Francia**	**NO**	**6.685.901**	**10,2%**
17	El Salvador	Sí	6.164.453	99,7%
18	Nicaragua	Sí	5.860.740	97,0%
19	**Italia**	**NO**	**5.704.863**	**9,4%**
20	**Marruecos**	**NO**	**5.500.997**	**17,3%**
21	Paraguay	Sí	4.724.610	69,5%
22	Costa Rica	Sí	4.267.298	99,2%
23	**Filipinas**	**NO**	**3.706.773**	**3,6%**
24	Puerto Rico	Sí	3.623.079	98,8%
25	Panamá	Sí	3.424.218	93,1%
26	Uruguay	Sí	3.250.165	98,9%
27	**Reino Unido**	**NO**	**3.110.880**	**4,9%**
28	**Alemania**	**NO**	**2.576.366**	**3,1%**
29	Guinea Ecuatorial	Sí	1.059.129	90,5%
30	**Canadá**	**NO**	**1.001.853**	**2,9%**

Martínez, Alberto (2014). "Ranking de países por número de hablantes de nativos del español". Retrieved from SpanishinTour.com.

1. How are these countries ranked?

2. Which country has the greatest number of Spanish-speakers?

3. Which country ranks second?

4. Look at the information printed in bold type. What do these countries have in common?

5. Which countries (from the NO list) do you think have the following as their first language:
   a. alemán
   b. francés
   c. filipino e inglés
   d. árabe y bereber
   e. portugués
   f. inglés
   g. italiano
   h. inglés y francés

Mi progreso intercultural

I can identify places where Spanish is spoken around the world.

I can recognize the importance of Spanish as a language of real-world and online communication.

 Paso 3

Give two reasons why Spanish is an important world language in the 21st century. Use evidence from the charts to support your answer.

1. _____

2. _____

Actividad 2

En mi comunidad

 Paso 1

Are there Spanish speakers in your community? When describing "your community" think about local families, neighborhoods, schools, places of worship, towns or larger cities. Are some Spanish-speaking countries especially well represented in your community?

 Paso 2

Using the map on the facing page, and those in the front of your textbook, make a list of countries around the world represented among members of your community. Be sure to list the countries' names in Spanish. Then share with a classmate the countries where some people in your community are from, using the model.

Modelo
. . . .

Delia Ortiz es de Cuba.

 Paso 3

How frequently is Spanish encountered in your community, your country, around the world and online? What are some places and situations in which you could use your developing Spanish skills, now and in the future? Answer these questions in the discussion forum in Explorer.

¿DÓNDE SE HABLA ESPAÑOL?

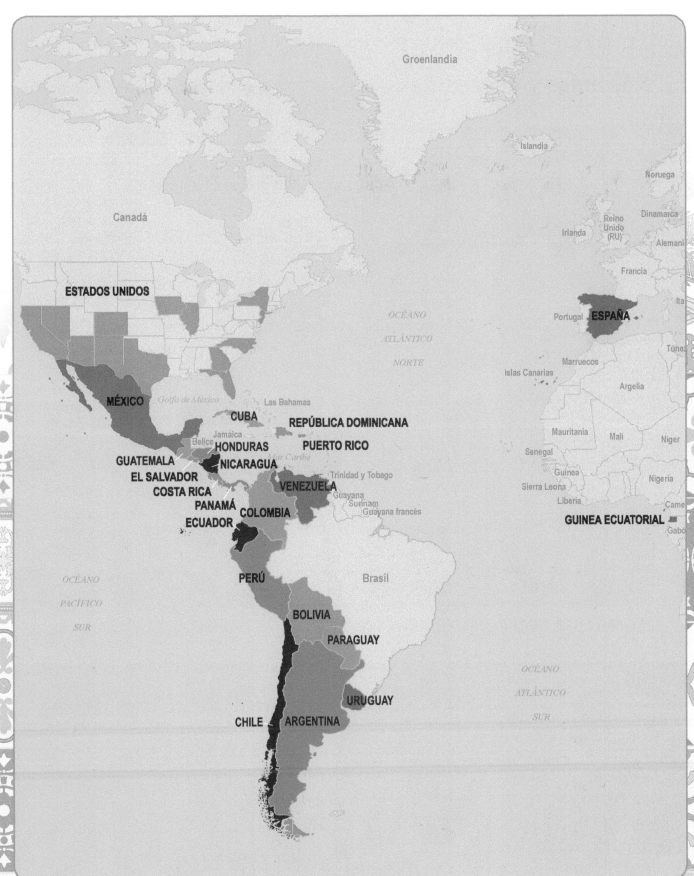

Comunica
Así se dice 1
🎧 ⊕ Saludos y despedidas

¿CÓMO TE LLAMAS?

¿CÓMO ESTÁS?

¿CÓMO ESTÁ USTED, PROFESOR?

¿DE DÓNDE ERES?

ADIÓS

Actividad 3

¡Mucho gusto!

 Paso 1 ¿Cómo te llamas?

Help your teacher get to know the members of your class. Answer his/her question following the model below.

Modelo

Profesor/a:	¿Cómo te llamas?
Estudiante:	Me llamo _____.
Profesor/a:	¡Mucho gusto!

Paso 2

Greet and ask the name of at least five of your classmates.

Modelo

Estudiante A:	¿Cómo te llamas?
Estudiante B:	Me llamo _____.
Estudiante A:	¡Mucho gusto!

How many languages can you recognize?

Actividad 4

Saludar a un amigo

Greet five different students in the class. If you don't know their names, add **¿Cómo te llamas?** If you know their name, simply follow the model.

Modelo

Estudiante A:	Hola, _____, ¿cómo estás?
Estudiante B:	Estoy bien, ¿y tú?
Estudiante A:	Estoy muy bien, gracias.

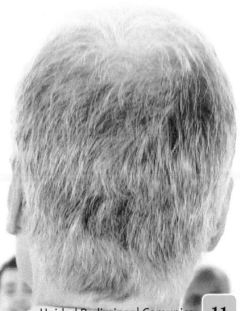

Enfoque cultural

Práctica cultural: Los saludos y la distancia personal

In many cultures, it is common to exchange handshakes, hugs, a backslap, or kisses when greeting someone and saying goodbye. The exact greeting and gesture depend on the region and the age, sex, or social status of the people involved. Spanish even has different ways of saying "you", depending on the region and level of formality or social distance. **Tú** or **vos** are used with friends and family, while **usted** is more appropriate for older people or formal settings. You will study these differences in later chapters. For now, it makes sense to observe people carefully to become familiar with the practices relating to greetings and physical space. Go to your *EntreCulturas 1* Explorer course discussion forum for this topic to answer the intercultural reflection questions below.

Reflexión intercultural

How do people greet each other where you live? What is the typical distance you maintain when speaking to someone your age? Someone older? Someone of a different sex? How does it feel when someone "violates" your personal space? Answer the questions in the discussion forum online in Explorer.

Actividad 5

Buenos días, profesor/Buenos días, profesora

Pretend that your classmate is your teacher. Greet your teacher addressing him as **profesor** or her as **profesora**, then reverse roles. Remember to use the **usted** form in your greeting.

Modelo

Estudiante:	Buenos días, profesor. ¿Cómo está usted?
Profesor:	Muy bien, gracias.

Mi progreso intercultural

I can recognize and use appropriate words, gestures and body language to greet people in different cultures.

Actividad 6

 Tu origen

Ask at least five other classmates where they are from. When they ask you, include your town, city, or state in your answer.

Modelo

. . . .

Estudiante A: ¿De dónde eres?

Estudiante B: Soy de _____.

Actividad 7

Asunción, Paraguay

🎧 ✦ **¿Saludo o despedida?**

Listen to the following statements and decide whether each one is a **saludo** *(greeting)* or a **despedida** *(goodbye)*.

	saludo	despedida
1.		
2.		
3.		
4.		
5.		

Además se dice

*The **Además se dice** ("you can also say…") segment will give you additional vocabulary throughout the book to express your ideas in Spanish.*

The phrase **¿Cómo estás?** is usually used as a greeting; the answer is almost always **¡Bien!** or **¡Muy bien!**, not a true report on how you really are. However, you can give a more accurate answer with the following expressions.

- bien   *fine*
- muy bien   *very well*
- más o menos   *so-so, O.K.*
- regular   *O.K., all right, not good (Esp.)*
- mal   *bad, not well at all*

Actividad 8

 ¡Adiós!

Practice saying goodbye to classmates. Wave to each classmate as you walk away, and vary the expressions you use.

Actividad 9

¡Mi primera conversación en español!

Combine all the expressions you have learned so far to have a complete conversation. Repeat with at least two classmates you don't know yet. Be sure to practice both A and B roles.

Modelo

Estudiante A:	¡Hola! Me llamo _____ ¿Cómo te llamas?
Estudiante B:	Me llamo _____.
Estudiante A:	Mucho gusto. ¿De dónde eres?
Estudiante B:	Soy de _____.
Estudiante A:	¡Interesante! ¡Adiós!
Estudiante B:	¡Nos vemos!

Mi progreso comunicativo

I can ask and answer questions to meet and greet a young person in an appropriate manner.

Así se dice 2

🎧 🌐 **El alfabeto español**

Felize

Listen to the Spanish alphabet. Notice both the name of the letter and how it sounds in a word.

A árbol	**B** bufanda	**C** coche	**Ch** chupete
D dedal	**E** euro	**F** flor	**G** guante
H helicóptero	**I** imán	**J** jalapeño	**K** kiwi
L luna	**LL** llave	**M** montaña	**N** nariz
Ñ piña	**O** ojo	**P** paraguas	**Q** quince
R rueda	**S** sandía	**T** tambor	**U** uvas
V volcán	**W** web	**X** xilófono	**Y** yoyo	**Z** zapato

Abecedario adapted from http://aulasptmariareinaeskola.es

Enfoque cultural

Producto cultural: El alfabeto español

Did you know that Spanish uses a letter that we do not have in English? It is the **ñ**. When you recite the Spanish alphabet it comes after the letter **n**. Are you familiar with the word *jalapeño*? If so, then you know the sound of the **ñ**. Its pronunciation is similar to the "ny" in English words like *canyon*. The mark over the **ñ** is called a *tilde*. You may have seen it on the keyboard of your computer. The letter **ñ** has come to symbolize the Spanish language used around the world.

Gerardo Posada

Conexiones

What other special characters and punctuation marks are used in written Spanish? Investigate how to include these characters when writing on the devices you use for Spanish class. Share your findings with your classmates in the discussion forum in your Explorer course.

Actividad 10

Escribe el nombre

Listen to these people introduce themselves and write each name as you hear it spelled.

1. _____   2. _____   3. _____   4. _____

Actividad 11

Nuestros video blogueros

Listen to our video bloggers say and spell their names. Write the name as you hear it spelled.

	Pais de orígen	Nombre del/de la video bloguero/a
1.	Colombia	— — — — — — —
2.	Costa Rica	— — — — —
3.	España	— — — — — —
4.	México	— — — — — — — —
5.	Paraguay	— — — — — — — — — — — —
6.	República Dominicana	— — — — —

Actividad 12

 ⊕ **¡Pronúncialo en español!**

Listen to these names in English and Spanish. How does the pronunciation differ? Practice saying the names.

Nombre en inglés	Nombre en español
Barbara	Bárbara
Ruben	Rubén
Oscar	Óscar
Patricia	Patricia
Ana	Ana
David	David
Victor	Víctor
Sebastian	Sebastián
Thomas	Tomás
Hugo	Hugo

Estrategias

Intercultural Strategy

Is your name hard for some people to pronounce? Has anyone ever mispronounced it? If so, how did it make you feel? Did you correct the person's mispronunciation?

It can be difficult to remember people's names if you are not very familiar with the language. If you meet someone and have trouble catching their name, you can ask them to spell it out with the question **¿Cómo se escribe tu nombre?** Write down the person's name, then practice saying it. You don't have to pronounce it perfectly, but your new acquaintance will appreciate that you made the effort!

Actividad 13

 Mi nombre/tu nombre

Practice spelling your first name using the Spanish alphabet, and writing your partner's name when you hear how it is spelled.

Modelo

Estudiante A: Me llamo _____ .
                 Se escribe __ __ __ ...

Estudiante B: Mi nombre es _____ .
                 Se escribe __ __ __ ...

 Mi progreso comunicativo

I can understand and write out some common names in Spanish when I hear them or hear them spelled.

I can spell out my first and last name using the Spanish alphabet.

Así se dice 3

🎧 🧭 El calendario

Enero de 2017

lunes	martes	miércoles	jueves	viernes	sábado	domingo
						① uno
2 dos	3 tres	4 cuatro	5 cinco	⑥ seis	7 siete	8 ocho
9 nueve	10 diez	11 once	12 doce	13 trece	14 catorce	15 quince
16 dieciséis	17 diecisiete	18 dieciocho	19 diecinueve	20 veinte	21 veintiuno	22 veintidós
23 veintitrés	24 veinti-cuatro	25 veinti-cinco	26 veintiséis	27 veintisiete	28 veinti-ocho	29 veintinueve
30 treinta	31 treinta y uno					

DÍAS FESTIVOS EN ESPAÑA, 2017

1 enero	Año Nuevo
6 enero	Epifanía del Señor
2 febrero	Fiesta de la Candelaria
25 febrero	Carnaval
28 febrero	Día de Andalucía
19 marzo	San José
26 marzo	Horario de Verano
9 abril	Semana Santa
14 abril	Viernes Santo
16 abril	Domingo de la Resurrección
17 abril	Lunes de Pascua
23 abril	Día de Aragón
23 abril	Día de San Jorge
1 mayo	Fiesta del Trabajo
2 mayo	Fiesta de la Comunidad
15 mayo	San Isidro
3 junio	Corpus Christi
5 junio	Lunes de Pentecostés
25 junio	Fiesta de Santiago Apóstol
13 agosto	Día de Cantabria
15 agosto	Asunción de la Virgen
12 octubre	Fiesta Nacional de España
29 octubre	Horario de Invierno
1 noviembre	Fiesta de Todos los Santos
9 noviembre	Almudena
6 diciembre	Día de la Constitución
8 diciembre	La Inmaculada Concepción
25 diciembre	Natividad del Señor

Febrero
Lu	Ma	Mi	Ju	Vi	Sá	Do
	①	②	3	4	5	
6	7	8	9	10	11	12
13	14	15	16	17	18	19
20	21	22	23	24	㉕	26
27	㉘					

Marzo
Lu	Ma	Mi	Ju	Vi	Sá	Do
		1	2	3	4	5
6	7	8	9	10	11	12
13	14	15	16	17	18	⑲
20	21	22	23	24	25	㉖
27	28	29	30	31		

Abril
Lu	Ma	Mi	Ju	Vi	Sá	Do
					1	2
3	4	5	6	7	8	⑨
10	11	12	13	⑭	15	⑯
17	18	19	20	21	22	㉓
24	25	26	27	28	29	30

Mayo
Lu	Ma	Mi	Ju	Vi	Sá	Do
①	②	3	4	5	6	7
8	9	10	11	12	13	14
⑮	16	17	18	19	20	21
22	23	24	25	26	27	28
29	30	31				

Junio
Lu	Ma	Mi	Ju	Vi	Sá	Do
			1	2	③	4
⑤	6	7	8	9	10	11
12	13	14	15	16	17	18
19	20	21	22	23	24	㉕
26	27	28	29	30		

Julio
Lu	Ma	Mi	Ju	Vi	Sá	Do
					1	2
3	4	5	6	7	8	9
10	11	12	13	14	15	16
17	18	19	20	21	22	23
24	25	26	27	28	29	30
31						

Agosto
Lu	Ma	Mi	Ju	Vi	Sá	Do
	1	2	3	4	5	6
7	8	9	10	11	12	⑬
14	⑮	16	17	18	19	20
21	22	23	24	25	26	27
28	29	30	31			

Septiembre
Lu	Ma	Mi	Ju	Vi	Sá	Do
				1	2	3
4	5	6	7	8	9	10
11	12	13	14	15	16	17
18	19	20	21	22	23	24
25	26	27	28	29	30	

Octubre
Lu	Ma	Mi	Ju	Vi	Sá	Do
						1
2	3	4	5	6	7	8
9	10	11	⑫	13	14	15
16	17	18	19	20	21	22
23	24	25	26	27	28	㉙
30	31					

Noviembre
Lu	Ma	Mi	Ju	Vi	Sá	Do
	①	2	3	4	5	
6	7	8	⑨	10	11	12
13	14	15	16	17	18	19
20	21	22	23	24	25	26
27	28	29	30			

Diciembre
Lu	Ma	Mi	Ju	Vi	Sá	Do
				1	2	3
4	5	⑥	7	⑧	9	10
11	12	13	14	15	16	17
18	19	20	21	22	23	24
㉕	26	27	28	29	30	31

Adapted from www.calendario365.es

Actividad 14

💬 Los números del 1 al 31

Working with a partner, count from 1 to 31 forwards and backwards, and again skipping odd then even numbers.

Actividad 15

  Las fechas

Listen and mark the dates you hear on the calendar provided to you by your teacher.

Actividad 16

Mi cumpleaños

¡Hola, Miguel! ¿Cuándo es tu cumpleaños?

Mi cumpleaños es el 24 de marzo.

  **Paso 1**

Practice with a partner saying your own birthday in Spanish.

Modelo

Estudiante A: Mi cumpleaños es el 19 de septiembre.

Estudiante B: Mi cumpleaños es el 28 de abril.

  **Paso 2**

¿Qué día cae mi cumpleaños? *What day does my birthday fall on?*

You need to check on which day of the week birthdays of several students fall. Listen to each date, locate it on the 2017 calendar from Spain and then write the day of the week the birthday falls on.

1. _____   2. _____   3. _____

4. _____   5. _____   6. _____

Mi progreso comunicativo

I can understand and say days, dates and months in Spanish.

Detalle gramatical

Las fechas

You can ask about the date of social events, in this case, a party:

—**¿Cuál es la fecha de la fiesta?**
What is the date of the party?

—**Es el 20 de mayo.**
It's May 20.

To express a date, Spanish uses the following structure:

el + number + **de** + name of month

Examples:
el 15 de noviembre
el 31 de julio

One exception: for the first day of the month we say **el primero** instead of the number **uno**.

Actividad 17

Las estaciones del año

Paso 1: Las estaciones y los meses

🔄 ✳️ Read **Enfoque cultural** Perspectiva cultural: Las estaciones and complete the grid below with the months that correspond to each season.

		Canadá	Argentina
la primavera	1.	marzo	septiembre
	2.	abril	octubre
	3.	mayo	noviembre
el verano	1.	junio	deciembre
	2.	julio	enero
	3.	agosto	febrero
el otoño	1.	septiembre	marzo
	2.	octubre	abril
	3.	noviembre	mayo
el invierno	1.	deciembre	junio
	2.	enero	julio
	3.	febrero	agosto

💬 **Paso 2: Estaciones y meses**

Your partner will say a month of the year at random. You answer with the season that the month belongs to in the climate of your region. See how many months and seasons you can name in one minute, then switch roles.

Modelo

. . . .

Estudiante A: abril

Estudiante B: primavera

Patagonia, Argentina

Además se dice

Las estaciones del año

la primavera	*(spring)*
el verano	*(summer)*
el otoño	*(fall)*
el invierno	*(winter)*

Enfoque cultural

Perspectiva cultural: Las estaciones

In some parts of the Americas, there are four distinct seasons in a calendar year: el verano, el otoño, el invierno and la primavera. Canada is in the Northern Hemisphere, and Argentina is in the Southern Hemisphere, so the seasons in these two locations are opposite. For example, April is a **primavera** month in Canada, but **otoño** in Argentina.

In some climates, especially in Central America, there are only two distinct seasons: the rainy season *(de mayo a noviembre)* and the dry season *(de diciembre a abril)*. In Costa Rica, for example these seasons are called **el invierno** and **el verano**, respectively. Answer the Reflexión intercultural questions in the forum in your Explorer course.

Julio (el invierno) en Bariloche, Argentina

Julio (el invierno) en Península Nicoya, Costa Rica

Reflexión intercultural

What kind of weather is associated with different times of the year where you live? Answer the following questions as a class or in the Explorer discussion forum.

1. Do you have a favorite season or month of the year?

2. What holidays and activities do you associate with that time of the year?

3. Is the weather an important part of your perspective on the month or season?

4. What is the weather like in December and January where you live? And in Argentina and/or Canada?

5. How might the differences in weather influence the year-end celebrations in different countries?

Mi progreso intercultural

I can recognize differing cultural perspectives on the seasons in areas with different climates.

Sor Juana Inés de la Cruz
el 12 de noviembre

Isabel Allende
el 2 de agosto

Actividad 18

¿Quién eres?

📖 Paso 1

Form groups of six students. Each person in the group should assume the identity of one of the famous people depicted in the images on this page, and memorize when his/her birthday is. Practice saying your identity to yourself with **Soy _____.**

🎧 ✹ Paso 2

Listen to the birth dates of the famous people. When you hear your character's birth date, say your identity and raise your hand. The first person to correctly say his/her identity on the right date gets a point for his/her team.

Modelo

. . . .

Profesor/a: Tu cumpleaños es el quince de enero.

Estudiante: ¡Sí, soy Martin Luther King!

Simón Bolívar
el 24 de julio

Miguel de Cervantes
el 29 de septiembre

Eva Perón
el 7 de mayo

Felipe de Borbón
el 30 de enero

Actividad 19

La fiesta de San Fermín

Ayuntamiento de Pamplona,
Autor: Pedro-Martín Balda

📖 **Paso 1: Un póster sobre San Fermín**

Look at the poster from Spain. It depicts a scene in the streets of a famous city during La Fiesta de San Fermín. Can you explain what happens?

Find the following:

1. the dates of La Fiesta de San Fermín

2. the city where the festival takes place

3. the name of the animal depicted in the poster

4. the word in Spanish for:
   fairs
   big
   exciting

▶ ✦ **Paso 2: Una canción de San Fermín**

You are going to watch a video created by Tío Spanish (Ainhoa Ferragud Basagoiti). The song you'll hear is sung by Spaniards to celebrate the famous fiesta depicted in the poster. As you watch, count off how many months are cited in the song.

🎤 **Paso 3: A cantar**

With a partner, practice the verses of the song you just heard, printed below. Can you sing the verses to the same tune heard in the video?

---

1 de enero

2 de febrero

3 de marzo

4 de abril

5 de mayo

6 de junio

7 de julio

¡San Fermín!

Enfoque cultural

Perspectiva cultural: El toro como icono cultural

The **encierro** ("running of the bulls") in the feast of San Fermín in Pamplona, Spain, is just one of many events around Spain, Portugal, and southern France that involve a millennia-old fascination with this animal in the Mediterranean area.

La corrida (bullfight) is another well-known icon of Spanish identity.

Corridas are often a part of many town festivals. However, in the 21st century, many Spaniards believe that this tradition perpetuates cruelty against animals, and one region, Cataluña, has abolished bullfights.

✺ Conexiones

What symbols are important to the identity of your community/state/country? Think of animals, flowers, or other mascots. Are there any symbols that are controversial (favored by some, found offensive or inappropriate by others)?

The Toros de Guisando bull statues, found near Ávila in central Spain, are almost 5000 years old.

El toro es un icono importante de la cultura española.

📝 ✺ Paso 4: A escribir

What festivals, holidays, or events are important in your culture? Create a list of the four most important events and dates, and try to express the name in Spanish. Use a dictionary or ask **¿Cómo se dice _____?** to get your teacher's help. Then compare your list with those of your classmates to see which events are repeated.

Modelo

1. La Navidad es el 25 de diciembre.

📝 Paso 5

Create a simple song or poem based on a date that is important in your culture. For example, the model below is about the United States Independence Day, the Fourth of July. If you prefer, use your birthday as inspiration for the poem.

Modelo

Primero de abril,
dos de mayo
tres de junio
cuatro de julio
¡Independencia!

Actividad 20

📖 ¿Qué año es?

Look at the image below. Can you find the Spanish expression for "Happy New Year"?

Καλή χρονιά
Feliç any nou
Szczęśliwego Nowego Roku
Feliz Año Novo
Feliz Año Nuevo
Gutes Neues Jahr
Heri ya Mwaka Mpya
sana sa'eedah
Sawatdee Pi Mai
Gott Nytt År
Xin nian yu kuai
Manigong Bagong Taon
Shana Tova
Bonne Année
Happy New Year
Felice Anno Nuovo
akemashite omedetou
С Новым Годом
Chuc mung nam moi

Actividad 21

🎧 ✴ Los números del 2000 al 2020

2000 2001 2002
2003 2004 2005
2006 2007 2008
2009 2010 2011
2012 2013 2014
2015 2016 2017
2018 2019 2020

Listen to the numbers 2000–2020, and use your finger to follow along in the image above. What expression do you hear for "two thousand"?

Los fuegos artificiales *(fireworks)* son parte de la celebración del Año Nuevo en Barcelona, España.

Actividad 22

🎧 ✳ Los Premios Grammy Latinos

Listen to the year that some famous songs won the Grammy Latino for **Canción del año** *(Song of the Year)*. When you hear the year, consult the table and write the name of the artist who recorded the song that year.

Modelo

Escuchas *(you hear)*: dos mil seis

Escribes: *(you write)*: 2006, Shakira con Alejandro Sanz ("La tortura")

Año	Canción del año	Artista
2000	*Dímelo*	Marc Anthony
2001	*El alma al aire*	Alejandro Sanz
2002	*Y solo se me ocurre amarte*	Alejandro Sanz
2003	*Es por ti*	Juanes
2004	*No es lo mismo*	Alejandro Sanz
2005	*Tú no tienes alma*	Alejandro Sanz
2006	*La tortura*	Shakira con Alejandro Sanz
2007	*La llave de mi corazón*	Juan Luis Guerra
2008	*Me enamora*	Juanes
2009	*Aquí estoy yo*	Luis Fonsi
2010	*Miente*	Camila
2011	*Latinoamérica*	Calle 13
2012	*Corre*	Jesse & Joy
2013	*Volví a nacer*	Carlos Vives
2014	*Bailando*	Enrique Iglesias
2015	*Hasta la raíz*	Natalia Lafourcade

Carlos Vives

Natalia Lafourcade

Actividad 23

Los años importantes de mi vida

Paso 1

When did the important events in your life happen? Fill out the **yo** column of the chart with the relevant years; write the numerals as well as the words en español.

Paso 2

Ask your partner when his/her important events happened by asking **¿En qué año...?** and pointing to an event from the list. Your partner should answer with a year in Spanish, e.g., **2005 (dos mil cinco)**. Jot down the year (use numerals) in the space provided. If the year matches what you wrote, say **Yo también**. Reverse roles so that now you have to respond to your partner's questions.

Los años importantes de mi vida	Yo	Mi compañero/a
the year you were born		
the year you started school		
the year you expect to graduate from high school		
the year you visited or hope to visit a new Spanish-speaking area		

⊕ **Enfoque cultural**

Práctica cultural: Los años

In English, we usually say years in hundreds (e.g., 1935 = nineteen thirty-five, 2015 = twenty fifteen). The years in Spanish are always expressed in thousands (**mil, dos mil,** etc.).

2017 dos mil diecisiete
(*two thousand seventeen*)

2025 dos mil veinticinco
(*two thousand twenty-five*)

1931 mil novecientos treinta y uno
(*one thousand nine hundred thirty-one*)

Conexiones

How do you say these dates in English: 1900, 1905, 1917, 2000, 2005, 2011, 2016? Is there more than one acceptable way to say some years? Give examples. Answer in the discussion forum in Explorer.

Explora

Campamento audiovisual

The activities in this section are based on an ad published on the web by Equip MediaCamp - Talleres Audiovisuales.

Antes de leer

Actividad 24

What kind of organized summer activities are available to young people where you live? Brainstorm with your class and list information about 3–5 programs offered in your area.

activities offered	duration	location

Al leer

Actividad 25

Paso 1: Visualización

1. Look at the ad. What catches your attention first?

2. What does the image tell you about the program advertised?

Paso 2: Predicciones

List four questions you expect to have answered by reading this ad.

3. The ad uses two languages, Spanish and English. Why do you think English is used in an ad for a summer camp in Spain?

Paso 3: Búsqueda de detalles

1. What are four types of audio and/or visual media students can experience at the camp?

2. What does the number 14 represent in this ad?

3. In which season does the camp take place? What words in the ad indicate this?

4. What do you think "de 9 a 13h" means in this ad?

5. What do you think the word **plaza** might mean in this ad?

6. List five true Spanish cognates (other than months) found in this promotion.

Watch the Reading Strategies video in Explorer for more tips to help you understand what you read in Spanish.

✷ Estrategia comunicativa: Los cognados

◯◯ **Cognates** are words in two languages that share a similar meaning, spelling, and pronunciation. Almost 40% of all words in English have a cognate word in Spanish. Recognizing these words will help you understand more when you read and hear Spanish. Compare the following examples:

English	español
telephone	teléfono
revolution	revolución
poem	poema
intelligent	inteligente

CAMPAMENTO AUDIOVISUAL
MEDIA CAMP 2014

MEDIA CAMP

CAMPAMENTO URBANO EN ZARAGOZA
UNA INMERSIÓN EN EL MUNDO AUDIOVISUAL
ACTIVIDADES AUDIOVISUALES
CINE   FOTOGRAFÍA   TV   RADIO

Campamento URBANO semanal desde el
22 de Junio al 5 de Septiembre

Horario de 9 a 13h
Servicio de guardería opcional
Edad: de 4 a 14 años

¡RESERVA TU PLAZA!
www.habitosdeestudio.com
976934763

C/ Belle Époque 25 (local)
Valdespartera, Zaragoza

ORGANIZADO POR:
HD HÁBITOS DE ESTUDIO   how audiovisual & multimedia

Vocabulario

I can greet and say goodbye (Así se dice 1)

¡Hola!	*Hello! Hi!*
Buenos días, profesor/profesora	*Good morning, professor*
Buenas tardes	*Good afternoon*
¿Cómo estás?	*How are you? (informal)*
¿Cómo está usted?	*How are you? (formal)*
Estoy bien. ¿Y tú?	*I'm fine. And you?*
¡Muy bien, gracias!	*Great, thanks!*

Además se dice

más o menos	*so-so, OK*
regular	*OK, all right*
mal	*bad, not well*
¡Adiós!	*Goodbye!*
¡Chao!	*Ciao!*
¡Nos vemos!	*See you!*
¡Hasta luego!	*See you later!*

I can exchange basic personal information (Así se dice 1,3)

¿Cómo te llamas?	*What's your name?*
Me llamo ____	*My name is ____*
Mi nombre es ____	*My name is ____*
¿De dónde eres?	*Where are you from?*
Soy de ____	*I'm from ____*
el cumpleaños	*birthday*
¿Cuándo es tu cumpleaños?	*When is your birthday?*
Mi cumpleaños es	*My birthday is…*
el ____ de ____ .	*the ____ of ____ .*
el primero de ____ .	*the first of (month)*

I can spell names (Así se dice 2)

¿Cómo se escribe…? (How do you spell…?)

el alfabeto

A	a	L	ele	V	uve
B	be	M	eme	W	doble uve
C	ce	N	ene	X	equis
D	de	Ñ	eñe	Y	ye
E	e	O	o	Z	zeta
F	efe	P	pe		
G	ge	Q	cu	**los dígrafos**	
H	hache	R	erre	CH	che
I	i	S	ese	LL	elle
J	jota	T	te		
K	ka	U	u		

Los números 1 a 31 (Así se dice 3)

1 uno	11 once	21 veintiuno
2 dos	12 doce	22 veintidós
3 tres	13 trece	23 veintitrés
4 cuatro	14 catorce	24 veinticuatro
5 cinco	15 quince	25 veinticinco
6 seis	16 dieciséis	26 veintiséis
7 siete	17 diecisiete	27 veintisiete
8 ocho	18 dieciocho	28 veintiocho
9 nueve	19 diecinueve	29 veintinueve
10 diez	20 veinte	30 treinta
		31 treinta y uno

I can express calendar time (Así se dice 3)

Los meses del año (The months of the year)

enero	*January*
febrero	*February*
marzo	*March*
abril	*April*
mayo	*May*
junio	*June*
julio	*July*
agosto	*August*
septiembre	*September*
octubre	*October*
noviembre	*November*
diciembre	*December*

Los días de la semana (The days of the week)

lunes	*Monday*
martes	*Tuesday*
miércoles	*Wednesday*
jueves	*Thursday*
viernes	*Friday*
sábado	*Saturday*
domingo	*Sunday*

Las estaciones (the seasons)

el verano	*summer*
el otoño	*autumn, fall*
el invierno	*winter*
la primavera	*spring*

Vive entre culturas

Cursos de verano

People all over the world often use their summer to travel to another country in order to improve their language skills.

Imagine you decide to go to Spain. You will need to choose a school and to read about the courses offered there. When you get there you will meet people from all over the world and will have to introduce yourself and say something about who you are.

In this **Vive entre culturas** segment, you will assess how well you use what you have learned so far to:

• read an ad

• understand Spanish speakers as they introduce themselves

• answer a few questions about yourself.

Miles de estudiantes viajan a otros países para estudiar idiomas.

Interpretive Assessment

⊕ Centro de estudios Método

Paso 1

This banner on the internet catches your eye. Write down three things you learn about Centro de Estudios Método. Now make a prediction: write three additional things you think you will learn when you read the full ad. You can access the graphic organizer in Explorer.

Paso 2

Read the full ad in your Explorer course. Were your predictions correct? Write down three additional things you learned.

   Nuevos compañeros

Two Spanish-speaking students are going to introduce themselves at the general meeting before the language courses begin at Centro de Estudios Método. Look at the chart to see what information you will hear about these students in their introductions. Then listen to the introductions and jot down the information that you hear.

	Estudiante 1	Estudiante 2
Nombre		
Origen		
Edad *(age)*		
Mes de su cumpleaños		

Interpersonal Assessment

💬 El primer día en el Centro de Estudios Método

Preparación

You have enrolled in a Spanish course in the Centro de Estudios Método with students from all over the world. The first day of class, the teacher asks each student some questions so you can get to know each other. What do you think the teacher will ask you? Make a list of possible questions, think about how you would respond, and share with your classmates.

💬 ✴ Presentémonos

Now, it's your turn! You will hear the teacher ask you some questions; answer each of them in Spanish. You will hear each question twice, then you will hear a beep indicating you should begin your response. A second beep will indicate you should stop speaking, and listen for the next question. If you don't understand a question, answer with: **Lo siento; no comprendo.** (*I'm sorry, I don't understand*).

UNIDAD 1
¿Quiénes somos? Identidades

Unit Goals

- Interact to express your identity, ask for and give personal information and express preferences about activities.

- Interpret images, video, audio, and print texts in Spanish to gain insights into identity.

- Present basic information about yourself.

- Investigate, explain and reflect on the role of language and music in shaping identity in Paraguay, in Texas and in your community as well.

Essential Questions

Who am I? How does what I do define who I am?

How am I similar to and different from young people in the Spanish-speaking world?

How do language and music shape identity?

There are many sides to our identity. We may be students, athletes, artists and volunteers. In this unit you will learn to talk with Spanish speakers about who you are, and start to develop another aspect of your identity: bilingual communicator connecting across cultures.

MARÍA LAURA RAMÍREZ GONZÁLEZ, NUESTRA VIDEO BLOGUERA DE PARAGUAY

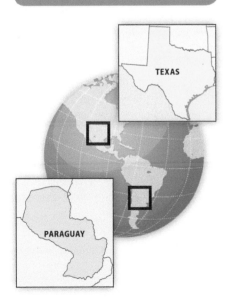

TEXAS

PARAGUAY

Comparaciones

 Paraguay y Texas

Población

Paraguay
6.8 millones

55% urbana
  45% rural

 ASUNCIÓN

Los Estados
Unidos y Canadá

Exploración
española de
Norteamérica
1500–1600

Cabeza de Vaca

Fundación de
las colonias
británicas en
Norteamérica

Guerra de
independencia
de Estados
Unidos

	1500–1600	hasta 1534	1534	1600–1750	1776–1783	1811

Paraguay

Varias tribus
habitan la región
que hoy es
Paraguay

Los españoles
llegan a Paraguay

PARAGUAY

Paraguay se
independiza
de España

Texas
27 millones
75% urbana
25% rural

TEXAS
PARAGUAY

HOUSTON

Texas se une
a los EE.UU.
como el estado
número 28

Canadá se separa
legalmente del
Reino Unido

Barack Obama
es el primer
presidente afro-
americano de
EE.UU.

1845	1865–1935	1954	1982	1989	1992	2008
	Paraguay pierde (*loses*) territorio en guerras con países vecinos (Argentina, Uruguay, Brasil)	El General Alfredo Stroessner toma el poder en Paraguay	Primeras elecciones democráticas libres en décadas	Nueva constitución paraguaya: el guaraní se declara lengua co-oficial con el español	Blanca Ovelar es la primera candidata mujer en un partido nacional	

Actividad 1

Productos de Paraguay y Texas

🔍 ⓪ Paso 1

Look at the images on this page. Which could represent aspects of Paraguayan identity? Which could represent Texas? Explain your answers.

⓪ Paso 2

What are some of the objects or places associated with the identity of people from the place you live?

The Paraguayan harp, the national instrument of Paraguay

Comunica

La bandera (flag) paraguaya.
¿Tiene colores en común
con la bandera de Texas?

Video blog
Soy María Laura

Actividad 2

Soy María Laura

🔍 **Paso 1: Preparación**

Look at the picture of María Laura. What kind of information do you think she has included in her video blog? What do you think the phrases in the speech bubbles mean?

◉ ✦ Paso 2: Escucha

Listen to the video blog recording and raise your hand when you think you hear María Laura say the words from the picture captions.

Mi progreso intercultural

I can recognize some similarities and differences between a Paraguayan teen and myself.

✎ ◉ ✦ Paso 3: Resumen

Listen and watch again. Based on what you see and hear, write two sentences about what you think Laura is telling us in her video blog.

◎ ✦ Paso 4: Comparación

How is María Laura similar to you and/or other young people in your community? How is she different? Share your observations in class and in *EntreCulturas 1* Explorer.

Así se dice 1

✦ ¿Quién soy?

Soy bilingüe.
Me gusta hablar
español e inglés.

A

Hello!

¡Hola!

Soy estudiante.
Me gusta estudiar.

B

Soy latino.
Me gusta vivir en
dos culturas.

C

Soy latina.
Me gusta vivir en dos
culturas también.

Soy guitarrista.
Me gusta tocar
la guitarra.

D

Soy poeta.
Me gusta escribir
poemas.

E

Soy atleta.
Me gusta practicar
deportes.

F

Actividad 3

🎧 ✦ ¿Quién soy?

Look at the photographs above. Then listen to the six
speakers, and write down the letter of the picture that
corresponds to the speaker's identity.

1. _____ 2. _____ 3. _____ 4. _____ 5. _____ 6. _____

Actividad 4

 ¿Eres bilingüe? Are you bilingual?

Your teacher will ask you a series of questions about your identity. Listen carefully and follow the model to respond.

Modelo

Profesor:	¿Eres bilingüe?
Estudiante:	Sí, soy bilingüe./No, no soy bilingüe.

Actividad 5

Mi identidad/tu identidad

  Paso 1

Look at the list of identities in the chart and choose **sí** or **no** in the first column (under **Yo**) to indicate if they correspond to your identity.

Identidades	Yo	Compañero/a 1	Compañero/a 2	Compañero/a 3
guitarrista	sí/no	no —	no	no
latino/latina*	sí/no	no	no	no
estudiante	sí/no	sí	sí	sí
bilingüe	sí/no	no	no	no
poeta	sí/no	no	no	no
atleta	sí/no	sí	sí	sí

*Use **latina** if the person is a girl or woman, and **latino** if the person is a boy or man.

  Paso 2

Ask questions to three of your classmates, following this pattern, and record their answers in the chart in Paso 1.

Modelo

Estudiante A:	¿Eres *guitarrista*?
Estudiante B:	No, no soy guitarrista.
Estudiante A:	¿Eres *estudiante*?
Estudiante B:	Sí, soy estudiante.

Además se dice

- actor/actriz*
- artista
- bailarín/bailarina*
- bloguero/bloguera*
- ciclista
- entrenador/entrenadora*
- gimnasta
- fotógrafo/fotógrafa*
- futbolista
- vegetariano/vegetariana*
- voluntario/voluntaria*

*If there are two forms listed, the first one refers to a boy or man, and the second one to a girl or woman. Note that the masculine forms often end in **-o**, and the feminine forms in **-a**. Words that end in **-ista** can refer to males or females.

Identidades adicionales

📖 Paso 1

How many of the other identities listed in **Además de dice** can you understand without using a dictionary? Practice saying them out loud.

✎ Paso 2

Write the identity represented in each photograph.

1. _fotógrafa_   2. _____   3. _____

4. _____   5. _____   6. _____

✎ Paso 3

Which of these additional words would you use to describe yourself? Write sentences with **Soy** _____.

Actividad 7

 Personas famosas

One's profession is often an important part of identity.
Can you match these famous Spanish speakers with their
identity? Converse with your partner, connecting the person's
name and identity with **es**, as in the model. Look up the
people you don't know, or consult a classmate to fill in the
gaps in your knowledge.

Modelo

Estudiante A: ¿Javier Bardem?

Estudiante B: Javier Bardem **es** actor.

Personas famosas	Profesiones
1. Lionel Messi	actor/actriz
2. Carlos Santana	artista
3. Pablo Picasso	entrenador/entrenadora
4. Shakira	músico/cantante
5. Gael García Bernal	futbolista
6. Selena Gómez	ciclista
7. Alberto Contador	
8. Penélope Cruz	
9. Ron Rivera	
10. Marc Anthony	

Mi progreso comunicativo

I can ask and answer
questions to share
information about identity.

Javier Bardem, actor español

Observa 1

¿Quién soy?

> Hablo español
> y guaraní. Y tú,
> ¿**eres** bilingüe?

> Sí, ¡**soy** bilingüe
> también!
> Hablo español
> y francés.

¿Qué observas?

📹 ✳ Read the dialogue above and notice the words in bold used to introduce identities (**eres**, **soy**). Can you figure out when to use **eres** and **soy**? Discuss with classmates and teacher, view the Observa 1 resources for this unit in your Explorer course, and check the **Síntesis de gramática** at the end of this section to help you find out.

Actividad 8

Veinte preguntas: Mi identidad

 Paso 1

Look at these words. Select and write five that describe your identity. Don't let anyone see your words!

actor/actriz

entrenador/entrenadora

pianista

artista

estudiante

poeta

atleta

fotógrafo/fotógrafa

profesor/profesora

bilingüe

bailarín/bailarina

futbolista

gimnasta

voluntario/voluntaria

bloguero/bloguera

guitarrista

ciclista

latino/latina

vegetariano/vegetariana

Paso 2

Working with a **compañero** or **compañera**, ask questions like the one in the model until you discover a word on your partner's list. Then switch roles and answer your partner's questions. NOTE: Read the **Detalle gramatical** on pronouns, and notice that you don't need them in this interchange!

Modelo

Estudiante A: ¿Eres atleta?

Estudiante B: Sí, soy atleta./No, no soy atleta.

Detalle gramatical

El verbo *ser*

The verb **ser** is one way to express identity in Spanish

(yo) soy	*I am*
(tú) eres	*you (familiar, informal) are*
(ella) es	*she is*
(él) es	*he is*
(---) es	*it is*

The words in parentheses above are subject pronouns, like **I, you, he, she** in English. But Spanish doesn't use these pronouns the way English does. If you study the examples in this chapter, you'll see that the verb alone tells you who is talking: **soy** = *I am*. Also, there is no subject pronoun for "it"! Just use the verb: **Es** = *it is*.

Mi progreso comunicativo

I can ask and answer questions about my identity.

Mi progreso comunicativo

I can write sentences to express other people's identity.

Actividad 9

¿Quién es...?

See how many sentences you can write about the identities of your **compañeros de clase** and your teacher. Use the following models.

Modelos

Sophia es artista.

El Sr. Brown no es estudiante.

El Sr. Brown es profesor.

Sophia es artista.

El Sr. Brown no es estudiante.

El Sr. Brown es profesor.

Así se dice 2

⊕ Mis actividades favoritas

Me gusta...

escuchar música y bailar

comer

escribir

hablar

jugar

navegar en/por internet

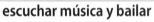

pintar

tocar un instrumento

trabajar

mirar películas

Actividad 10

 ¿Quién soy?

Listen to the speakers share their favorite activity, and select the correct identity.

1. **a.** futbolista   **b.** guitarrista

2. **a.** fotógrafa   **b.** voluntaria

3. **a.** ciclista   **b.** actor

4. **a.** gimnasta   **b.** bailarina

5. **a.** poeta   **b.** estudiante

6. **a.** atleta   **b.** artista

7. **a.** pintor   **b.** entrenador

Ella es bailarina.

Actividad 11

¿Lógico o ilógico?

Which of these sentences are logical? Rewrite the illogical sentences so they make sense.

1. Soy atleta; me gusta tocar el piano.

2. Soy artista; me gusta pintar.

3. Me gusta escribir poemas; soy poeta.

4. Soy entrenador; me gusta tocar la guitarra.

5. Soy vegetariana; me gusta comer hamburguesas.

6. Soy actriz; me gusta trabajar en la comunidad.

Enfoque cultural

Perspectiva cultural: Richard Blanco, un hombre de múltiples identidades

Richard Blanco is the first Latino poet to read a poem at a U.S. presidential inauguration (Barack Obama, 2012). Born in Madrid to Cuban parents, his family moved to the U.S. when he was an infant; and he was raised and educated in Miami, Florida. In 2015 Richard was honored again when he was asked to read his poem "Cosas del mar"/"Matters of the Sea" at the reopening of the American embassy in Havana, Cuba.

Conexiones

Research the life and career of Richard Blanco. How does he self-identify both personally and professionally? How are poets celebrated in our community?

El poeta hispano Richard Blanco recitó un poema durante la inauguración del Presidente Obama en 2013.

Actividad 12

📖 ✦ ¿Qué me gusta?

Which activity is associated with each person described below? Select the logical option.

1. Soy capitán del Real Madrid. Me gusta _____ al fútbol.

   a. escribir   b. tocar   c. jugar

2. Soy bailarina del Ballet Folklórico de México. Me gusta _____.

   a. surfear   b. bailar   c. hablar

3. Soy estudiante en la Universidad de Miami. Me gusta _____ biología.

   a. estudiar   b. pintar   c. comer

4. Soy Fernando Botero, el artista más famoso de Colombia. Me gusta _____.

   a. estudiar   b. jugar   c. pintar

El Ballet Folklórico de México es una expresión de la cultura mexicana.

5. Soy el famoso poeta Richard Blanco. Soy bilingüe. Me gusta _____ poemas y me gusta _____ español e inglés.

   a. surfear/participar

   b. escribir/hablar

   c. trabajar/pintar

6. Soy voluntario para Hábitat para la Humanidad. Me gusta _____ en la comunidad.

   a. bailar   b. trabajar   c. jugar

7. Soy Carlos Santana. Me gusta _____ la guitarra.

   a. comer   b. participar   c. tocar

8. Soy vegetariano. No me gusta _____ hamburguesas.

   a. estudiar   b. vivir   c. comer

Soy voluntario para Hábitat para la Humanidad.

Observa 2
Mis actividades favoritas

Pablo, ¿*te gusta* jugar al tenis?

No, no **me gusta**.

Bueno, **¿te gusta** jugar al golf?

Sí, **me gusta** mucho.

¿Qué observas?

Read the dialogue and notice the words in bold. Can you figure out when to use **me gusta** and **te gusta**? Discuss with classmates and teacher, view the Observa 2 resources for this unit online in Explorer, and check the **Síntesis de gramática** at the end of this section to help you find out.

Actividad 13

Veinte preguntas: ¿Qué actividad te gusta?

[A|Z] **Paso 1**

Look at these words. Select and write five (5) activities you like to do. Don't let anyone see your words!

Actividades

comer hamburguesas/verduras	jugar
practicar deportes/gimnasia/yoga	escribir
mirar películas	tocar la guitarra
escuchar música	montar en bicicleta
trabajar en la comunidad/ en un campamento de fútbol	estudiar
participar	pintar
hablar español	¿...?

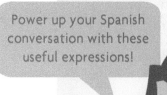

Power up your Spanish conversation with these useful expressions!

Expresiones útiles: Reacciones

You can react and express interest in what people tell you in Spanish by using the following expressions.

¡Qué interesante!	*Interesting!*
¡Qué bueno!	*Great!*
¡Qué pena!	*Too bad!*

Paso 2

Work with a **compañero** or **compañera**. Ask and answer questions like the ones in the model. Include some of the useful expressions in the sidebar at the right to react to your partner's answer.

Modelo

. . . .

Estudiante A: Emily, ¿te gusta practicar deportes?

Estudiante B: Sí, me gusta practicar deportes.

Estudiante A: Ah, eres atleta. ¡Qué bueno!

. . . .

Estudiante A: Jacob, ¿te gusta tocar la guitarra?

Estudiante C: No, no me gusta tocar la guitarra.

Estudiante A: Ah, no eres guitarrista.

Actividad 14

Un/a nuevo/a compañero/a de cuarto

You are going to a language immersion camp next summer, and you have to pick a roommate for your cabin.

📖 **Paso 1**

Look at the notes posted on the camp website by four possible roommates to find out about their interests. Select the one most compatible with you. Copy the phrases that indicate things you have in common.

¡Hola! Me llamo Ignacio Sánchez Villalobos. Soy de Málaga, España. Tengo 15 años y me gusta surfear, practicar yoga y hacer gimnasia.

No me gusta pintar, escribir poemas o tomar fotos.

Mi nombre es Natalia Romero Maldonado.

Soy de Asunción, Paraguay y tengo 14 años. Me gusta hablar inglés y practicar francés, pero no me gusta practicar deportes.

✒ ✦ Paso 2

Write a note to the student you have chosen to be your roommate. Introduce yourself and include the following information. You can use their notes as a model.

- your name *Tyler Galle Tyler Galle Tyler Galle*

- your age (tengo __15__ años)

- origin (where you are from) *Soy de Carmel, Indiana*

- 3 things you like to do *jugar beisbol, comer, hablar*

- 3 things you don't like to do *pintar, practicar matematicas, bailar*

1. Estoy cansado.
2. Me llamo Tyler.
3. A mi me gusta jugar beisbol.
4. Soy de Indiana.
5. Mi favorito deporte es beisbol.
6. Yo soy dos hermanos.

¡Hola! Mi nombre es Alejandro Bottaro. Tengo 16 años, y soy de Buenos Aires, Argentina. Me gusta escribir música, bailar y montar en bicicleta. Soy vegetariano, no me gusta comer hamburguesas o pizza.

¡Hola! Soy Daniela Martínez, y tengo 15 años. Soy de Brownsville, Texas. Me gusta jugar al fútbol, básquetbol y pintar, pero no me gusta mucho bailar o tocar instrumentos.

Así se dice 3

✦ Preguntas y respuestas

Entrevista con una turista

¿Cómo te llamas? — Me llamo Michelle González.

¿De dónde eres? — Soy de Texas.

¿Cuántos años tienes? — Tengo 15 años.

¿Cuándo es tu cumpleaños? — El 29 de mayo.

Hablas bien español. **¿Quién** es tu profesor? — Es el señor Smith.

¿Por qué estudias español? — Porque me gusta viajar a otros países.

¿Cuál es tu país favorito? — Paraguay, ¡por supuesto!

Actividad 15

 ✦ **Conversaciones con nuevos amigos**

Match the questions on the left with the logical answers on the right.

Conversación con Diego

1. ¿Cómo te llamas?
2. ¿Cómo se escribe Diego?
3. ¿De dónde eres?
4. ¿Cuántos años tienes?

a. Se escribe D-I-E-G-O.
b. Soy de El Paso.
c. Tengo dieciséis años.
d. Me llamo Diego.

Conversación con Graciela

1. ¿Cómo estás?
2. ¿Quién eres?
3. ¿Qué idiomas hablas?
4. ¿Qué estudias?
5. ¿Cuándo es tu cumpleaños?

a. Hablo español y guaraní.
b. Soy estudiante de medicina en la Universidad Nacional de Asunción.
c. Es el primero de mayo.
d. Estoy bien, gracias. ¿Y tú?
e. Soy Graciela.

Detalle gramatical

¿Qué? vs. ¿Cuál?

The English question "what?" is expressed with **¿Qué?** when giving a definition. We use **¿Cuál(es)?** for all other cases. **¿Cuál(es)?** can also be translated as "Which one(s)"?

El mate en una guampa, un recipiente hecho de un cuerno (horn).

¿Cuál es tu bebida favorita?	**What** *is your favorite drink?*
¡El mate, por supuesto!	*Mate, of course!*
¿Qué es el mate?	*What is mate?*
Es un té típico de Paraguay y otros países.	*It's a typical tea from Paraguay and other countries.*

Actividad 16

🎧 ✳ Respuestas posibles

Listen to these questions and choose the logical answer.

1. a. Me llamo Jorge.   b. Se escribe J-O-R-G-E.   c. Soy atleta.

2. a. Soy María.   b. Soy estudiante.   c. Soy de Dallas.

3. a. Soy José.   b. Soy artista.   c. Soy de Chile.

4. a. Tengo dos hamsteres.   b. Tienes diecisiete años.   c. Tengo catorce años.

5. a. Estoy muy bien.   b. Soy latino.   c. Me llamo Manuel.

6. a. Hablas español e italiano.   b. Tengo quince años.   c. Hablo español e inglés.

7. a. Me gusta jugar al tenis.   b. Te gusta jugar al golf.   c. Me gusta hablar español.

Actividad 17

💬 ✳ Entrevista

Write down five questions in Spanish that will allow you to find out interesting information about your classmates. Then interview each other to get to know each other better. Keep practicing until you can ask and answer questions confidently. Then, record your interview in your Explorer course.

✳ Mi progreso comunicativo

I can ask and answer a few questions to get to know another person.

Observa 3

Preguntas y respuestas

> Hola. ¿Cómo te **llamas**?

> Me **llamo** Ariana.

> Y ¿cuántos años **tienes**?

> **Tengo** cinco años.

> ¿Qué **haces**?

> **Soy** bloguera.

> ¡Qué interesante! ¿Y cuántos idiomas **hablas?**

> **Hablo** tres idiomas: español, inglés y portugués.

> ¡Impresionante!

¿Qué observas?

▶️ ✳️ Read the dialogues above and notice the words in bold used to ask and answer questions. Do you notice any patterns? Discuss with classmates and teacher, view the Observa 3 resources for this unit in Explorer, and check the **Síntesis de gramática** at the end of this section to help you understand.

Actividad 18

 ¿Cuántos años tienes? Un sondeo (*survey*)

Are you and your classmates the same age? Ask five of them this question to find out.

Modelo

. . . .

Estudiante A: ¿Cuántos años tienes?

Estudiante B: Tengo catorce años.

Estudiante A: Ah, yo tengo quince años.

. . . .

Estudiante A: ¿Cuántos años tienes?

Estudiante C: Tengo quince años.

Estudiante A: Ah, ¡yo también!

Actividad 19

¿Qué idiomas hablas?

 Paso 1

What languages have you heard in the media, or spoken in your home, school, or community? List the languages you think you have heard, and write in others that you have heard that are not on the list.

Además se dice

¿Hablas español?

María Laura from Paraguay speaks two languages, *español y guaraní*. Here are the names of some other languages you may have heard. Add to the list any other languages you or your friends speak or want to learn more about.

alemán	árabe
chino	español
francés	guaraní
inglés	italiano
polaco	portugués
tagalo	vietnamita

⊕ Estrategias

Listening strategy

When listening to Spanish, relax! You won't understand everything. Your goal for now is to understand a few familiar words and phrases as you listen. With practice, you will understand more.

Watch the listening strategies video in Explorer for more tips to help you understand spoken Spanish.

💬 ⊕ Paso 2

Is your class multilingual? Ask your classmates questions to find out what languages they speak. Follow the model, paying careful attention to the different forms of the verb **hablar** (**hablo**, **hablas**). Include an appropriate expression such as *¡Qué interesante! ¡Qué pena!* or *¡Qué bueno!* to acknowledge your classmate's answer.

Modelo

italiano

Estudiante A:	¿Hablas **italiano**?
Estudiante B:	No, no hablo italiano.
Estudiante A:	Ah, ¡qué pena!

inglés

Estudiante B:	¿Hablas **inglés**?
Estudiante A:	Sí, hablo inglés.
Estudiante B:	¡Qué bueno!

Actividad 20

Landfill Harmonic: la música y la basura*

🌐 Paso 1

The video you are about to see is a trailer for a documentary film from Paraguay about the relationship of garbage *(basura)* from a landfill and music. Can you guess what that relationship is? Write down two ideas and share with a partner.

La orquesta de Cateura toca música clásica con instrumentos producidos localmente.

*LandfillHarmonic (2012), *Teaser of the upcoming documentary film "Landfill Harmonic"*, Retrieved from https://www.youtube.com/watch?v=fXynrsrTKbl.

ⒶⓏ Paso 2

You will hear the following words in the video. Before watching the video, list all the words that relate to music and verify with your class.

instrumentos	estómago	violín	
tocar	personas	chelo	vida
orquesta	feliz	música	casa
basura	ñoqui	comunidad	

▶️ 🧭 Paso 3

Watch the video, listen carefully, and complete the information about Ada and Juan Manuel in the chart.

Nombre	Edad *(age)*	Instrumento
Ada	Tengo ____ años	Toco el chelo/la flauta/el violín
Juan Manuel . . . (Bebi)	Tengo ____ años	Toco el chelo/la flauta/el violín

🔗 Paso 4

Un documental sobre mi comunidad

You have been asked to create an inspirational documentary film about your community. Write a brief proposal for the film including the topic and two scenes you would include. Begin by outlining your proposal in the chart. Share with a partner and take notes about your classmate's proposal.

Lugar	Tema	Escenas
Cateura, Paraguay	los instrumentos reciclados de la basura	1. el basurero 2. la orquesta

Síntesis de gramática

1. Verbs in Spanish

In this unit, you have seen that verbs in Spanish change their form depending on the subject of the sentence:

— ¿**Habl<u>as</u>** español?
Do <u>you</u> speak Spanish?

— Sí, **habl<u>o</u>** español, y francés también.
Yes, <u>I</u> speak Spanish, and French too.

The form used for **yo** usually ends in **-o**, and the **tú** form ends in **-as** or **-es**. Some verbs do not follow this pattern; they are irregular. In this unit, you have seen three forms of the verb **ser** *(to be)*; all the present tense forms are given below:

		SINGULAR			PLURAL	
1st Person	(yo)	**soy**	*I am*	(nosotros)	**somos**	*we are*
2nd Person	(tú)	**eres**	*you are (informal)*	(vosotros)	**sois**	*you (plural) are*
	(usted)	**es**	*you are (formal)*	(ustedes)	**son**	*you (plural) are*
3rd Person	(él, ella)	**es**	*he, she is*	(ellos, ellas)	**son**	*they (people) are*
	-----	**es**	*it is*	-----	**son**	*they (things) are*

2. Questions

Questions with a yes/no answer in Spanish sound just like the statement, but with rising intonation at the end. You can optionally add a subject pronoun (**yo, tú,** etc.) after the verb to emphasize who is doing the action.

— ¿Hablas español?
Do you speak Spanish?

— ¿Eres **tú** guitarrista?
Are <u>you</u> a guitar player?

Note that there are no words in the Spanish question that correspond to English *do* or *does*.

Information questions require a question word or phrase (**¿Qué?, ¿Cómo?, ¿Cuántos años?**, etc.). In this type of question, the question phrase goes first, followed by the verb:

— ¿Cuántos años tienes?
How old are you?

— Pablo, ¿de dónde eres?
Pablo, where are you from?

Again, a pronoun (**yo**, **tú**, etc.) can be added after the verb for emphasis. Note that question words always require a written accent mark, and Spanish uses an inverted question mark to show where the question begins.

3. Likes and dislikes

In Spanish, you can ask about a friend's likes and dislikes using **¿Te gusta** _____**?**, with the infinitive form of a verb (**-ar, -er, -ir**) in the blank. To answer the question, use **Me gusta** _____.

To make the sentence negative, add **no** before **te gusta** or **me gusta**.

— **¿Te gusta** pintar?
Do you like to paint?

— Sí, **me gusta pintar**, pero **no me gusta** escribir poemas.
Yes, I like to paint, but I don't like to write poems.

Vocabulario

I can talk about who I am
(Así se dice 1)

¿Quién soy?	Who am I?
el actor/la actriz	*actor*
el/la artista	*artist*
el/la atleta	*athlete*
el bailarín/ la bailarina	*dancer*
bilingüe	*bilingual*
el/la bloguero/a	*blogger*
el/la ciclista	*cyclist*
el/la compañero/a de clase	*classmate*
el/la entrenador/a	*trainer, coach*
el/la estudiante	*student*
el/la fotógrafo/a	*photographer*
el/la futbolista	*football (soccer) player*
el/la gimnasta	*gymnast*
el/la guitarrista	*guitarist*
el poeta/ la poeta	*poet*
el/la vegetariano/a	*vegetarian*
el/la voluntario/a	*volunteer*

I can say what I like to do
(Así se dice 2)

Mis actividades favoritas	
bailar	*to dance*
comer	*to eat*
escribir poemas	*to write poems*
estudiar	*to study*
escuchar música	*to listen to music*
hablar	*to speak, talk*
jugar (al baloncesto)	*to play (basketball)*
mirar películas	*to watch movies*
navegar en/por internet	*to surf the web*
pintar	*to paint*
practicar deportes	*to practice sports*
tocar un instrumento	*to play an instrument*
trabajar	*to work*
vivir	*to live*

I can ask a few questions to get to know another person (Así se dice 3)

Palabras interrogativas	Question words
¿Cómo?	How? What?
¿Cuál?	Which one? What?
¿Cuándo?	When?
¿Cuánto/a?	How much?
¿Cuántos/as?	How many?
¿(De) dónde?	Where (from)?
¿Por qué?	Why?
¿Qué?	What?
¿Qué te gusta hacer?	What do you like to do?
¿Cómo te llamas?	What's your name?
¿Por qué estudias español?	Why are you studying Spanish?
¿De dónde eres?	Where are you from?
¿Cuál es tu deporte favorito?	What is your favorite sport?
¿Cuántos años tienes?	How old are you?
¿Cuándo es tu cumpleaños?	When is your birthday?

Expresiones útiles

también	also
¡Yo también!	Me too!
¡Qué interesante!	Interesting!
¡Qué bueno!	Great!
¡Qué pena!	Too bad!

I can say what languages I speak

¿Qué lenguas hablas?	What languages do you speak?
alemán	German
chino	Chinese
español	Spanish
francés	French
guaraní	Guarani
inglés	English
italiano	Italian
portugués	Portuguese
ruso	Russian
vietnamita	Vietnamese

En camino

Actividad 21

 ## Identidades

Think of four people you know well and who are different from each other. Can you think of words and sentences you have learned in Spanish to talk about their identities? List as many as possible for each person.

you	a member of your family	a classmate	another classmate	an adult in your community

Actividad 22

¿Quién eres?

Paso 1

Write as many questions as you can that you could ask of a classmate you don't know yet.

Paso 2

Pair up with a student in your class whom you have not yet met. Use the questions from Paso 1 to find out as much as you can about him/her.

Actividad 23

  **Presentación PechaKucha**

You have decided to compete for a state-wide scholarship to help fund the cost of going to a Spanish-speaking country as part of an exchange program. In order to introduce yourself to the scholarship committee (made up of Spanish teachers), you have decided to create a slide show that describes you, the activities you like, and how you self-identify.

Your presentation should include at least:

- four slides containing only images (photographs, drawings, symbols, etc.)
- your narration for two slides
- a minimum of eight sentences
- ninety seconds in length.

Actividad 24

El nuevo estudiante

 Paso 1

You will hear a dialog between a newly arrived Spanish-speaking exchange student and his bilingual guidance counselor at a high school in Texas. Look at the grid below, listen for the required information, and fill in the cells.

	Nombre	Apellido *(last name)*	Origen	Edad *(age)*	Deporte	Lenguas
Estudiante						
Consejero *(counselor)*	X		X	X		X

 Paso 2

How is the student in the dialog similar and/or different from you and other students at your school? If this student were coming to your community, what school activities, groups or classes do you think he would enjoy? List at least two people you think he should meet, and three classes, clubs or activities you would recommend, and explain your choices.

Mi progreso comunicativo

I can introduce myself and provide some details about myself.

Mi progreso intercultural

I can recognize some similarities and differences between young people from the Spanish-speaking world and myself.

Explora

Essential Question: How do language and music shape identity?

Overview

People around the world study new languages and enjoy music from different cultures. In this segment you will explore ads promoting language study in Paraguay and Texas, and hear some music that will help you gain insight into these two cultures. Finally, explore language learning and musical identity in your own community.

Read this bilingual sign from an airport terminal What do the pictures, arrows, letters and numbers communicate? In what other places would you expect to find bilingual signs?

Los idiomas y la identidad

Gráficos

These graphs were prepared based on information published on the web by the Centro Virtual Cervantes and the U.S. Census.

Mi progreso intercultural

I can recognize some similarities and differences between bilingualism in Paraguay and Texas.

 **Actividad 25**

Los idiomas que hablamos

  Paso 1

Are you or some people you know bilingual or multilingual? For each person you know, make a list of (1) languages they speak and (2) how they learned their languages. Compare your list with your classmates to see how many different ways people can become bi- or multi-lingual.

 Paso 2

Look at the pie graphs below. Write at least three sentences about languages in Paraguay and Texas, and how these places are similar and/or different.

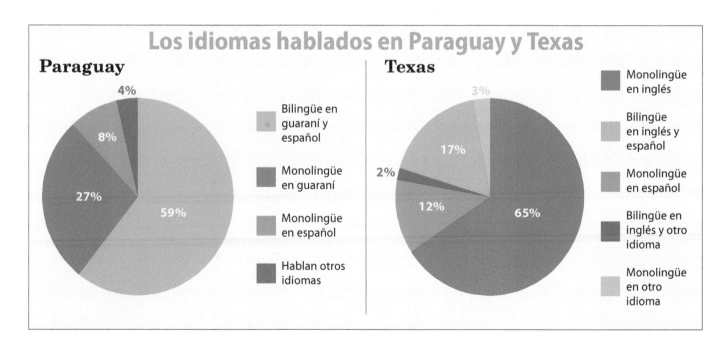

Los idiomas hablados en Paraguay y Texas

Paraguay

- 59% Bilingüe en guaraní y español
- 27% Monolingüe en guaraní
- 8% Monolingüe en español
- 4% Hablan otros idiomas

Texas

- 65% Monolingüe en inglés
- 17% Bilingüe en inglés y español
- 12% Monolingüe en español
- 3% Bilingüe en inglés y otro idioma
- 2% Monolingüe en otro idioma

Actividad 26

Anuncio: Aprende guaraní

This ad was published online by the Instituto Superior de Estudios Humanísticos y Filosóficos de Paraguay.

Mba'éichapa
¡Hola! ¿Qué tal?

porã ha nde
Bien, ¿y vos?

📖 Paso 1: Visualización

You are going to read the ad "Aprender guaraní de forma fácil, divertida y práctica", which appeared on a website published in Paraguay. Before you read the ad, work with a partner to answer the following questions:

1. What catches your attention first?

2. Describe the image and the layout of information on the page.

📖 Paso 2: Predicciones

Study the large words in the illustration "Curso de guaraní coloquial" to answer these questions:

1. Who might be interested in reading this ad? *People practicing Guarani*

2. What kind of information would they expect to find in the ad? *Who, where, how much*

Aprender GUARANÍ de forma fácil, divertida y práctica

Instituto Superior de Estudios Humanísticos y Filosóficos "San Francisco Javier" Itapúa 148 c/ Sacramento - Asunción, Paraguay Tel. 021290549

sábados de 14 a 17 hs.

Matrícula: 100.00 Gs.

Curso introductorio para la expresión oral y escrita en guaraní.

3 cuotas de 150.00 gs.

Curso de guaraní coloquial

Más información: (021)290-549/(0982)77-60-22

ISEHF (2014), "Aprender GUARANÍ de forma fácil, divertida y práctica", Adapted from http://www.isehf.edu.py/?p=1648.

📖 Paso 3: Búsqueda: Search for details

You are interested in the course advertised in this ad. Can
you find the following information? Jot down the information
you find, but be careful—not all the information is included.

1. The name of the class	*Curso de Guaraní abg vid*
2. The name of the textbook	
3. What you will learn in the course	*Guaraní*
4. The day classes are held	*Sábados*
5. How many months the course lasts	
6. How to find out more information	*Call the number*

📖 Paso 4: Palabras clave

Find the Spanish words/phrases in the ad to express
the following:

1. learn	*Aprender*
2. class or course	*Curo*
3. practical	*práctica*
4. oral expression	*expresión oral*

Jajoecha peve
Hasta luego

📖 Paso 5: ¡Usa la lógica!

Answer the following questions and share with your
classmates.

1. What does "14 a 17 hs" mean in the context of the ad?

2. In this ad the word **guaraní** refers to two different things.
   What are they?

Mi progreso comunicativo

I can understand the main
ideas and some details
from an ad for a language
program.

Después de leer

Actividad 27

🌐 Perspectivas culturales

As you read the ad, were you able to "read between the lines" to pick up on some cultural perspectives of people in Paraguay? Work with a partner to answer the following questions, then compare cultural perspectives about language learning and use in Paraguay and your community.

1. Why do you think the Instituto Superior chose the class times advertised for this course?

2. How is the class in the ad similar to your Spanish class? How is it different?

3. What are some reasons a person in Paraguay would want to take this class?

4. What are some of the reasons you decided to study Spanish?

5. When others make an effort to learn your language, what does that tell you about them?

Actividad 28

  Investiga

What opportunities are there to learn languages in your community other than at your school? Is there a community college or language institute? What languages are offered? Find websites, ads, flyers or other promotional materials announcing language learning opportunities. Share with your class using the model.

Modelo

En _____, ofrecen *(they offer)* clases de _____
y _____.

En Portland State University, ofrecen clases de vietnamita y ruso.

La música y la identidad

Una canción popular: "El pájaro campana"

✥ Mi música

Working with two or three classmates, answer these questions.

1. Make a list of the kinds of music (styles, artists, etc.) that you enjoy the most.

2. Is there a special musical style or musical instrument that people associate with your community or region—Cajun music in Louisiana, bluegrass music in Kentucky, etc.? What are some of the characteristics of this music: instruments, rhythm, theme of lyrics? Do you personally identify with this music? Does the music remind you of where you are from? Upload a link and a brief description of this music to the discussion forum in Explorer.

✥ Investiga

Look at the photograph of a typical instrument from Paraguay, **el arpa paraguaya**. Then explore the website Paraguayanharps.com, and write three things you learned about the instrument and/or the company.

El pájaro campana es el ave nacional de Paraguay.

Actividad 31

▶️ ✦ El canto (*song*) del pájaro campana

1. According to the photo caption at the right, how does the **pájaro campana** interact with others? What words does the text use to indicate the bird's behavior?

2. Use the links in Explorer to listen to recordings of "El pájaro campana". Do you think the music accurately reflects the bird's behavior, as described in the caption?

3. Now search the Internet for the terms "pájaro campana Paraguay," and note how many results you find. What does the quantity of results tell you about the importance of this symbol for Paraguayans' national identity? What symbols would you be likely to find in a search for your region's identity?

La canción "El pájaro campana" imita la vocalización del ave en la naturaleza. Empieza (it begins) con el canto de un pájaro. Otro pájaro contesta (answers), y después la música se convierte en un coro o una sinfónica de pájaros.

―――――――――――

"Dueling Harp" Rendition of Classic "Pájaro Campana" by Martin Portillo and Marcelo Rojas, CFV10179, Image Courtesy of Smithsonian Folkways Recordings, (p) (c) 2009. Used by permission.

Actividad 32

↩️ ✦ Símbolos nacionales

1. Review your answers in the previous activity about how the **pájaro campana** interacts with others of its species. Since this bird is a national symbol, what might this tell you about how Paraguayans see themselves (i.e., their national identity)?

2. Choose one of the options below, or add your own perspective on this Paraguayan symbol.
   a. Es importante cantar más fuerte (*louder*) que otros pájaros.

   b. Somos miembros de una comunidad, y la comunicación es importante.

   c. La música es más importante que la naturaleza.

América

This song was recorded by Los Tigres del Norte.

Actividad 33

Antes de leer y escuchar

 Paso 1: Mis experiencias

Working in groups of four, answer the following questions.

1. Do you listen to music with lyrics in Spanish? List several Latino or Spanish-language musical artists popular in your community.

2. What different styles of Latin music are you familiar with? Give specific examples.

Paso 2: Investiga

Read "La música de los Tigres del Norte" in your Explorer course, and research the group using the Internet, your library, and/or other resources. Then share with a partner at least two interesting facts you learned.

Actividad 34

A escuchar y leer

1. Listen to "America" to determine its tone. Which of these adjectives describe the "feeling" of the song? Sad, happy, romantic, angry, lively, depressing?

2. Complete the following phrase, repeated several times in the song:

    _____ *América* _____ _____.

3. Listen again while reading the lyrics, found in Explorer. As you listen and read, underline the cognates you find.

AMERICA, written by Enrique Franco. Published by TN Ediciones Musicales. Copyright Secured. Used by permission, all rights reserved.

©Dwight McCann

Enfoque cultural

Producto cultural: Los mapas expresan la identidad

How many continents did you learn that there are in the world? In many English-speaking countries, students learn that there are seven: Africa, Antarctica, Asia, Australia, Europe, North America and South America. But in Latin American schools, students are taught that there are six: África, América, Antártida, Asia, Europa y Oceanía. In fact, in Latin America to be "americano/americana" means something different from being an "American" in the USA. It means that you are from any one of the countries which make up the Americas: North America, Central America and the Caribbean, or South America.

Conexiones

Go to the appropriate Explorer discussion forum to answer the Reflexión intercultural below.

Actividad 35

América: ¿una o más?

After reading the **Enfoque cultural** above, prepare two versions of the world map. One should show the six continents typically represented in Spanish, each a different color and labeled with Spanish names. The other map should have the seven continents and colors, with labels in English.

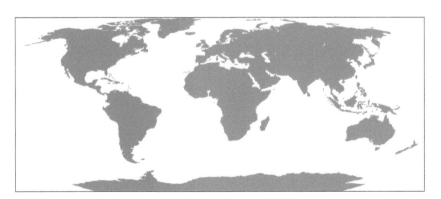

Mi progreso intercultural

I can recognize different perspectives on the meaning of the word *América*.

Reflexión intercultural

Why do you think **los latinoamericanos** see two continents as one? What do these continents share? The shape of the map of Texas is very recognizable. Are there maps that express identity where you live?

Share your observations in Explorer.

En mi comunidad

¡Exploremos la comunidad!

LANGUAGES IN OUR COMMUNITY

Madame Boucher habla francés

Lenguas habladas en casa en el Estado de Texas
(PERSONAS MAYORES DE 5 AÑOS)

- 65% Inglés
- 29% Español
- 5% Vietnamita
- 1% Otras lenguas

United States Census (2015), American Fact Finder, Community Facts.
Retrieved from http:/ factfinder.census.gov/faces/nav/jsf/pages/index.xhtml.

ENTRADAS

- SOPA DE TORTILLA
- GUACAMOLE
- QUESOS FUNDIDOS
- ENSALADA DE NOPALES
- ENSALADA DE POLLO
- ENCHILADA ·MOLE ·ROJA ·VERDE
- JALAPEÑO RELLENO
- CALABACITAS RELLENAS
- CHILES ENNOGADA
- NACHOS CON GUACAMOLE

PLATOS FUERTES

- TIRAS RANCHERAS
- FAJITAS DE POLLO
- PLATO TOLUCA
- PLATO VEGETARIANO
- POLLO FLOR DE CALABAZA
- POLLO CHIPOTLE
- TINGA DE GUAJOLOTE
- COCHINITA PIBIL
- PLATO PASTOR
- POLLO CON MOLE
- CAZUELITA (PARA 2 PERSONAS)
- ENTREMES MEXICANO (PARA 2 PERSONAS)

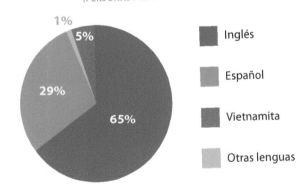

Menú del restaurante
"El buen sabor"

📖 ✦ Paso 1: Preparación

What languages are present in your community? As a class, prepare a list of people to talk to and places to explore, considering the following:

Family members, neighbors and friends

Classmates, teachers and school staff

US Census Factfinder data

Radio and television stations

Local newspapers and magazines

Local shops and restaurants

Churches and community centers

_____

_____

👥 🌐 Paso 2: La investigación

Select one or more of the areas in Paso 1 to explore, and bring back to class your evidence of languages in your community.

📝 Paso 3: La creación

Work with your group or class to create your visual presentation. Write at least a short caption in Spanish for each visual element.

🎤 Paso 4: La galería de presentaciones

Present your results to your classmates, another class in your school, or use technology to share with a class at another campus or in another country.

Reflexion intercultural

🌐 ✦ Answer these questions also available in your Explorer course in the form of a discussion forum.

1. Did anything your class discovered about languages in your community surprise you?

2. What are some situations in which you might encounter Spanish speakers in your community?

3. How will knowing some Spanish affect your interactions?

Mi progreso intercultural

I can recognize ways in which languages and language learning impact me and my community.

Vive entre culturas
Un intercambio estudiantil

Essential questions:

- Who am I? How does what I do define who I am?

- How am I similar to and different from some young people in the Spanish-speaking world?

Your school has been chosen to participate in an exchange program bringing students from Latin America and Spain to your community. You have volunteered to host one of the students in your home for three weeks.

Interpretive Assessment

¿Quiénes son los estudiantes extranjeros?

Get acquainted with Isaac and Marina, two of the exchange students, by watching the video blogs they have sent to your school.

▶️ 🧭 Paso 1: A conocer a Isaac y Marina

Watch each video blog of Isaac and Marina. Using the graphic organizer in your Explorer course, mark the words you hear. Compare your list with a **compañero/a de clase**.

▶️ 🧭 Paso 2: Información esencial

Watch the video blogs again to learn everything you can about Isaac and Marina. Note what you learn on your organizer. You may need to infer some of the details.

📖 ▶️ Paso 3: ¿Quién habla?

Using the checklist in Explorer, identify the characteristics of each video blogger.

Based on what the two students said in their video blogs, which student would you like to host in your home during his or her three-week stay in your community?

CENTRAL
SAN AN

ENROLLM
FOREIGN EX

Name: *Isaac M.*

Age: ___

Home Address: C

City: *Palmares*

Country of Birth

Number of Sibl

Brothers ___

Languages (co

CENTRAL HIGH SCHOOL
SAN ANTONIO, TEXAS

ENROLLMENT FORM FOR
FOREIGN EXCHANGE STUDENTS

Name: *Marina F.*

Home Address: *General Martínez Campos 20*

City: ___

Country of Birth: *Dominican Republic*

Number of Siblings: ___

Brothers ___ Sisters ___

Number of pets: ___

Languages (conversational proficiency):

___ ___ ___ ___

, vasco

Interpersonal Assessment

 ✦ **Email: Permíteme presentarme**

Write an email to introduce yourself to one of the exchange students, following the instructions in Explorer.

Presentational Assessment

🎤 ✦ **Mi primer video blog**

You will create a video blog to share with the family you will stay with when you and your classmates travel to Spain or Costa Rica next summer. Follow the directions in Explorer to create and share your video.

⊙ 🖊 ✦ **Comparaciones culturales**

Of the three video bloggers you have met in this unit, who is the most similar to you? Copy and complete the sentences and share with a **compañero/a de clase** in the discussion forum in Explorer.

Modelo

Yo soy similar a María Laura/Isaac/Marina porque *(because)* yo soy _____ y él/ella también.

Yo soy similar a María Laura/Isaac/Marina porque me gusta _____ y a él/ella también le gusta.

UNIDAD 2
La vida en la escuela

Unit Goals

- Exchange information about your life at school, including people, places, calendars, schedules, and student activities.

- Interpret images, videos, schedules, and calendars to gain insights into what school life is like in Costa Rica.

- Present information about your own life at school.

- Investigate and reflect on how a country's educational system mirrors cultural values and perspectives.

What places, people, and activities define student life?

How is student life at my school similar to and/or different from student life at a school in Costa Rica?

How do schools reflect the values of their communities?

CONOCE A ISAAC MORALES ROJAS, NUESTRO BLOGUERO DE COSTA RICA.

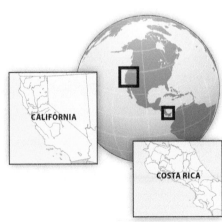

When you meet people your age who speak Spanish, you will want to talk about your life at school. In this unit, Isaac will show you around his school in Costa Rica in his video blog. Learning about schools and education in other places will help you understand how to make students new to your community feel comfortable in your school.

Comparaciones: Costa Rica y California 84

Discover some ways Costa Rica and California are similar and different by exploring a timeline and images relating to the importance of education.

Comunica: La vida en la escuela 87

Learn to ask and answer questions about people, places, and things at school, the school day and calendar, and school activities.

Síntesis de gramática y vocabulario 116

Identify school supplies (definite articles and gender), express the places and people there are at school (using **hay,** indefinite articles and the quantifiers **muchos/muchas**), tell about classes and schedules (**¿A qué hora?**) and talk about some activities and school (**-ar** verbs in present tense).

Explora 124

Read school calendars and schedules, and view images and video blogs to gain insights into school life in Costa Rica. Reflect on the educational values reflected in schools in Costa Rica and in your community.

Vive entre culturas 134

Imagine you are going to set up a "sister school" relationship with a Costa Rican school. View and interpret a promotional video to select a partner school, write an email to exchange information about your school, and create an audiovisual presentation about your school day.

Comparaciones

✦ Costa Rica y California

Costa Rica
4.8 millones

77% urbana

33% rural

California (Estados Unidos)	1502	1533	1723	1808	1821	1847	1850

California (Estados Unidos)

Hernán Cortés llega a lo que hoy es Baja California

La "Alta California", parte de México, se independiza de España

California se une a los EE. UU. como el estado número 31

Costa Rica

1502 Cristóbal Colón llega a Costa Rica en su 4º viaje

1533

1723 Gran erupción del volcán Irazú destruye la ciudad de Cartago

1808 Se introduce el café, que se convierte en un cultivo de gran importancia económica

1821 Costa Rica se independiza de España el 15 de septiembre

1847 Un decreto nacional permite por primera vez la educación de mujeres

1850

California
38.8 millones

95% urbana

CALIFORNIA REPUBLIC

5% rural

CALIFORNIA

COSTA RICA

California vive la "fiebre del oro" y atrae a gente de todo el país

La mujer obtiene el derecho a votar

Se firma La Carta de las Naciones Unidas en San Francisco, estableciendo esta organización

Barbara Boxer

California es el primer estado con dos mujeres en el Senado de los Estados Unidos: Barbara Boxer y Dianne Feinstein

Dianne Feinstein

| 1848–55 | 1911 | 1945 | 1948 | 1987 | 1992 | 2010 | 2014 |

El presidente José María (Don Pepe) Figueres Ferrer elimina el Ejército (army)

El presidente Óscar Arias Sánchez recibe el Premio Nobel de la Paz

Laura Chinchilla Miranda es la primera mujer elegida como presidenta de Costa Rica

Costa Rica llega a los cuartos de final en la Copa Mundial de Fútbol

Actividad 1

Productos de Costa Rica y California

Paso 1

Look at the images. Can you identify those related to education in Costa Rica? In California? What do they have in common? How do they differ?

Paso 2

How do the images compare to schools you have attended? List three ways they are similar, and three ways they are different.

Comunica

Essential Questions: What places, people and activities define student life? How is my life at school similar to and/or different from student life at a school in Costa Rica?

La carreta de madera (*wood*) es un símbolo nacional de Costa Rica.

La bandera (*flag*) costarricense. ¿Qué tiene en común con la bandera de California?

Costa Rica es famosa por sus buenos cafés.

Video blog
Soy Isaac

**Vista del distrito central
de Palmares, Costa Rica.**

Parque Central de Palmares

Iglesia católica de Palmares

Actividad 2

¡Saludos desde el Colegio San Agustín!

🔍 ✴ **Paso 1: ¡Bienvenidos a mi colegio!**

You are going to hear Isaac from Palmares, Costa Rica, talk about his school, el Colegio Bilingüe San Agustín. First, watch the video without sound. Based on the images you see, which of the following aspects do you think Isaac talks about? Then listen and discover which of your predictions were correct.

- las asignaturas/las materias *(subjects)*
- la comida *(food)*
- los profesores
- el tiempo libre *(free time)*
- el uniforme
- las zonas *(school grounds)*

El uniforme escolar

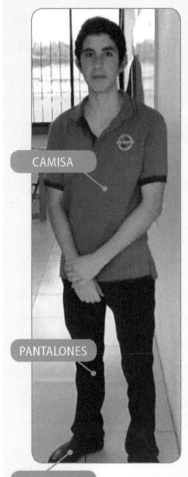

CAMISA

PANTALONES

ZAPATOS

🔍 ✦ Paso 2: Comparaciones

What do you see in the video that is similar to and different from your school?

▶ ✦ Paso 3: ¿De qué color es?

You will hear three colors in Isaac's video blog: **negro**, **verde**, **azul**. Match these colors with the items he points out.

1. camisa
2. pantalones
3. zapatos

a. ▢ azul
b. ▢ verde
c. ▢ negro

▶ ✦ Paso 4: ¿Cierto o falso?

Read these statements in Spanish, and confirm the meaning with your teacher. Then relisten to Isaac's blog, and tell whether each one is true (**cierto**) o false (**falso**), according to what he says.

1. Isaac asiste *(attends)* a una escuela bilingüe.

2. A Isaac le gusta *(Isaac likes)* mucho estudiar inglés.

3. Isaac estudia ciencias.

4. A Isaac le gusta jugar fútbol.

5. A Isaac le gusta ver televisión.

6. El uniforme de Isaac tiene *(has)* el nombre de la escuela.

7. Isaac pregunta: ¿Cuántas asignaturas tienes?

8. Isaac se despide de nosotros *(says goodbye to us)*.

Reflexión intercultural

✦ How is Isaac's school similar to and/or different from schools in your community? Share your observations in class and in *EntreCulturas 1 Explorer*.

✦ **Mi progreso intercultural**

I can recognize some similarities and differences between school life in Costa Rica and in my community.

Así se dice 1

✦ ¿Qué necesitamos para la clase?

> ¿Qué necesitas para la escuela?

> Tengo la mochila, pero necesito útiles.

Un billete (*bill*) de 5.000 colones. El colón es la moneda de Costa Rica.

OFERTAS ÚTILES ESCOLARES

lápices
(paquete
de 20)

El lápiz es más barato en paquetes

₡2.000

hojas de papel
(paquete de 100)

₡1.000

bolígrafos
(paquete
de 6)

₡1.000

La mochila cuesta ocho mil colones

mochila

₡8.000

carpeta
(paquete
de 10)

₡2.000

libros de texto

₡5.000–12.000

diccionario
inglés-español

₡7.000

Los cuadernos son perfectos para la clase de inglés

cuadernos
(8 x 100 hojas)

₡4.000

tijeras **₡1.000**

Las tijeras son para la clase de arte.

tablet

₡80.000

computadora

₡200.000

calculadora

₡9.000

agenda
escolar

₡2.000

Actividad 3

¿Qué hay en tu mochila?

First, read the list of school supplies below. Then, as you watch the video, tell which items Paola and María Laura have in their backpacks.

Paola

- libros
- cuadernos
- calculadora
- estuche *(pencil case)*
- tijeras
- bolígrafo
- lápices
- un libro para leer
- agenda escolar

María Laura

- diccionario
- libros
- cuadernos
- calculadora
- táblet
- lápiz
- bolígrafo
- borrador *(eraser)*

Actividad 4

¿Qué necesitas?

Paso 1

Look at the list of required supplies for Colegio Juan Santamaría below. Copy the items that you have in your backpack today by writing **Tengo** *(I have)* in front of them to make a sentence.

Modelo

Tengo una calculadora.

Tengo 3 carpetas.

etc.

Mi progreso comunicativo

I can write a list of school supplies I need to purchase.

Colegio Juan Santamaría.

Lista de útiles necesarios

- ☐ 3 lápices
- ☐ 2 bolígrafos
- ☐ hojas de papel
- ☐ cuaderno
- ☐ calculadora
- ☐ 3 carpetas
- ☐ agenda escolar
- ☐ libro de texto

Además se dice

Los números de 30 a 100

30 treinta
31 treinta y uno
32 treinta y dos
…
40 cuarenta
50 cincuenta
60 sesenta
70 setenta
80 ochenta
90 noventa
100 cien/ciento

Use **cien** before nouns (**cien estudiantes, cien dólares**), and **ciento** before other numbers (**ciento cuatro**, 104; **ciento cuarenta y cuatro**, 144)

Other numbers you should be able to recognize:

200 doscientos
300 trescientos
400 cuatrocientos
500 quinientos
600 seiscientos
700 setecientos
800 ochocientos
900 novecientos
1.000 mil
5.000 cinco mil
8.000 ocho mil
10.000 diez mil

Paso 2

Now ask a partner about the items on the list, using the **modelo** to guide you.

Modelo

Estudiante A: ¿Tienes (*do you have*) _____?

Estudiante B: Sí, tengo.
No, no tengo./Necesito (*I need*) _____.

Actividad 5

¿Qué cuesta más?

Check the prices of the items on the school materials ad in **Así se dice 1** (page 90) and tell which costs more.

1. los lápices/los bolígrafos

2. la computadora/la táblet

3. la mochila/las tijeras

4. la agenda escolar/la calculadora

Actividad 6

¿Qué necesito?

A new student who speaks Spanish needs to get school supplies. Write shopping lists with the items needed in four of your classes.

la clase de español	la clase de arte	la clase de matemáticas	la clase de ciencias

Enfoque cultural

Práctica cultural: Vocabulario regional

Regional varieties of Spanish have distinct names for common vocabulary, just as with dialects of English (U.S. *truck* = British *lorry*). Most of these variants are understood everywhere, and the context usually makes the intended meaning clear. You should learn to recognize a variety of regional words in Spanish, and when you speak or write, use the words associated with the places you are interested in.

el ordenador (España)
la computadora (elsewhere)

la pluma (México)
el lapicero (Costa Rica)
la birome (Argentina)
el bolígrafo (elsewhere)

el salón de clase (México)
el aula (elsewhere)

⬡ Conexiones

Can you cite any regional expressions or expressions used by a specific social group in the English-speaking world? What stereotypes or preconceived ideas occur to you when you hear these expressions?

Actividad 7

💬 ¿De quién es? *(Whose is it?)*

In groups of four, contribute two items per person from your backpacks to a pile, without looking at who contributed each item. Then, take turns guessing the owner of each item, following the model.

Modelo

Estudiante A:	¿Es de Jacob el bolígrafo?
Estudiante B:	Sí, es de Jacob./No, es de Michelle.
Estudiante C:	¿Es de Emma la calculadora?
Estudiante D:	Sí, es de Emma/No, es de Jacob.

Detalle gramatical

Possession with DE

The expression *definite article* + *noun* + **de** + *person* is one way to indicate possession:

La clase **de** Isaac es grande.
Isaac's class is big.

Los libros **de** Wanda son pesados.
Wanda's books are heavy.

El ordenador **de** la profesora es un Mac.
The teacher's computer is a Mac.

Note how in Spanish the object possessed comes first, followed by **de** and the owner. Spanish does not have a possessive structure like **'s** in English.

Observa 1

Escuelas diferentes

En el Colegio Bilingüe San Agustín, Costa Rica

1 *La soda* (comedor) *es pequeña.*

2 *El pasillo es largo.*

Los estudiantes son bilingües.

3 *Los profesores son amables.*

El director es simpático.

En diferentes colegios de California, EE. UU.

4 *El auditorio es histórico.*

5 *El edificio es moderno.*

La biblioteca (library) *es grande.*

6 *El campo deportivo es importante.*

El gimnasio es grande.

7 *Las aulas* (classrooms) *son modernas.*

¿Qué observas?

▶ ✦ Look at the words in bold preceding the nouns, which all correspond to "the" in English: **el, la, los, las**. Can you figure out the pattern of when to use each one? Discuss the examples with your classmates and teachers, view the **Observa 1** resources for this unit in your Explorer course, and check the **Síntesis de gramática** at the end of this section of the unit.

Actividad 8

¿Masculino o femenino?

 Paso 1

Listen to your teacher say the following nouns, and say the number of the photo that corresponds to the meaning.

a. auditorio

b. soda

c. campo deportivo

d. profesores

e. aulas

f. edificio

 Paso 2

Listen to these words again, paying special attention to the ending. Show that you understand the gender of the word by repeating it with its article: **el** or **los** for masculine nouns or **la** or **las** for feminine nouns.

Actividad 9

Personas y lugares

 **Paso 1**

Write the definite article (**el, la, los,** or **las**) used to identify these people and places in a school.

a. _____ edificio más importante es _____ biblioteca.

b. _____ auditorios son pequeños *(small)*.

c. _____ directores son de Costa Rica.

d. _____ gimnasio es muy grande.

e. _____ directora se llama Margarita Muñoz Piña.

f. _____ estudiantes son de muchos estados diferentes.

g. Me gustan mucho _____ aulas de mi colegio.

h. _____ campo deportivo es artificial.

 Paso 2: ¿Es verdad?

Rewrite the sentences in **Paso 1** to make them true for your school.

Expresiones útiles: Expressing location

You can use the verb **estar** with the preposition **en** and a place to describe location of people or objects:

¿Dónde **estás**?
Where are you?

Estoy en el aula 14.
I'm in room 14.

Mi progreso comunicativo

I can express where my school activities take place.

Actividad 10

¿Dónde estás durante el día?

 Paso 1

Write a list indicating where you are each period of your school day. Use the preposition **en** with a definite article and a place. If you have different schedules on different days, make more than one list.

Modelo

Período 1:	Estoy en el aula 14.
Período 2:	Estoy en el laboratorio de lenguas.
Período 3:	Estoy en la biblioteca.

Paso 2

Now exchange your information with a partner to compare your schedules.

Modelo

| *Estudiante A:* | ¿Dónde estás en el período 1? |
| *Estudiante B:* | Estoy en el aula 14. |

Actividad 11

¡Educación para todos!

Paso 1

In Costa Rica, various organizations participate in campaigns to collect school supplies (**útiles escolares**) for students who cannot afford to buy them. Look over the ad on the facing page, and answer these questions.

ÚTILES ESCOLARES
Campaña de donación 2016

DEL 11 AL 22 DE ENERO

Queremos que toooodos los niños estén listos para empezar el colegio.

¡Los niños son el futuro del país!

Un pack escolar incluye:

- dos cuadernos A4 (rayado)
- tres bolígrafos (rojo, negro, azul)
- dos lápices

- caja de lápices de colores
- tijeras
- sacapuntas
- regla de 20cm

Mi progreso comunicativo

I can understand a simple written ad in Spanish.

Mi progreso comunicativo

I can create a simple written promotional message.

1. What **útiles** are mentioned in the ad? Which of these would a student need in your school?

2. When does the campaign take place?

3. What is the purpose of the ad?

4. What items typically needed in your school are **not** mentioned in the ad?

Paso 2

Using this ad as a model, sketch or digitally create an ad in Spanish for your community in which you solicit donations of the school supplies that you mentioned in **Paso 1**. Include at least the following elements:

- the name of your school
- the dates of the campaign

- the list of útiles needed

DONACIÓN

Mi progreso intercultural

I can identify some shared values between my community and a community in the Spanish-speaking world.

Reflexión intercultural

What values are reflected in the **Campaña de donación 2016**? What activities in your community are expressions of similar values?

Así se dice 2

✦ Mi día en la escuela

La clase de historia **empieza** a las 7:00.

Horario	Asignatura	Lugar
7:00-9:00	Historia	Aula 9
9:00-9:20	Recreo	Aula 7
9:20-11:20	Francés	Cafetería
11:20-12:10	Almuerzo	Aula 12
12:10-14:10	Matemáticas	
14:10-14:30	Recreo	Aula de computadoras
14:30-16:30	Informática	

Horario	Asignatura	Lugar
7:00-9:00	Matemáticas	Aula 14
9:00-9:20	Recreo	
9:20-11:20	Francés	Aula 7
11:20-12:10	Almuerzo	Cafetería
12:10-14:10	Geografía	Aula 8
14:10-14:30	Recreo	
14:30-16:30	Química	Laboratorio 1

Hay un recreo **por la mañana**, y otro **por la tarde**.

Tengo la clase de matemáticas a las 7:00 en el aula 14. ¿Y tú?

Yo tengo matemáticas por la tarde, de las 12:10 a las 2:10.

Y francés de las 9:20 a las 11:20 en el aula 7.

¡Tengo francés por la mañana también!

Actividad 12

 ¿Dónde tienen las actividades?

Look at the two schedules on the smart phones. Listen to your teacher say classes or activities from the these students' schedules, and say where the class or activity takes place.

Actividad 13

  Clasifica las actividades

Which classes offered at your school fall into these categories? Write as many as you can in the first row below (**en mi escuela**). In the second row, add as many other possibilities as you can think of. Use the vocabulary in the **Estrategias** sidebar, and look up any other items you'd like to include.

	Humanidades	Lenguas	Ciencias	Artes
En mi escuela				
En otras escuelas				

Estrategias

Communicative strategy: Los cognados

Learning to recognize cognates will help you expand your vocabulary quickly. For example, **geología** looks like the English word *geology*.

Can you guess these classes and activities by noting their similarity with English words?

Otras asignaturas y actividades en la escuela

el álgebra

las artes visuales

la banda

el coro

el deporte

la educación cívica

la educación física

la música

Cognates don't always sound like their English counterparts, but with some practice, you will find that cognates will boost your ability to communicate.

Detalle gramatical

¿A qué hora?

To tell at what time events happen, we use the phrase **a la(s)** with a number. Use **la** with times that start with 1:00 and **las** with other numbers. The colon is read as **y**, the quarter hour can be **y quince** or **y cuarto**, and the half hour can be **y treinta** or **y media**.

La clase empieza **a las** 3:30 (a las tres y media). *Class begins at 3:30.*

Tengo química **a las** 10:15 (a las diez y cuarto). *I have chemistry at 10:15.*

A duration of time *(from … to…)* is given with **de la(s) _____ a la(s) _____.**

Tengo geometría de la 1:00 (la una) a las 2:20 (las dos y veinte). *I have geometry from 1:00 to 2:20.*

Actividad 14

Mi horario

A new exchange student is going to "shadow" you all day to learn about your school. Pick a representative day of the week, fill out your schedule, then narrate what classes you have at what times, and in what locations. Record your schedule in Explorer.

7:00		13:00	
7:30		13:30	
8:00		14:00	
8:30		14:30	
9:00		15:00	
9:30		15:30	
10:00		16:00	
10:30		16:30	
11:00		17:00	
11:30		17:30	
12:00		18:00	
12:30		18:30	

Modelo

A las 8:00 tengo la clase de geografía en el aula 32.

De las 9:00 a las 9:50, tengo la clase de español en el aula de computadoras.

Mi progreso comunicativo

I can present information about my school day orally.

Actividad 15

La mejor hora para la clase

Paso 1

Are you a morning person, or do you do better in certain subjects in the afternoon? When is the best time of day for the subjects you are taking? List your classes according to your preference.

Clases por la mañana	Clases por la tarde
Da lo mismo *(it doesn't matter)*	

Paso 2

Is it better to take certain classes at a particular time of day? Using the information from **Paso 1,** interview your partner to find out his/her preferences. Try to elaborate your answer with one of the **motivos** *(reasons)* provided, or add your own.

Modelo

—¿Te gusta la clase de matemáticas por la mañana?—

Sí, me gusta, porque… /No, no me gusta, porque…

Expresiones útiles: Giving reasons

Use the conjunction **porque** *(because)* followed by a sentence to give a reason or explanation.

porque estoy descansado/descansada *(I'm rested)*

porque estoy cansado/cansada *(I'm tired)*

porque el profesor es dinámico/la profesora es dinámica

porque la clase es aburrida *(boring)*

porque me duermo *(I fall asleep)*

porque tengo muchos amigos en la clase

porque ¿ … ?

Observa 2

¿Qué hay en mi colegio?

En el Colegio Calderón (Costa Rica)

Hay **un** gimnasio grande.

Hay **una** cafetería.

Hay **muchas** aulas.

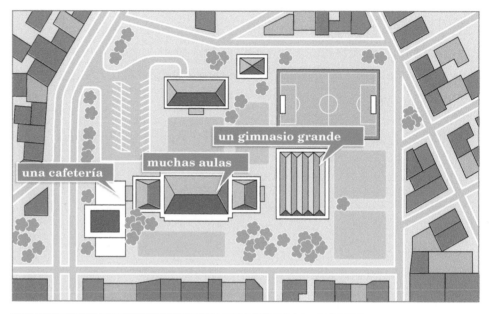

En Tustin High School (California, EE. UU.)

Hay **un** campo de fútbol americano.

Hay **una** piscina olímpica.

Hay **muchos** edificios.

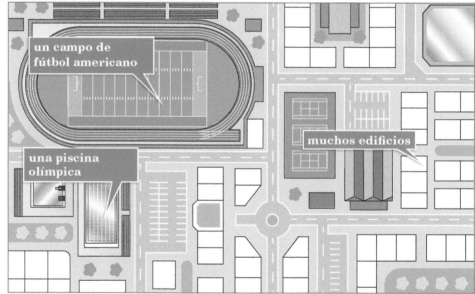

¿Qué observas?

Look at the words in bold preceding the places in these schools: **un**, **una**, **muchos**, **muchas**. Can you figure out when to use **un** vs. **una**? **Muchos** vs. **muchas**? Discuss the examples with your classmates and teacher, view the **Observa 2** resources for this unit in Explorer, and check the **Síntesis de gramática** at the end of the **Comunica** section of the unit.

Actividad 16

📖 ¿Hay uno o muchos?

How many people and facilities from this list are there at your school? Combine a quantity word from the left with the nouns at the right to describe where you study. Be careful to match the ending of the quantity word with the gender and number of the noun. You can look up and add other words as well.

Modelo

En mi escuela, hay **muchas profesoras**.

	biblioteca(s)
un	cafetería(s)
una	campo(s) deportivo(s)
muchos	edificio(s)
muchas	gimnasio(s)
	laboratorio(s) de lenguas
	pasillo(s)
	profesor(es)/profesora(s)
	secretario(s)/secretaria(s)
	¿ ... ?

En mi escuela, hay...

Actividad 17

✎ Mi escuela ideal

Describe the things you'd like to have in your ideal school. Include a quantity by using **un**, **una**, **muchos**, **muchas**. Try to add a phrase to explain your choices, as in the model.

Modelo

En mi escuela ideal, hay muchos campos deportivos, porque me gusta jugar deportes.

Actividad 18

Un nuevo colegio

Michael, from California, and Gabriela, from Costa Rica, met last year at a summer camp, then kept in touch through chat when they returned home. Michael just changed to a new school, and Gabriela is inquiring about his experience.

Estudiantes del colegio trabajan en un proyecto para la clase.

GabiCR: MikeUSA:

> Hola Miguel, ¿cómo estás?

>> Muy bien, gracias. Estoy en una nueva escuela este año.

> ¿Una escuela nueva? ¿Te gusta?

>> Sí, me gusta. Hay muchos estudiantes que son mis amigos.

> ¿Qué más hay en la escuela? ¿Hay clases interesantes?

>> Tengo clases difíciles este año, pero el colegio es fenomenal. Hay muchas aulas modernas, una biblioteca con tecnología nueva, y hay una cafetería con comida deliciosa.

> ¡Qué suerte! Uf, no hay comida deliciosa en mi cafetería.

>> Ja ja ja. Oye, tengo que hacer mi tarea.

> Yo también. Tengo un proyecto de biología. ¡Hasta luego, Miguel!

>> ¡Adiós, Gabi! Bss.

✏️ Paso 1

Read the text chat, and list at least four things that Gabriela learns about Michael's new school.

⊚⊚ Paso 2

Name one difference between Michael's and Gabriela's schools.

✏️ Paso 3

Write at least three sentences to compare your school to Michael's, following the model.

Modelo

Mi escuela es similar al colegio de Miguel porque hay _____.

Mi escuela es diferente del colegio de Miguel porque (no) hay _____.

Así se dice 3

◈ ¿Qué hacemos en la escuela?

Las actividades de los estudiantes

caminar a la escuela

tomar el autobús

almorzar en la soda

bailar durante las ceremonias

cantar el himno nacional
de Costa Rica

regresar a casa

Las actividades de los profesores

enseñar estudios sociales

ayudar a los estudiantes

Otras actividades en la escuela

estudiar inglés en un colegio bilingüe

llevar *(wear)* uniforme todos los días

hablar con los compañeros entre *(between)* clases.

trabajar en equipo *(in teams)*

jugar al futbolín *(foosball)* con los amigos

prestar atención *(pay attention)* al profesor

participar en un intercambio *(exchange)* cultural

usar las computadoras

Actividad 19

 ⊕ **Lo que nos gusta hacer en la escuela**

Listen to each statement as students describe activities they like to do in school, and write the number of the corresponding picture.

A. _____   B. _____   C. _____   D. _____   E. _____   F. _____

Actividad 20

📖 **¿En qué parte del colegio?**

Match the phrases in the two columns to write logical sentences about what Costa Rican students do in different parts of the school.

Modelo

Los estudiantes **suelen nadar** *(typically swim)* en la piscina.

1. Los estudiantes suelen almorzar	en el aula de computadoras
2. Los estudiantes suelen jugar al básquetbol	en la soda
3. Los estudiantes suelen navegar por internet	en el aula
4. Los estudiantes suelen escuchar al profesor	en la biblioteca
5. Los estudiantes suelen estudiar	en el gimnasio

Detalle gramatical

El infinitivo en español

In Spanish, the most basic form of verbs (action words) is **el infinitivo** *(the infinitive)*, the form that usually corresponds to the English verb preceded by "to". The Spanish infinitive is just one word, and it always ends in **-ar**, **-er**, or **-ir**:

- estud**iar**   *to study*
- hac**er**   *to do, make*
- escrib**ir**   *to write*

You have already learned to use the infinitive with **me gusta/te gusta** to express activities you like to do.

- ¿Te gusta **jugar al** fútbol? *Do you like to play soccer?*
- Me gusta **tocar** la guitarra. *I like to play the guitar.*

Actividad 21

📖 ¿Quién lo dice?

Read the following statements about different aspects of school life. Who would most logically make these statements? Some statements may correspond to more than one person.

A. un/una estudiante

B. un profesor/una profesora

C. el director/la directora (principal)

D. el/la guardia de seguridad (the security guard)

1 "Ayudo a mis estudiantes cuando tienen dificultades."

2 "Tomo el autobús a la escuela."

3 "Soy el jefe (boss) de la escuela."

4 "Presto atención al profesor cuando estoy en clase.

5 "Llevo uniforme de lunes a viernes."

6 "Enseño matemáticas, mi asignatura favorita."

7 "Juego al futbolín con mis compañeros de clase."

8 "Hablo con mis compañeros de clase sobre la tarea (about the homework)."

9 "Trabajo en la escuela."

Actividad 22

¡Firma aquí!: ¿Qué te gusta hacer?

💬 🧭 Paso 1

Read the following questions, and make sure you understand the meaning. Then circulate among your classmates, and find five different people who answer **sí** (different question for each student). Each time a classmate answers yes, have them sign their name next to the number of the question on a separate sheet of paper.

Modelo

Estudiante A: ¿Te gusta llevar uniforme?

Estudiante B: Sí, me gusta llevar uniforme.
                    No, no me gusta llevar uniforme.

1. ¿Te gusta estudiar español?

2. ¿Te gusta hablar con tus compañeros entre clases?

3. ¿Te gusta almorzar en la cafetería?

4. ¿Te gusta jugar al básquetbol en el gimnasio?

5. ¿Te gusta cantar el himno nacional?

6. ¿Te gusta caminar a la escuela?

7. ¿Te gusta estudiar ciencias?

8. ¿Te gusta ayudar a tus compañeros de clase?

9. ¿Te gusta participar en los clubes?

10. ¿Te gusta hablar con el director/la directora?

Paso 2

Using the responses that you collected, write sentences to describe your compatibility with your classmates. Use the models as your guide.

Modelo

Jacob y yo somos compatibles porque nos gusta navegar por internet.

Además se dice

Más actividades académicas

aprender idiomas

leer libros

Mi progreso comunicativo

I can ask and respond to questions relating to personal preferences about school activities.

Observa 3

Una entrevista con Isaac, estudiante de intercambio

Isaac, de Palmares, Costa Rica, is spending a year at Buena Vista High School in California. The school website interviewed him and published the exchange in this article.

Buena Vista High School

¿Quién eres?

BVHS Hola, ¿cómo te **llamas**?

Isaac Me **llamo** Isaac.

BVHS ¿De dónde eres?

Isaac Soy de Costa Rica. **Estudio** inglés y español en el Colegio Bilingüe San Agustín.

BVHS ¡Qué chiva! ¿**Estudias** otras lenguas?

Isaac Sí, **estudio** portugués en una academia.

¿Y tu escuela?

BVHS Isaac, dime, ¿tu escuela es diferente a un colegio en los Estados Unidos?

Isaac Sí, es un poco diferente, por ejemplo, nosotros **llevamos** uniforme todos los días. **Almorzamos** en la soda al aire libre, no en una cafetería. También **cantamos** el himno nacional una vez por semana.

¿Cómo te movilizas?

BVHS ¿Cómo **llegas** al colegio?

Issac También es diferente. **Camino** al colegio, pero mis amigos **toman** el transporte escolar, el autobús.

¡Qué perfil internacional!

BVHS Los intercambios son importantes en tu colegio bilingüe, ¿verdad?

Isaac Sí, es verdad. Tengo compañeros que **participan** en un intercambio en Inglaterra. Ellos **visitan** lugares históricos, **practican** inglés, **cantan** el himno nacional de Costa Rica y **bailan** bailes folclóricos en las ceremonias. **Estudian** en Inglaterra con una profesora que **acompaña** al grupo. Ella es bilingüe y **enseña** a los estudiantes ingleses un poco sobre la cultura de Costa Rica.

¿Qué observas?

▶️ ✴️ In the interview, notice the words in bold that specify actions (verbs). Look carefully at the endings, and try to figure out from the context who is doing each action. Do you notice any patterns? How many different endings do you notice? Discuss your observations with your **compañeros de clase** and with your teacher. View the **Observa 3** resources in Explorer for this unit and check the **Síntesis de gramática** at the end of the section for more information.

Actividad 23

📖 ✴️ ¡Yo también!

Read the following quotes from Isaac's interview (on the left), and choose a response on the right that is true for you.

1. "Estudio portugués"
   - a. ¡Yo estudio portugués también!
   - b. Yo sólo estudio español.

2. "Llevamos uniforme todos los días."
   - a. ¡Nosotros llevamos uniforme también!
   - b. No llevamos uniforme en mi escuela.

3. "Almorzamos en la soda."
   - a. ¡Almorzamos en la soda también!
   - b. Almorzamos en la cafetería o fuera (outside) de la escuela.

4. "Cantamos el himno nacional."
   - a. ¡Cantamos el himno también!
   - b. No cantamos el himno en mi escuela.

5. "Camino al colegio."
   - a. ¡Yo también camino al colegio!
   - b. No camino; tomo el transporte escolar.
   - c. No camino; voy en carro a la escuela.

6. "Mis compañeros participan en un intercambio."
   - a. ¡Mis compañeros también participan en un intercambio!
   - b. Todos mis compañeros estudian aquí.

7. "Mis compañeros practican inglés."
   - a. ¡Mis compañeros también practican inglés!
   - b. Mis compañeros practican español.

8. "Mi profesora enseña la cultura de Costa Rica".
   - a. ¡Mi profesora enseña cultura también!
   - b. Mi profesora enseña sólo español.

Detalle gramatical

Subject pronouns

You have already seen the pronouns **yo**, **tú**, **él**, **ella**, and **usted** (Unidad 1). Spanish has additional pronouns that serve as subjects of the sentence:

Nosotros estudiamos en EE. UU., pero **ellos** estudian en Inglaterra.
We study in the U.S., but they study in England.

—¿Quién participa en un intercambio?
—**Ellas**.
Who is participating in an exchange?
They are. (Those girls are.)

Ustedes son de Costa Rica, ¿verdad?
You all are from Costa Rica, right?

We do not normally need these pronouns, because the verb tells who the subject is (the **-mos** ending indicates **nosotros**, for example).

For more information on how to translate "you," and a complete list of pronouns, see the **Síntesis de gramática.**

Actividad 24

¿Quién lo hace? *(Who does it?)*

Underline the verb (the action word) in each sentence. Identify the subject, if it is mentioned. If not, say which subject pronoun could be used.

Modelo

<u>Los estudiantes</u> del Colegio San Agustín <u>participan</u> en un intercambio.——→ los estudiantes.

<u>Participamos</u> en un intercambio. ——→ nosotros

1. ¿Por qué no cantas el himno nacional?

2. Estudio para el examen de historia.

3. Ramón y sus amigos juegan al béisbol en el verano.

4. Siempre caminamos a la escuela por el parque.

5. ¿Mira usted muchas películas de ciencia ficción?

6. Hablo con mis amigos en la cafetería todos los días.

7. Victoria estudia sola *(alone)*.

8. Héctor y yo pintamos un graffiti 3D.

Actividad 25

💬 ✳ ¿Qué haces tú en la escuela?

Working with a **compañero/a de clase**, find out as much as you can about his/her school experience by asking these yes-or-no questions. Add any additional questions you would like to know about.

Modelo

¿Caminas a la escuela?
Sí, camino a la escuela./No, no camino a la escuela.

1. ¿Cantas en un coro?

2. ¿Practicas un deporte?

3. ¿Estudias inglés y español?

4. ¿Ayudas a tus compañeros?

5. ¿Participas en muchas actividades?

6. ¿Tomas el autotbús?

7. ¿ … ?

Actividad 26

✳ ¿Cuándo lo hago?

Fill in the graphic organizer in your Explorer course with at least six sentences that describe the the time of day you engage in different activities in school. Use the present tense **yo** form of **-ar** verbs you have learned, or look up additional vocabulary to describe your routines.

Modelo

No llevo uniforme escolar los sábados o los domingos.

Carrera a campo traviesa.

✳ Mi progreso comunicativo

I can ask and answer questions about life at school in oral conversations.

**Expresiones útiles:
Las partes del día**

por la mañana
in the morning

al mediodía
at noontime

por la tarde
in the afternoon

por la noche
in the evening

los sábados
on Saturdays

los domingos
on Sundays

Actividad 27

📑 Prepara tu entrevista

You would like to interview a new exchange student in your school. Prepare your interview by writing at least six potential questions for your new classmate. Be sure to include two kinds of questions: yes-or-no, which only require a verb in the **tú** form, and information questions, which need a question word like **¿Qué?**, **¿Cómo?**, **¿Dónde?**, etc.

Modelo

estudiar:

¿Estudias mucho?

¿Qué estudias?

Soy de Cañas Guanacaste. ¿Y vos?

Enfoque cultural

Práctica cultural: ¿Cómo se dice "you" en Costa Rica?

You have seen that different regions have their unique vocabulary for everyday objects and other aspects of language can also vary geographically. In Costa Rica, Spanish speakers use a range of forms to address another person directly ("you"), depending on the locale and the age and status of the participants in the conversation. While **tú** is understood in every Spanish-speaking area, you might hear **vos** or **usted** in Costa Rica to address friends and children. Each of these pronouns has its own distinct forms (verb, object of preposition, possessives):

Marcos, ¿qué estudi**as** este semestre? (tú)

Marcos, ¿qué estudi**ás** este semestre? (vos)

Marcos, ¿qué estudi**a** este semestre? (usted)

As a learner of Spanish, you should focus on learning **tú** for familiar contexts and **usted** for older people and in professional contexts. You can learn **vos** if you are interested in Central America or other regions where it is common (Argentina, Paraguay, Uruguay).

Conexiones

In standard English, we have only one pronoun, *you*, to address our conversation partner. How do people address a group in colloquial or regional varieties of English? Think about your interactions with friends, teachers, and adults at your school.

Actividad 28

 Un día típico en el colegio

Write a blog entry in which you describe a typical day in your school. Include your classes as well as extracurricular activities.

¡OJO! Pay special attention to the verb endings, which tell who does each action. Use the verbs provided in the list below, and look up others that you may need.

Por la mañana, …

Por la tarde, …

> ayudar, bailar, caminar, cantar, entrenar, estudiar, hablar, montar en bicicleta, navegar por internet, practicar deportes, terminar, tocar, trabajar

Mi progreso comunicativo

I can list in writing a few of the activities I regularly do at school.

Muchos estudiantes estudian en la biblioteca o participan en actividades, como la orquesta.

Síntesis de gramática

Gender and Number

In Spanish, nouns (the words that name persons, places, or things) have an inherent gender, either masculine or feminine. For people and animals, the grammatical gender usually matches the biological sex (**el profesor**, a man, is masculine, **la profesora**, a woman, is feminine). However, unlike English, even inanimate objects and abstract things have gender: **el lápiz** (*pencil*) is masculine, and **la verdad** (*truth*) is feminine.

masculine nouns	feminine nouns
el bolígrafo	la calculadora
el lápiz	la ciencia
el papel	la educación
el estudiante	la estudiante
el profesor	la profesora

You must memorize the gender of a noun as a part of its meaning. Sometimes the ending of the word can help. Words ending **-ción**, for example, are always feminine (**la atención**, **educación**, **la información**).

Grammatical *number* tells us how many of a noun there are: singular indicates one, and plural more than one of the noun in question. To make a noun plural, add **-s** to a word that ends in a vowel, add **-es** to a word that ends in a consonant or some accented vowels:

vowel-final words	consonant-final words, some accented vowels
el bolígrafo → los bolígrafos	el lápiz → los lápices
la calculadora → las calculadoras	el profesor → los profesores
el sofá → los sofás	el bambú → los bambúes

Note that some spelling changes may apply:

- a final **-z** changes to **-c-** before **-es**.

- adding the syllable **-es** may require a change in the written accent mark (**nación/naciones**, **examen/exámenes**).

The definite article

In Spanish, the definite article (similar to *the* in English) has four forms, **el, los, la, las,** depending on the gender (masculine or feminine) and number (singular or plural) of the noun.

el borrador (masc. sing.)	*the eraser*	**los** borradores (masc. pl.)	*the erasers*
la escuela (fem. sing.)	*the school*	**las** escuelas (fem. pl.)	*the schools*

For nouns that refer to male and female humans or animals, **los** is used to indicate a mixed gender group: **los profesores** can refer to an all male group or any combination of male and female teachers. **Las profesoras** would refer to a group of only female teachers.

Sometimes Spanish must use the definite article where English does not:

La educación es muy importante.
Education is very important.

Yo voy a **la** clase de español.
I am going to Spanish class.

Feminine words that begin with a stressed **a-** sound take the singular article **el: el álgebra, el agua, el aula**. But these words are really feminine, as the plural shows: **las aguas, las aulas**.

Subject pronouns

The table below gives the complete list of subject pronouns in Spanish. Remember that these pronouns are used only for emphasis or to answer a question. In other cases, the verb ending indicates who is carrying out the action, and the pronoun can be omitted from the sentence.

yo	*I*	**nosotros** **nosotras**	*we*
tú*	*you (informal)*	**vosotros*** **vosotras***	*you, y'all, you guys (Spain)*
vos*	*you (informal)*		
usted*	*you (formal)*	**ustedes***	*you (Spain, formal); you (L.Am. informal and formal)*
él **ella**	*he* *she*	**ellos** **ellas**	*they*

Areas where **vos** may be heard instead of **tú**

*Spanish has many words for "you"; choosing the right one depends on the region and the level of respect or social distance you want to show the person you are addressing.

The Spanish verb

The basic form of the verb (action word) in Spanish is the infinitive, which can end in **-ar**, **-er** or **-ir** (e.g., **cantar**, **beber**, **escribir**). This is the form we typically look for when looking up verbs in a dictionary. The infinitive has many uses; so far you have used it with **me/te gusta**.

To talk about habitual actions or general truths, we use a form of the verb called the present indicative tense. For infinitives that end in **-ar**, this tense has the same endings as the sample verb **hablar** below:

yo	habl**o**	nosotros/as	habl**amos**
tú	habl**as**	*vosotros/as*	*habl**áis***
vos	*habl**ás***		
usted	habl**a**	ustedes	habl**an**
él	habl**a**	ellos	habl**an**
ella	habl**a**	ellas	habl**an**

Siempre **hablo** español con mi familia.

*I always **speak** Spanish with my family.*

No **estudiamos** latín en mi escuela.

*We don't **study** Latin in my school.*

¿**Vos tomás** el autobús al colegio?

*Do **you take** the bus to school?*

These same present tense forms are used in questions; note that there is not a separate word that corresponds to the English *do/don't/does/doesn't*.

Estos estudiantes conversan entre las clases.

Vocabulario

I can say what things I have and I need for school. (Así se dice 1)

Tengo...	*I have*
Necesito...	*I need*
¿Qué necesitas?	*What do you need?*
¿Cuánto cuesta?	*How much does it cost?*
¿Cuánto cuestan?	*How much do they cost?*

la agenda escolar	*assignment notebook*
el bolígrafo	*pen*
la calculadora	*calculator*
la carpeta	*folder*
la computadora	*computer*
el cuaderno	*notebook*
el diccionario	*dictionary*
la escuela	*school*
la hoja de papel	*sheet of paper*
el lápiz/los lápices	*pencil; pencils*
el libro de texto	*textbook*
la mochila	*backpack*
el papel	*paper*
el paquete	*package*
la táblet	*tablet computer*
las tijeras	*scissors*

El uniforme escolar

la camisa	*shirt*
el escudo	*logo; crest; emblem*
la falda	*skirt*
los pantalones	*pants*
los zapatos	*shoes*
blanco/a	*white*
negro/a	*black*
verde	*green*

Los números de 30 a 1000

treinta	30
cuarenta	40
cincuenta	50
sesenta	60
setenta	70
ochenta	80
noventa	90
cien/ciento	100
doscientos	200
mil	1.000

I can exchange information about classes and schedules and tell about my school. (Así se dice 2)

Las asignaturas y actividades

el almuerzo	*lunch*
la ciencia	*science*
los estudios sociales	*social studies*
la geografía	*geography*
la historia	*history*
la informática	*computer science*
las matemáticas	*math*
la química	*chemistry*
el recreo/el receso	*break (between classes)*

Los lugares en la escuela

hay	*there is/there are*
un/una	*a/an/one*
unos/unas	*some*
muchos/muchas	*many*
el auditorio	*auditorium*
el aula; el salón de clase	*classroom*
la biblioteca	*library*
el comedor/la soda (C.R.)	*cafeteria*
el campo de fútbol	*soccer field*
el colegio (C.R.)	*high school*
el edificio	*building*
el gimnasio	*gymnasium*
el laboratorio	*laboratory*
la oficina	*office*
el pasillo	*hallway*
la piscina	*swimming pool*

El horario de clases

¿A qué hora?	*(At) what time?*
La clase empieza a…	*The class begins at…*
La clase termina a…	*The class ends at…*
el horario	*schedule*
entre clases	*between classes*

Expresiones útiles: Las partes del día

por la mañana	*in the morning*
al mediodía	*at noontime*
por la tarde	*in the afternoon*
por la noche	*in the evening*
los sábados	*on Saturdays*
los domingos	*on Sunday*

I can talk about things I do at school. (Así se dice 3)

Lo que hacen los estudiantes y los maestros

almorzar (o → ue)	*have lunch*
ayudar	*help*
caminar	*walk*
cantar	*sing*
enseñar	*teach*
estudiar	*study*
llevar	*wear; to bring*
participar	*participate*
prestar atención	*pay attention*
regresar a casa	*go back home*
tomar	*take*
trabajar en equipo	*work in teams*
usar	*use*

Más vocabulario escolar

el autobús	*bus*
la ceremonia	*ceremony*
el compañero de clase/ la compañera de clase	*classmate*
el director/la directora	*principal*
el himno nacional	*national anthem*
el intercambio	*exchange*
el maestro/la maestra	*teacher (particularly in elementary school)*
el profesor/la profesora	*teacher*
el secretario/la secretaria	*secretary*

En camino

Actividad 30

En el colegio: Paola, Christian y yo

▣ ✦ Paso 1

Paola and Christian are going to talk about their schools. First, look at the topics they will mention in the table below. Then, as you watch and listen, list in the appropriate category the aspects they mention.

	Horas/ horarios	Asignaturas	Útiles escolares	Las partes de la escuela
Paola				
Christian				
Yo				

◎ Paso 2

Now, list words that relate to your own school in the row marked **yo**. Then write at least four sentences noting similarities and differences between Paola's or Christian's school and your own.

Modelo

En el colegio de Paola, hay _____, pero en mi colegio, no.

Paola y yo llevamos _____ en la mochila, pero ella no tiene _____.

Paola estudia _____, pero yo no.

Paola, nuestra bloguera de la República Dominicana

Christian, el bloguero de México

Actividad 31

Horarios compatibles

Follow the **Pasos** below to set up a study group with at least three of your classmates.

  **Paso 1**

Write out a list of all your weekly commitments (classes, music lessons, sports, church, etc.). Include the activity, the time of day and the day of the week.

Modelo

Tengo _____ de _____ a _____ los _____.

Tengo fútbol de las 3:00 a las 5:00 los lunes y los jueves.

 **Paso 2**

¿Tienes tiempo? Based on your schedule and commitments, identify two or three times when you are available for a study group. Then, ask three other classmates questions based on your schedule to find available times. Be sure to jot down the answers that will help you find a common time.

Modelo

Estudiante A: ¿Tienes tiempo de las 5:00 a las 6:00 los miércoles?

Estudiante B: Sí, está bien. *or*
                    No. Tengo clase de piano.

 **Paso 3**

Compile your results, and write a note to your teacher indicating the names of the students in your group and the time you can meet together, for example, **Mi grupo estudia de las 4:00 a las 5:00 los lunes.**

Mi progreso comunicativo

I can present information about my school and extracurricular activities in writing.

Mi progreso comunicativo

I can interact orally to exchange information about my activities.

Explora

Essential Question: How do schools reflect the values of their communities?

Overview

Schools educate students, prepare them for the future, and transmit cultural values. In this segment, you will explore how the Costa Rican educational system reflects that country's unique values and prepares students to contribute to society. Finally, you will reflect on how schools in your community reflect values and prepare you for the future.

Los uniformes son importantes para la identidad de muchos estudiantes.

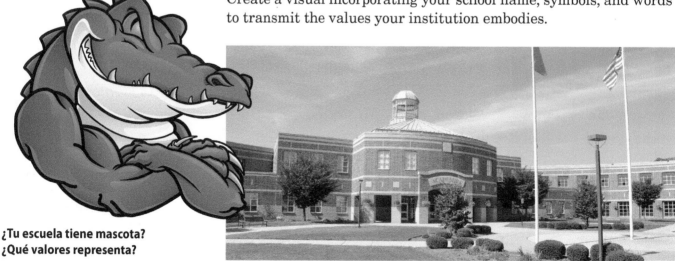

¿Tu escuela tiene mascota?
¿Qué valores representa?

La importancia de la educación

Gráficos

These graphs about literacy rates and education spending were prepared using information published by the CIA World Factbook.

La alfabetización (*literacy*) es una prioridad importante para el futuro de un país.

Actividad 32

 Costa Rica: Un país único

Study the two graphs below and write three facts you learn from each of them. Then write two sentences telling what you can infer about Education in Costa Rica based on the information in the graphs.

Tasa de alfabetización de adultos mayores de° 15 años

- Costa Rica: 98%
- Panamá: 95%
- Honduras: 89%
- El Salvador: 87%
- Nicaragua: 83%
- Guatemala: 82%

° *(older than)*

Gasto *(expenditures)* % del Producto Interno Bruto (PIB)*

	La educación 	Las fuerzas armadas
Costa Rica	6.9%	0%
Los Estados Unidos	5.2%	4.35%

PIB = GDP, the Gross Domestic Product, the total of goods and services produced in a country.

Mi progreso comunicativo

I can identify key details from charts and graphs, and make inferences about cultural perspectives.

Actividad 33

Los uniformes

🌐 Paso 1: ¿Un símbolo importante?

Why do certain organizations (schools, hospitals, restaurants, police, military, etc.) have uniforms? Make a list of advantages and disadvantages with a partner, keeping in mind the larger perspective of who else in your community/culture wears uniforms, and why. Share your results with the class.

📖 🔍 Paso 2: Los componentes del uniforme escolar costarricense

Public school students in Costa Rica all wear uniforms, as decreed by the Ministerio de Educación Pública (MEP) de Costa Rica. The colors and details may vary, but all public school uniforms must meet the minimum guidelines in the list at the right. Using

El uniforme colegial
Blusa/camisa (2 unidades)
Calcetín (2 unidades)
Enagua/falda/pollera o pantalón (1 unidad)
Zapatos
Escudo de la institución

the photos and contextual clues in the list, figure out the meaning of each component of the uniform in the box and in the list in **Paso 3**.

Isaac (Costa Rica)

María Laura (Paraguay)

Melissa (Colombia)

▶️ 🌐 ✴️ Paso 3: Hablan los blogueros

View and listen to three **blogueros** describe their uniforms.
List the components that you hear each one mention.

	Isaac	María Laura	Melissa
blusa	❏	❏	❏
camisa	❏	❏	❏
chaqueta	❏	❏	❏
escudo	❏	❏	❏
falda/pollera	❏	❏	❏
pantalón	❏	❏	❏
medias *(knee socks)*	❏	❏	❏
zapatos	❏	❏	❏
tenis	❏	❏	❏

▶️ ✴️ Paso 4: ¿Les gustan los uniformes?

Listen and watch the videos again. How do the three
students feel about their uniforms? Do they seem proud,
indifferent, or annoyed?

**En 1948, el antiguo cuartel militar
(*former military headquarters*) se
transforma en el Museo Nacional de
Costa Rica.**

Enfoque cultural

Perspectiva cultural: Uniformes escolares, no militares

Figueres Ferrer

En el año 1948, el presidente José María ("Don Pepe") Figueres Ferrer decide que Costa Rica no necesita ejército *(army)*. El país elimina las Fuerzas armadas y usa el presupuesto *(budget)* militar para la educación, la cultura y la seguridad pública. Hay fuerza pública (o policía) en Costa Rica, pero no hay soldados. Hoy, cuando visitantes *(visitors)* importantes llegan a Costa Rica, no hay bandas con uniformes militares en el aeropuerto. Hay un grupo de estudiantes en uniformes escolares para darles la bienvenida *(to welcome them)*.

**Estudiantes costarricenses le dan la
bienvenida (*welcome*) al presidente
estadounidense Barack Obama.**

🔗 ✴️ Conexiones

Why do you think Costa Rica made this decision in 1948? What advantages and disadvantages might come from such a decision?

Mi progreso intercultural

I can compare cultural practices and perspectives reflected in the use of uniforms in my community and in Costa Rica.

Reflexión intercultural

What groups of people in your community wear uniforms? What cultural values are reflected in the use of uniforms in your school, community and country? How does this compare to what you have learned about Costa Rica? Answer the questions in the Forum in Explorer, and share your observations with your classmates.

La educación y los valores

Actividad 34

Centro Educativo Futuro Verde

The information was published on the web by the Costa Rican school Centro Educativo Futuro Verde (2016).

Centro Educativo Futuro Verde

Centro Educativo Internacional Bilingüe

| Inicio | Sobre FV | Académica | Información | ¡Involúcrese! |

2016 Año Escolar

Año escolar empieza:
Miércoles 10 de febrero

Año escolar termina:
Viernes, 16 de diciembre

Horario

Las clases comienzan a las 7:40 a.m.

Los estudiantes deben de llegar no más tarde de las 7:30 a.m. para homeroom y para asegurar que estén preparados para el inicio de clases. Las clases terminan a las 3:00 p.m.

Vacaciones:

Semana Santa: 21–25 de marzo

Vacaciones de 15 días: 27 de junio–15 de julio

Vacaciones de invierno: 26 de septiembre–12 de octubre

Distribución de trimestres:

Trimestre I: 3 de febrero – 6 de mayo

Trimestre II: 09 de mayo – 26 de agosto

Trimestre III: 29 de agosto – 16 de diciembre

Paso 1: Visualización y predicciones

Observe the images and organization of the web site to answer these questions:

1. What catches your attention first on this web page?

2. What do the images communicate about the school?

3. What do you expect to learn by studying in this program?

📖 🔎 Paso 2: Búsqueda de detalles

Read the web page carefully to answer the following questions:

1. During which months are students in school?

2. Which months are students on vacation?

3. How long is the school day? What time does it begin and end?

4. Which of the three vacation periods during the school year is longest? How many days does it last?

5. How is the school year divided? Is it similar to or different from your school system?

🌐 Paso 3: Conclusiones

Observe the photograph of the mural painted on a wall at Futuro Verde.

1. What does it tell you about the school's values?

2. What kind of images and/or artwork are present at your school? What values do they represent?

Enfoque cultural

Práctica cultural: Pasantías laborales

Most Costa Rican high school students graduate when they complete the 11th grade. However, those students who choose to attend a **colegio técnico** complete an additional year of studies that prepare them for jobs in business, services, agriculture, and industry. Students in a **colegio técnico** often spend a portion of the school day in a workplace (hospital, business, etc.) doing a **pasantía**, a type of internship. The **pasantía** experience should have the following characteristics:

1. provides a work experience relevant to the student's specialty area of study

2. minimum age of 16 years old at the start of the internship

3. must take place during school year (between March and October), not during the summer vacation.

🔗 ⊛ Conexiones

In what ways do schools in your community prepare students for work after high school? If you could participate in a **pasantía**, what type of placement would you seek?

Actividad 35

📖 ✦ El horario de Gabriela

Gabriela studies at the Colegio Técnico Profesional de Tronadora and participates in a **pasantía** internship. What can her schedule tell you about her educational experience?

1. Identify the times, days and place of Gabriela's **pasantía**. How many hours per week are spent in the workplace?

2. What kind of skills do you think Gabriela gets from this experience?

3. Which other classes in Gabriela's schedule do you think provide valuable knowledge and skills for her future career? Explain.

Mi progreso comunicativo

I can identify key details and understand cultural practices when reading authentic print materials.

**Ministerio de Educación Pública -
Colegio Técnico Profesional de Tronadora**

Académica	Lección	Lunes	Martes	Miércoles	Jueves	Viernes
7:00/7:40	1	Pasantía Clínica municipal	Comunicación oral	Comunicación Empresarial	Inglés	Español
7:40/8:20	2	Pasantía Clínica municipal	Comunicación oral	Comunicación Empresarial	Religión	Español
8:20/9:00	3				Español	Edu. Física
9:00/9:20		RECREO				
9:20/10:00	4	Pasantía Clínica municipal	Comunicación oral	Comunicación Empresarial	Matemáticas	Edu. Física
10:00/10:40	5	Pasantía Clínica municipal	Comunicación oral	Comunicación Empresarial	Matemáticas	Cívica
10:40/11:20	6					Química
11:20/12:10		ALMUERZO				
12:10/12:50	7	Destrezas computacionales	Pasantía Clínica municipal	Música	Psicología	Comunicación oral
12:50/13:30	8	Destrezas computacionales	Pasantía Clínica municipal	Biología	Estudios Soc.	Comunicación oral
13:30/14:10	9			Biología	Estudios Soc.	
14:10/14:30		RECREO				
14:30/15:10	10	Destrezas computacionales	Pasantía Clínica municipal	Biología	Química	Comunicación oral
15:10/15:50	11	Destrezas computacionales	Pasantía Clínica municipal	Inglés	Química	Comunicación oral
15:50/16:30	12			Inglés	Guía	

En mi comunidad

Los valores de mi escuela

Centro Educativo **Futuro Verde**

Centro Educativo Internacional Bilingüe

| Inicio | Sobre FV | Académica | Información | ¡Involúcrese! |

Nuestra visión:

Ser una institución progresista, internacional y bilingüe con una comunidad dedicada, de apoyo y humanitaria que se esfuerza por promover pacíficamente un mundo armonioso.

Inspiración.
Dedicación.
Innovación.

Juntos, hacemos el futuro

Actividad 36

La educación

📖 **Paso 1: Los valores**

Read the web page published by the Escuela Futuro Verde, and list all the cognates you recognize. Circle the words on your list that you think refer to the values that inspired the school's founders.

Paso 2: La investigación

What is your school's vision, mission, motto, or philosophy? Collect and read documents and statements from your current school, schools you have attended in the past, and/or nearby schools, colleges or universities.

 Paso 3: Imágenes icónicas

1. Describe the images of school mascots that you see at the right. What characteristics do they represent to you?

2. Does your school have a logo, mascot, or seal that is used to identify it?

3. Why do you think these images were selected to represent your school?

4. In a group, write a list of five words or a short sentence in Spanish that summarizes for you the values your school seeks to represent. How many of these words are cognates in Spanish?

Paso 4: Nuestra visión

To communicate your school's identity and values to a group of Spanish-speaking exchange students, create a poster or digital image incorporating your school logo, mascot, or seal, together with a short phrase or lists of words in Spanish that summarize the values your school seeks to transmit to students.

El escudo del Colegio Bilingüe San Agustín, la escuela de nuestro bloguero Isaac.

Mi progreso comunicativo

I can create a written presentation communicating school values.

Vive entre culturas

Un programa de hermandad con una escuela en Costa Rica

Essential questions:

- What places, people, and activities define student life?

- How is student life at my school similar to and/or different from student life at a school in Costa Rica?

Your school has decided to participate in a sister school program with a school in Costa Rica. Two schools are interested in linking with yours and have sent promotional videos.

Interpretive Assessment

📖 ✦ Paso 1: Los factores importantes

Before you watch the videos, study the list of aspects below. How important are these in your choice of a partner school? Rate each aspect on a scale of 1 (not important) to 5 (very important).

- programas bilingües

- las materias ofrecidas

- las aulas

- los laboratorios de ciencias

- el laboratorio de lenguas

- programas actualizados *(up-to-date),* como la robótica

- la calidad del personal *(staff)*

- las instalaciones deportivas *(sports)* y actividades físicas

- las actividades extra escolares *(extra-curricular)* y culturales

- las residencias estudiantiles

- la biblioteca

- la cafetería o soda

- la seguridad *(safety)*

- las zonas verdes

- la ubicación *(location)*

- los valores *(values)*

Paso 2: Nuestras opiniones

In groups of four, compare your answers in **Paso 1.** Identify five factors the group agrees are important.

Modelo

. . . .

Para mí, el/la _____ es importante.

Para mí, los/las _____ son importantes.

Paso 3: Dos escuelas en Costa Rica

Watch the videos from two Costa Rican schools. Using the graphic organizer from your Explorer course, check off the features that each school offers. Then use the information you gathered to decide which is a better partner school for you.

Interpersonal Assessment

¡Somos escuelas hermanas!

Your school has just initiated a sister school relationship with a school in Costa Rica. Each student in the Spanish program has been given an e-pal in your sister school. Write an email, following the guidelines in your Explorer course.

Presentational Assessment

Un día en mi vida escolar

To get to know each other better, you, your classmates, and students at your sister school in Costa Rica are going to share with each other **Un día en mi vida escolar** (*A Day in the Life of My School*). Create a PechaKucha-style visual presentation. Follow the instructions in Explorer.

UNIDAD 3
Mi familia es tu familia

Unit Goals

- Exchange information about home life and family.

- Interpret short texts about family structure and activities.

- Prepare and present a collection of images and descriptions to share information about your home, family, and friends.

- Explore traditions, languages, people, and the geography of Spain and Colorado.

Who makes up my family?

What places and activities bring us together as a family?

How is my family similar to and different from families in the Spanish-speaking world?

MARINA FERRARA HERNÁNDEZ, NUESTRA VIDEO BLOGUERA DE ESPAÑA

Family and traditions make us unique and define who we are. Often when you meet new people your age, you want to talk about your family and the things that you do together. In this unit, you will meet Marina from Spain, who will introduce you to her family through her video blog. You will also hear from other bloggers who will introduce you to their families and traditions.

Las relaciones intergeneracionales cambian con la tecnología.

La playa es un destino de vacaciones popular entre las familias españolas.

Comparaciones
🧭 España y Colorado

Personas por familias

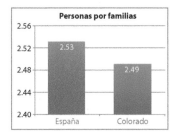

España	2.53
Colorado	2.49

España
47 millones

78% urbana

22% rural

 Colorado (Estados Unidos)

Los indígenas pueblo habitan Mesa Verde

La expedición de Coronado nombra la región "Colorado" por el color rojo del río

Fundación de la Universidad de Colorado

Colorado se une a los EE. UU. como estado No. 38

Helen Robinson

Helen Robinson: primera mujer elegida al Senado de Colorado

c. 600	1218	1492	c. 1540	1876	1898	1913

España

Fundación de la Universidad de Salamanca

Cristóbal Colón llega a las Américas

Guerra Hispano-estadounidense

Colorado
5 millones

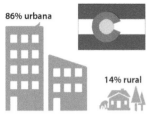

86% urbana

14% rural

COLORADO

ESPAÑA

Comienzos de la industria del esquí: estaciones en Estes Park, Loveland

La población hispana de Colorado alcanza el 20%

Los Broncos de Denver ganan el Super Tazón

1931	1936–1939	1975	1986	1992	2010	2014	2016

Clara Campoamor: primera mujer elegida al Parlamento de España

Guerra Civil Española

Muerte del dictador Franco; transición a la democracia

España entra en la Unión Europea

Juegos Olímpicos en Barcelona

Felipe VI a los 46 años, se convierte en el nuevo rey de España tras la abdicación de su padre, Juan Carlos I

Clara Campoamor

Actividad 1

Productos de España y Colorado

🔍 🌐 ⟲ Observe the images below. Which ones could represent aspects of family traditions or geography in Spain? Which ones represent your community, and which ones might be universal? Share your observations with a **compañero/a de clase** and then with the rest of the class.

Comunica

Essential Questions:

- Who makes up my family?
- What places and activities bring us together as a family?

Esta familia de Málaga, España, tiene tres hijos. ¿Cuántos hijos hay en tu familia?

Una madre enseña a sus hijos a hacer panellets, un postre típico catalán.

Video blog
Soy Marina

Actividad 2

Soy Marina, ¿os acordáis de mí?

🔍 💬 ✴️ **Paso 1: Preparación**

¿Os acordáis de *(do you remember)* Marina? Look at these photos from her album. Write three things you think she might mention in her video blog based on these photos and the captions.

1 *Hola, soy Marina. ¿Os acordáis de mí?*

2 *Tengo una familia mediana (medium-sized).*

3 *Mi gato se llama Billy.*

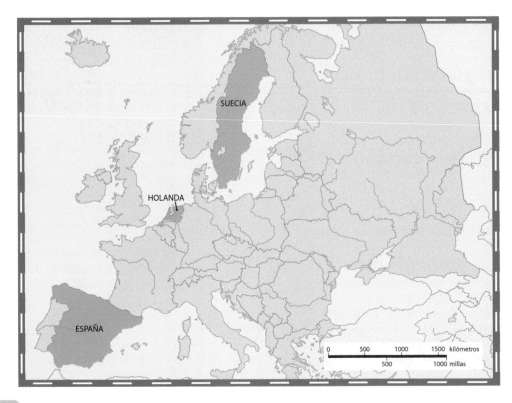

Marina tiene parientes en España, Holanda y Suecia. Miren estos países en este mapa de Europa. ¿Cómo se dicen en inglés?

◉ ✦ Paso 2: Escucha

1. What words do you know in Spanish to talk about members of the family? Make a list with a classmate.

2. Now compare your list with the one at the right. Before you listen to and view the video blog by Marina, confirm the meaning of all these words, and listen to your teacher's pronunciation of them so that you will recognize them when you hear them.

madre　　**hermana**

hermano

gato　　　**abuelos**

perro　　**padre**

3. Watch and listen to Marina's video blog. Which family members in the list does she mention?

📖 ◉ ✦ Paso 3: Resumen

Read the following sentences, and make sure you understand their meaning. Then, listen again to Marina's video blog, and indicate whether each statement is true or false, based on the photos you've seen and what she says. Correct the false information, listening to the blog again if you need to.

1. Marina vive *(lives)* con su padre y su madre.

2. Marina tiene tres hermanos.

3. Marina tiene un hermano mayor *(older)*.

4. La hermana de Marina vive en España.

5. Marina tiene un animal doméstico en la casa.

6. El hermano mayor de Marina vive en Suecia.

Casas antiguas en el centro de Madrid.

España, Holanda y Suecia son países miembros de la Unión Europea.

Así se dice 1
✤ Esta es mi familia

Una reunión familiar de Marina, la bloguera de España

Mi Familia

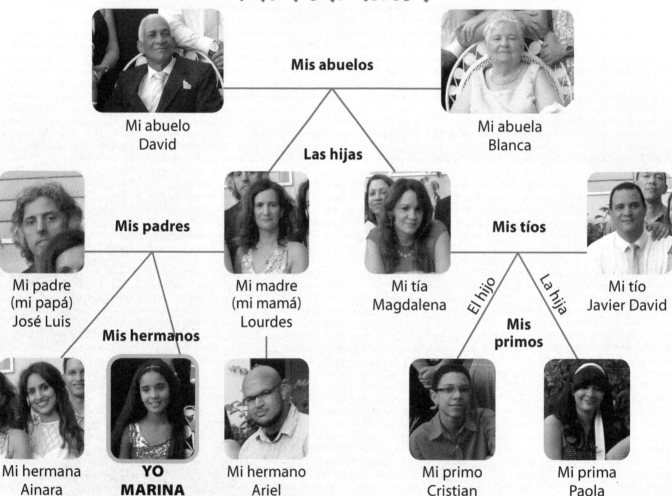

Mis abuelos

Mi abuelo
David

Mi abuela
Blanca

Las hijas

Mis padres

Mis tíos

Mi padre
(mi papá)
José Luis

Mi madre
(mi mamá)
Lourdes

Mi tía
Magdalena

Mi tío
Javier David

Mis hermanos

El hijo

La hija

Mis primos

Mi hermana
Ainara

**YO
MARINA**

Mi hermano
Ariel

Mi primo
Cristian

Mi prima
Paola

David es **el esposo** de Blanca, y Blanca es **la esposa** de David.

Marina es **la nieta** de Blanca y David, y Ariel es **su nieto**.

Cristian es **el sobrino** de Lourdes y José Luis,
y Paola es **su sobrina**.

Mi gato Billy

Actividad 3

🔍 🔤 ¿Quién es quién?

Decide if each sentence about Marina's family is true or false, based on the information in the family tree. Rewrite the false sentences to make them true.

1. José Luis es el padre de Marina.

2. Magdalena es la hermana de Lourdes.

3. Cristian es el primo de Paola.

4. Ariel es el hijo de Javier David.

5. Magdalena es la tía de Marina.

6. Blanca tiene cinco nietos.

7. Magdalena es la hija de Blanca.

8. Lourdes y José Luis son los abuelos de Cristian.

Actividad 4

Mi familia y tu familia

💬 Paso 1

Interview a classmate about his or her own family, a fictional family, or a famous family. Use the following questions:

1. ¿Tienes una familia grande, mediana o pequeña?

2. ¿Tienes abuelos? ¿Cómo son?

3. ¿Tienes hermanos? ¿Cuántos hermanos tienes?

4. ¿Tienes primos? ¿Cuántos primos tienes en total?

5. ¿Hay mascotas en tu casa? Si hay, ¿qué mascota tienes?

✍️ Paso 2

Sum up the information you found out about your classmate's family. Provide as much detail as you can.

Modelo

Emma tiene una familia pequeña. Tiene una hermana, y no tiene primos.

Mi progreso comunicativo

I can ask and tell about family members and pets.

Actividad 5

Una familia dominicana

🎧 Paso 1: ¿Qué escuchas?

Read the list of family words below, then listen as your teacher reads a note from Paola, our video blogger from la República Dominicana, in which she tells us about her family. Put a check mark next to the vocabulary words you hear in Paola's description.

1. __✓__ familia

2. __✓__ madre

3. __✓__ tíos

4. __✓__ gata

5. _____ perro

6. __✓__ hermano

7. __✓__ abuelos

8. __✓__ prima

9. _____ hermanos

10. _____ hijos

📹 📝 🧭 Paso 2: Conoce mejor a Paola

You heard your teacher read about Paola, and now you will hear Paola tell you about her family. As you watch the video, take notes in the graphic organizer provided in your *EntreCulturas 1* Explorer course. Share what you heard first with a partner, then with the class.

📹 🧭 Paso 3: Una sorpresa *(surprise)*

Paola tells us about an interesting family connection at the end of her description. To whom is she related?

Este abuelo juega con sus nietas en la Plaza de España (Sevilla).

 ⊕ **Paso 4: ¿Qué tienes en común con Paola?**

Write Paola an email in which you introduce your family or a fictional family to her and explain what the two families have in common.

Modelo

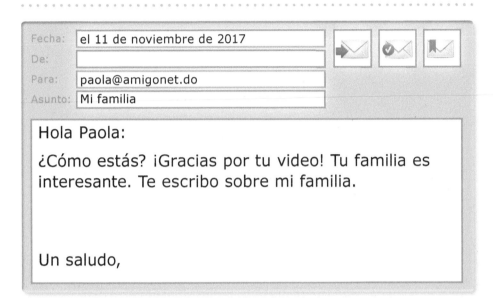

Fecha:	el 11 de noviembre de 2017
De:	
Para:	paola@amigonet.do
Asunto:	Mi familia

Hola Paola:

¿Cómo estás? ¡Gracias por tu video! Tu familia es interesante. Te escribo sobre mi familia.

Un saludo,

Mi progreso comunicativo

I can write simple messages to compare information about my family and others.

Esta madre soltera juega con su hija en el parque.

Enfoque cultural

Práctica cultural: Nuevos modelos de familia

From 1975 to the present, Spain transformed itself from a dictatorship to democracy and a member of the European Union (see timeline in the chapter opener). The traditional Catholic family of the 20th century is less common than before, and Spanish families resemble the structures we find in other European countries and the U.S. Divorce and remarriage are more frequent, and same-sex marriage is legal. **Familias monoparentales** *(single-parent families)* are growing in number, and **parejas de hecho** *(unmarried couples)* commonly head households and raise children.

Spanish has precise or legal vocabulary for the complex relationships in these new family models (left column below), but people tend to use labels that show the emotional relationship (right column):

el padrastro *(step-father)*	el esposo de mi madre
la madrastra *(step-mother)*	la esposa de mi padre
la pareja de hecho *(partner)*	la pareja de mi padre/madre
el hermanastro / la hermanastra *(step-brother/step-sister; half-brother/half-sister)*	mis hermanos / los hijos de mi padre/madre
el/la medio/a hermano/a *(half-brother/half-sister)*	mi hermano/a

 ⊕ **Conexiones**

What types of family structures have you seen depicted on television shows or in movies? How do the characters refer to family members? How do they compare to the Spanish equivalents?

Actividad 6

Mi nombre y apellidos

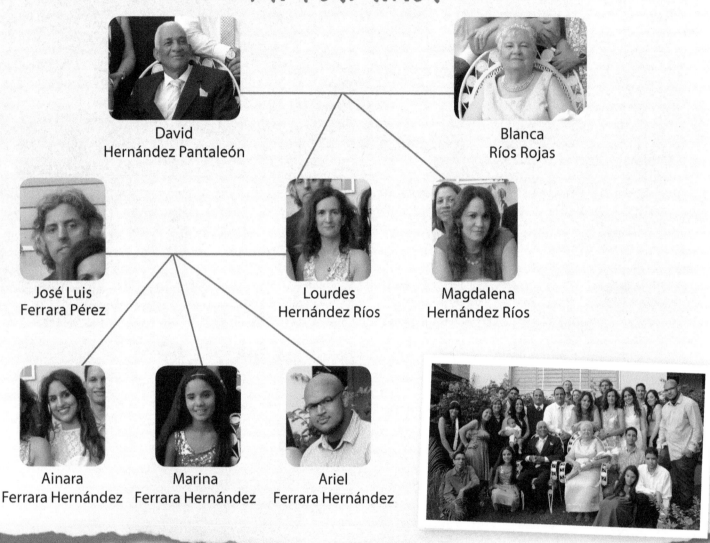

Mi Familia

David
Hernández Pantaleón

Blanca
Ríos Rojas

José Luis
Ferrara Pérez

Lourdes
Hernández Ríos

Magdalena
Hernández Ríos

Ainara
Ferrara Hernández

Marina
Ferrara Hernández

Ariel
Ferrara Hernández

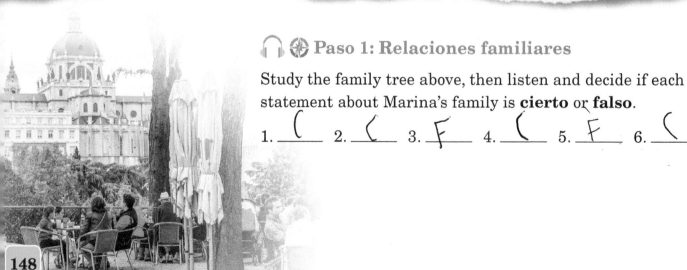

🎧 ✦ Paso 1: Relaciones familiares

Study the family tree above, then listen and decide if each statement about Marina's family is **cierto** or **falso**.

1. ___C___   2. ___C___   3. ___F___   4. ___C___   5. ___F___   6. ___C___

🔍 📖 Paso 2: Mis apellidos

Study the two last names of each person in the family tree. Can you find a pattern? What two names are children given in Spain? Read the **Enfoque cultural** on **Los apellidos** to confirm your answer.

Enfoque cultural

Práctica cultural: Los apellidos

In Spain and in many Latin American countries it is common to give a child two given names (**nombres**). For example, a girl named María Paula García Elizondo would go by "María Paula", and her nickname might be based on both names, "Maripau." María Paula's given names will be accompanied by her two surnames (**apellidos**)—first her father's family name (García, **el apellido paterno**), then her mother's (Elizondo, **el apellido materno**).

◇ ⊕ Conexiones

Do you know of anyone who uses both their mother's and father's last names? How is their complete name written? What local customs do you know about regarding how people get their names?

"Soy María Ángeles Sánchez Millán, o Marián. Mi bisabuela (great grandmother), en la foto, es María Ángeles Villalobos del Olmo. Mi abuela también se llama María Ángeles."

Reflexión intercultural

⊕ Are you named after family members of a previous generation? How do names of your family members and friends reflect family ties?

Otros miembros de la familia

el/la bebé   *baby*

el/la bisabuelo/a
great-grandfather/mother

el/la esposo/a
husband/wife

el/la sobrino/a
nephew/niece

DATOS PERSONALES:

1. Nombre	
2. Apellido paterno	
3. Apellido materno	
4. Fecha de nacimiento	
Día	
Mes	
Año	
5. Edad	
6. Sexo Varón ❑ Mujer ❑	

Mi progreso intercultural

I can understand how family and given names reflect identity in some Spanish-speaking cultures.

Expresiones útiles: Cómo describir a las personas

alegre
happy

callado/a
quiet

divertido/a
fun

educado/a
polite

gracioso/a
funny, comical

honesto/a

impaciente

mayor (que)
older (than)

menor (que)
younger (than)

ordenado/a
organized

serio/a

soltero/a
unmarried; single

Observa 1

¿Cómo son las personas de mi familia?

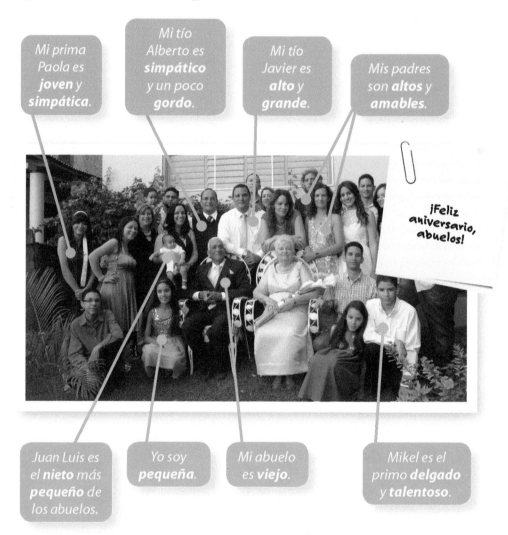

Mi prima Paola es **joven** y **simpática**.

Mi tío Alberto es **simpático** y un poco **gordo**.

Mi tío Javier es **alto** y **grande**.

Mis padres son **altos** y **amables**.

¡Feliz aniversario, abuelos!

Juan Luis es el **nieto** más **pequeño** de los abuelos.

Yo soy **pequeña**.

Mi abuelo es **viejo**.

Mikel es el primo **delgado** y **talentoso**.

¿Qué observas?

▶️ 🌐 Look at the words in bold that Marina uses to describe the members of her family. Can you figure out when to use *simpático* vs. *simpática*? *Pequeño* vs. *pequeña*? *Alto* vs. *altos*? Also, where are these descriptive words (adjectives) placed—before or after the noun they describe? Discuss the examples with your classmates and teachers, view the **Observa 1** resources for this unit in Explorer, and check the **Síntesis de gramática** at the end of this section of the unit.

Actividad 7

¿Cómo son?

📖 **Paso 1**

Combine a phrase from the left-hand column with a description in the right-hand column to make sentences that Marina could say about her family. ¡OJO! The descriptions are possible only if they agree in gender and number.

1. Mi familia
2. Mis hermanos
3. Mis tías
4. Mi abuela
5. Mis primos
6. Mi gato Billy

a. son altos.
b. es baja.
c. es dominicana.
d. son españoles.
e. son flacos.
f. es grande.
g. son mayores.
h. es menor que su hermano.
i. es pequeño.
j. son simpáticas.

✏️ **Paso 2**

Write sentences like those in **Paso 1** to reflect a fictional or famous family situation. You can use vocabulary from **Así se dice 1, Otros miembros de la familia,** or look up other words you need. Make sure you include adjectives that agree in gender and number with the nouns!

Estrategia

¿Cómo se dice?

If you don't know how to express an idea in Spanish, you can ask a bilingual speaker to give you the equivalent by using the question
¿Cómo se dice _____ en español?

If you don't understand a word in Spanish, a similar question can get you the translation you need:
¿Cómo se dice _____ en inglés?

Of course, these questions are not useful with monolingual Spanish speakers! Later on, we will study other strategies for getting your ideas across when you don't yet have all the vocabulary you need.

Detalle gramatical

Los adjetivos

You may have noticed already that Spanish adjectives (words that describe nouns) are just like articles in that they have more than one form: **Buenos días, buenas tardes**.

Most adjectives (like **bueno/a**) have four forms: **-o, -a, -os, -as**.

Adjectives that end in **-e** only have two endings (**-e, -es**); they do not distinguish masculine and feminine, showing only plural agreement:

Mis primas son inteligentes, y mis primos son súper altos.

These two patterns cover most adjectives in Spanish. See the **Síntesis de gramática** for a complete explanation.

Actividad 8

🎧 ✦ ¿De quién hablo?

Listen to the speaker describe different members of her family. Of the four possibilities below, who could she be referring to? Listen carefully to the gender and number of the adjective to figure it out. More than one answer may be possible!

a. La tía Maricarmen

b. El tío Alberto

c. Los abuelos

d. Las primas Sofía y Lucía

Modelo

....

(You hear)   Es simpática.

(Refers to)   La tía Maricarmen

1. ___*b*___   2. ___*c*___   3. ___*d*___

4. ___*b*___   5. ___*a*___   6. ___*d*___

Actividad 9

💬 Lluvia de adjetivos

Working in groups of four, one student chooses one of the images to the left and creates a phrase (article + noun + adjective) to describe it. The next person in the group has to repeat the first student's phrase and add an adjective. Then the next two students repeat the entire phrases as built so far and add additional descriptions. Take turns starting the game.

Modelo

....

Estudiante A: Los abuelos buen**os**

Estudiante B: Los abuelos mayor**es** y buen**os**

Estudiante C: Los abuelos mayor**es**, buen**os** y simpátic**os**

Estudiante D: Los abuelos mayor**es**, buen**os**, simpátic**os** y alegr**es**

Actividad 10

¿Conoces a estas familias?

How well do you know famous families? In this activity, you will write an anonymous description of a famous family - real or fictional. Then, your teacher will read descriptions out loud to see if the class can guess which family it is.

 Paso 1: Prepara tu descripción

Create your description by writing out the answers to the following questions. Do not use any names or other obvious identifying information.

1. ¿Cuántas personas hay en la familia?

2. ¿Quiénes son? (el padre, la hermana, etc.)

3. ¿Cuántos años tiene cada persona?

4. ¿Cómo son los miembros de la familia? Escribe una descripción, con adjetivos.

Paso 2: Adivina

Now listen as your teacher reads family descriptions at random. Can you identify your classmates' families?

Expresiones útiles: Descripciones físicas

Tiene el pelo rubio.
He/she has blond hair.

Tiene los ojos negros.
He/she has dark brown eyes.

azul *blue*
castaño/a *brown*
de color café *brown*
negro/a *black*
verde *green*

Es pelirrojo/a.
He/she is a red-head.

Es guapo/a.
He/she is handsome/pretty.

Es moreno/a.
He/she is dark-complected.

Mi progreso comunicativo

I can describe the members of my family.

Enfoque cultural

Perspectiva cultural: Familias icónicas

Conexiones

Esta es la familia real *(royal family)* de España. Felipe VI es rey de España desde *(since)* 2014. Hay cuatro personas en la familia del rey. Felipe es el padre. Es delgado y muy alto. Su esposa se llama Letizia. Es joven es rubia y atlética. Tienen dos hijas, Leonor y Sofía. La abuela de las niñas también está en la foto, y también se llama Sofía.

What prominent families are in the public eye in your community?

Así se dice 2

✥ Mi casa, mi hogar

Mi hogar ideal es…

1 una casa

2 un apartamento o piso

Mi casa ideal está en…

3 la ciudad

4 el pueblo

5 el campo

6 el barrio

7 una calle tranquila

8 una avenida

La casa de mis sueños tiene…

9 una cocina grande y moderna

10 un comedor para las fiestas familiares

11 una sala informal, con espacio para la pantalla plana

12 dos baños grandes

13 un dormitorio para cada persona de la familia

14 una terraza con vistas

15 un jardín

16 un garaje para el coche

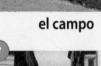

Enfoque cultural

Práctica cultural: Los espacios donde vivimos

The names of the parts of a house vary across the Spanish-speaking world:

Dónde vivimos
piso/apartamento/departamento

Lugares para dormir
el dormitorio/la habitación/el cuarto

Espacios que compartimos *(we share)*
la sala (de estar)/el salón/el líving (Argentina, Chile)
el patio/el jardín/el solar/la yarda (U.S.)

Los edificios altos

la planta baja	*bottom/ground floor*
la primera *(first)* planta	*second floor*

In some cases the variants are regional synonyms, but in others they reveal interesting details about the local culture. For example, **la yarda** in U.S. Spanish refers to a typical North American suburban yard. Since most Spaniards live in **pisos**, with no outdoor green space of their own, **el jardín** in Spain suggests a public park or common garden area. In Costa Rica or Venezuela, **el solar** is the green space around a freestanding house.

Conexiones

Which parts of the houses/apartments in your community are unique to the culture or region? How does the design of houses/apartments in the community affect how people interact with family and neighbors?

Actividad 11

¿Dónde en la casa?

List the parts of the house where you can do each activity.

1. estudiar
2. comer
3. hablar por teléfono
4. mirar películas
5. tocar un instrumento
6. jugar videojuegos
7. navegar por internet
8. bailar
9. convivir *(be together)* con la familia
10. estar solo/a *(alone)*

La casa estilo ranch es típica de muchas ciudades norteamericanas. Viene de la casa de un rancho del oeste de Estados Unidos.

Actividad 12

 ¿Quién vive aquí?

Which dwellings in the left-hand columns would be good for the people at the right? There may be more than one option.

1. un piso de un dormitorio en la ciudad

2. una casa de cuatro habitaciones en el campo

3. un apartamento con dos baños

4. un piso con garaje y un parque en el barrio

a. una familia con tres hijos

b. una mujer soltera

c. una pareja mayor

d. un estudiante de 22 años

e. un padre soltero con dos hijas

Enfoque cultural

Práctica cultural: Salir del "nido del hogar" *(Leaving the nest)*

En muchos países hispanohablantes, los hijos pueden vivir en casa de sus padres hasta *(until)* terminar la universidad. No hay mucha presión por salir del hogar e independizarse. En muchas ocasiones los hijos de 30 años todavía viven en casa.

⟲ ✦ Conexiones

What is the custom in your community? Typically, how old are young people when they become independent? What are the reasons for leaving home?

Mi progreso intercultural

I can compare across cultures who makes up a family and how long people live together at home.

Reflexión intercultural

✦ How long do you plan to live at home with your parents? Interview adult family members and acquaintances to find out what motivated them to leave home. How do those experiences compare with what you have learned about young people in the Spanish-speaking world?

Record your reflections in the forum in Explorer and comment on three classmates' posts.

Actividad 13

La casa de Paola

 Paso 1

Watch Paola, the blogger from Santo Domingo, la República Dominicana, as she gives a video tour of her house, without the sound. Write down as many details in Spanish as you can about what you think she may be saying.

 Paso 2

Now watch and listen to Paola's tour, to see how many details you were able to predict in **Paso 1**.

Actividad 14

Una nueva casa

🎧 Paso 1

Susana has just moved into a new apartment, and she describes it in the conversation with her friend Eva. Listen and indicate which elements on the list she mentions.

el baño   el comedor

la cocina   el dormitorio de Susana

el garaje   el patio

la terraza

🎧 Paso 2

Listen again, and describe in detail the elements of the house Susana mentions.

Expresiones útiles: Hablando de la familia

Viven cerca de mí.
They live close to me.

Viven lejos de mí.
They live far away from me.

Nos vemos mucho/poco.
We see each other a lot/ little.

Mi progreso comunicativo

I can ask and answer questions about family members and where they live.

Actividad 15

¿Dónde viven tus parientes?

 Paso 1

Answer the following questions about your extended family members. If you do not have an extended family, answer with information about a family that you know well.

1. ¿Dónde viven? ¿A qué distancia de tu casa están?

2. ¿En qué tipo de casa viven?

3. ¿Quiénes viven en la casa?

4. ¿Cuántos años tienen los hijos que viven en la casa?

 Paso 2

Compare your answers with those of five other classmates. Are there any patterns? Summarize them in Spanish to present to the class.

Modelo

En general, mis abuelos/tíos/primos viven cerca/lejos de mí.

Actividad 16

¡Vamos a compartir *(share)* casa!

Paso 1: Los elementos importantes

You are going to share a vacation house with a Spanish-speaking friend and his/her family. Working on your own, make a list of five elements (rooms or features) that you absolutely must have in your house. Look up any additional vocabulary you need, or ask your teacher.

Paso 2: ¡Negociemos!

Working with a partner, role play and negotiate a common list of five things that you will have in a house that you will share. Use the **Expresiones útiles** to negotiate with them.

Mi progreso comunicativo

I can talk about where I live.

Expresiones útiles: Cómo llegar a una solución común

Yo prefiero ____.
I prefer ____.

Mi propia habitación
My own room

Para mí es importante ____.
For me ____ is important.

¿Qué tal si tenemos…?
What if we have…?

¡No seas tonto/a!
Don't be silly!

De acuerdo.
Agreed.

Susana tiene razón.
Susana is right.

Observa 2
¿Dónde está?

La terraza está **al fondo** del piso.

El dormitorio está **detrás** del baño.

La sala está **al lado** de la cocina.

La cocina está **a la derecha** de la entrada.

El baño está **a la izquierda** de la entrada.

El pasillo está **en medio** del piso.

¿Qué observas?

Look at the words in bold in these descriptions. Can you figure out the meaning of the location words (prepositions)? Use the drawing to help you infer the meaning. What verb is used with these prepositions to express location? Discuss the examples with your classmates and teacher, view the **Observa 2** resources for this unit in Explorer.

Actividad 17

🔤 El diseño perfecto

What is the most logical place for these rooms in a house? Combine these sentence fragments to make logical sentences, adding the appropriate places after the preposition. Be careful when you combine **a** or **de** + the article **el**.

los baños		al fondo de
la cocina		al lado de
el comedor		a la derecha de
el dormitorio de los padres		a la izquierda de
el dormitorio de los adolescentes	está	detrás de
el dormitorio de los niños pequeños	están	en medio de
el patio		
la terraza		

Modelo

La cocina está al lado del comedor.

Detalle gramatical: El verbo estar

You have already seen some forms of the verb **estar** in greetings (**¿Cómo estás? Estoy bien.**) It is also used to express the location of things and people:

El baño **está** cerca del dormitorio.
The bathroom is near the bedroom.

Mis abuelos **están** en la cocina con mamá.
My grandparents are in the kitchen with Mom.

Below are the present tense forms of **estar**:

estoy	estamos
estás	estáis
está	están

Detalle gramatical: Las contracciones

The prepositions **a** and **de** combine with the masculine singular article **el** to form contractions:

a + el = al

de + el = del

Está a la derecha **del** comedor.
It's to the right of the dining room.

Hay una hamaca **al** fondo de la terraza.
There's a hammock at the rear of the terrace.

Note that the other articles do not form contractions: **a la, de los,** etc.

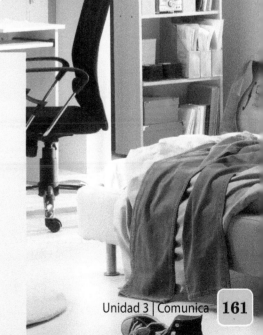

Actividad 18

¿Qué casa es?

Working in groups of four, take turns describing these floor plans in Spanish. As you describe one, your partners will try to guess which one it is, then switch roles.

Bougainvillea, rural Spain

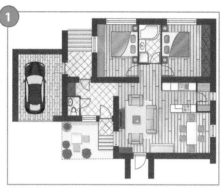

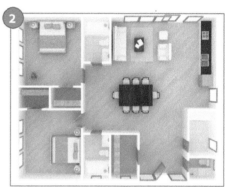

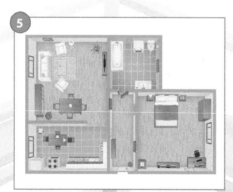

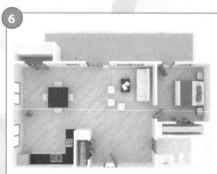

Actividad 19

La casa de mis sueños (dreams)

 Paso 1

Draw a rough floor plan of your dream house or apartment, and label the rooms in Spanish.

Paso 2

Work with a **compañero/a**, but don't show him/her your floor plan. Take turns asking and answering questions to see if each of you can reproduce the other's design.

Modelo

. . . .

Estudiante A: ¿Qué hay en tu casa?

Estudiante B: Hay _____, _____ y _____.

. . . .

Estudiante A: ¿Dónde está _____?

Estudiante B: Está al lado/a la derecha/etc. de la cocina.

Actividad 20

Preguntas importantes

You are going to live with a Spanish family for three weeks in the summer. You like all the families you have the option of staying with, but their housing options are very different. What questions would you ask to find out the information important to you about a place to live? Write as many different questions as you can.

Modelo

. . . .

¿Tiene _____?

¿Hay _____?

¿Cuántos/cuántas _____ tiene?

¿Dónde está _____?

¿Está cerca/lejos de _____?

Mi progreso comunicativo

I can talk about places in the house.

Ask questions to keep a conversation going.

⊛ Estrategias

Conversation strategies

Practice talking about your family, so that when you meet Spanish speakers, you can converse with confidence. Have some pictures to share, and be sure to ask lots of questions to keep the conversation going. Watch the Conversation Strategies video in your Explorer course for more tips!

Así se dice 3

✦ ¿Qué te gustaría hacer mañana?

andar en bicicleta

ayudar a los abuelos

comer juntos

dar un paseo

explorar la ciudad

hacer deporte

ir al cine

salir con amigos

ver la televisión

Además se dice

Otras actividades

asistir a conciertos
go to concerts

correr
run/jog

hacer camping
go camping

leer cómics
read comics

hacer tareas domésticas:
do chores:

cuidar a los niños *babysit, watch the kids*	poner la mesa *set the table*
dar de comer a los animales *feed the animals*	ir de compras *go shopping*
hacer la cama *make the bed*	

merendar
have a snack

nadar en la piscina
swim in the pool

pasear al perro
walk the dog

visitar museos
visit museums

Actividad 21

🔤 ¿Qué actividad es?

Which activity is associated with the items in each list below?

1. hamburguesa, pizza, paella, bocadillo *(sandwich)*

2. *Los juegos del hambre: Sinsajo, Hobbit: La batalla de los cinco ejércitos, La trilogía Divergente: Leal*

3. correr, andar en bicicleta, jugar al básquetbol

4. preparar la comida, hacer la cama, limpiar la cocina

5. el parque, las calles, el tráfico

6. programas, anuncios *(commercials)*, series

La paella es un plato icónico de España.

Actividad 22

Actividades que me gustan

✺ Paso 1: ¿Con quién haces las actividades?

Make three lists of activities: (1) things you like to do alone, (2) things you do with friends, and (3) things you do with your family. Which activities are on all three lists?

📝 Paso 2: ¿Adónde vas para hacer esta actividad?

Where could one go to do the activities in **Paso 1**? Choose a logical place from this list, or add other ideas of your own.

al parque	a la casa de los amigos	a la casa de los abuelos
a mi habitación	al gimnasio	al cine
a una reserva natural	al centro de la ciudad	

Modelo

....

Voy **al parque** para andar en bicicleta.

Voy **a la casa de mis amigos** para leer cómics juntos.

Detalle gramatical: El verbo *ir*

The verb **ir** *(to go)* has the present tense forms below:

voy	vamos
vas	vais
va	van

It is frequently used with the preposition **a** and a place to tell where one is going, and the preposition **para** plus infinitive to tell the purpose of the trip:

Voy al gimnasio para hacer ejercicio.
I go to the gym to work out.

Expresiones útiles: Un deseo para el futuro

You have already learned to express your general likes and dislikes with **(no) me gusta**. The phrase **me gustaría** (*I would like*) is used to talk about a desire or wish for the future:

Me gustaría salir con mis amigos el viernes.
I'd like to go out with my friends on Friday.

¿Te gustaría ir con nosotros?
Would you like to go with us?

Mi progreso comunicativo

I can propose activities to do with others.

Paso 3: ¿Qué te gustaría hacer el fin de semana?

Ask three **compañeros/as** which of the activities in **Paso 1** they would like to do this weekend. If they answer yes, ask a follow up question to find out who they would like to do the activity with or where they'd like to go.

Modelo

Estudiante A: Este fin de semana, ¿te gustaría dar un paseo?

Estudiante B: Sí, me gustaría mucho./No, no me gustaría.

Estudiante A: ¿Con quién?

Estudiante B: Me gustaría dar un paseo con mis amigos.

Estudiante A: ¿Dónde?

Estudiante B: Me gustaría dar un paseo con mis amigos en el parque.

Actividad 23

¡Llegan las vacaciones!

Paso 1: Las actividades

Read the list of vacation activities. Which ones do you think Juan Carlos, a fifteen-year-old Spaniard, would like to do on his next vacation?

1. andar en bicicleta
2. ayudar en casa
3. comer
4. cuidar a los niños
5. dar de comer a las mascotas (*pets*)
6. dar un paseo
7. explorar los parques
8. ir de compras
9. hacer la tarea
10. pintar
11. preparar la comida
12. poner la mesa
13. ver la televisión

⊛ **Paso 2: Las vacaciones de Juan Carlos**

Listen to Juan Carlos talk about his vacation, and list the activities you hear. Were your predictions correct?

 Paso 3: Tus vacaciones

Now write at least six sentences about what you would like to do on the next school break. Where would you like to go? Who would you like to do the activities with?

Modelo

. . . .

Durante las próximas vacaciones, <u>me gustaría explorar</u> un parque nacional con mi familia.

Actividad 24

Mi fin de semana ocupado *(busy)*

Paso 1: ¿Vamos al cine?

Your cousins want you to go to the movies this weekend. Your parents have agreed to let you go once that you finish all your chores. List your obligations during the week and on the weekend, using the expression **tener que** + infinitive.

Mis obligaciones en la semana	Mis obligaciones los fines de semana

 Paso 2: Preguntas y respuestas

Compare your list of chores with those of three classmates. Who has to do more?

Modelo

. . . .

Estudiante A: ¿Qué tienes que hacer en la casa?

Estudiante B: Tengo que pasear al perro todos los días.

Expresiones útiles: Obligaciones y excusas

The most common way to express obligations and chores is with the expression **tener que** + *infinitive*:

Tengo que ayudar en la casa.
I have to help around the house.

Notice that we conjugate only the first verb (**tener → tengo/tienes**/etc.) to show who has the obligation or intention, while the second verb remains in the infinitive.

These phrases are also useful in giving excuses:

Lo siento.
I'm sorry.

No puedo.
I can't.

Tengo que estudiar.
I have to study.

Tengo que cuidar a mi hermano menor.
I have to watch my little brother.

Observa 3

¿Qué hacen los españoles en familia?

Según varias encuestas, las familias españolas participan en una variedad de actividades cuando están juntos:

> 66 *Los viernes* ***cenamos*** *juntos y* ***vemos*** *películas en casa. Los sábados mi hermano y yo* ***leemos*** *cómics.* 99

Alejandro Muñoz Losada, 16 años

> 66 ***Salimos*** *con amigos o parientes los sábados, y los domingos* ***comemos*** *con los abuelos.* 99

Carmen Sánchez Carballo, 15 años

> 66 *Somos muy activos.* ***Hacemos*** *manualidades y* ***jugamos*** *deportes.* 99

Nerea Acuña Núñez, 14 años

Otras respuestas:

> "***Nadamos*** *en la piscina,* ***hacemos*** *camping o* ***vamos*** *de picnic".*

> "***Hacemos*** *tareas domésticas—* ***limpiamos*** *la casa,* ***organizamos*** *cosas…"*

> "*No* ***hacemos*** *nada. Mi familia es muy aburrida".*

> "***Visitamos*** *museos y* ***asistimos*** *a conciertos de música actual".*

Pero los gustos varían con la edad:

Los niños de 6 a 12 años **ven** películas en casa.

Los adolescentes **usan** videojuegos y consolas, o **salen** con sus amigos.

Los padres **visitan** museos o **asisten** a conciertos.

¿Qué observas?

🧭 Look at the verbs in bold in the quotes, which tell us that the people doing the actions are **nosotros**. Can you figure out the pattern of when to use the **-amos**, **-emos** or **-imos** endings? (Hint: Make sure you know how to spell the infinitive of each verb.) Now look at the **ellos** form of verbs that end in **-an**, **-en**. What patterns do you see here? Discuss the examples with your classmates and teachers, view the **Observa 3** resources for this unit in Explorer, and check the **Síntesis de gramática** at the end of this section of the unit.

Actividad 25

¿Quién lo hace?

  Paso 1: Las actividades

Listen to these sentences, which describe activities that different people do. Tell who does each one by naming the subject pronoun that corresponds to the verb you hear: **yo, tú, ella, nosotros, vosotros, ellos.**

1. _____ 2. _____ 3. _____ 4. _____

5. _____ 6. _____ 7. _____ 8. _____

Paso 2: ¿Con quién?

Listen to each sentence again, and based on the activity, add a phrase that tells who the speaker might do the activity with.

Modelo

....

(*you hear*) Comes en restaurantes baratos…

(*you write*) con los amigos.

Detalle gramatical: Formas irregulares de YO

Some verbs have an irregular form in the first person singular **(yo)**. You have already seen some of these in previous lessons. The verbs in bold below have regular forms for the other persons in the present tense.

- **dar: doy** (das, da,…)
- estar: estoy
- **hacer: hago** (haces, hace,…)
- ir: voy
- **poner: pongo** (pones, pone,…)
- **salir: salgo** (sales, sale,…)
- ser: soy
- **ver: veo** (ves, ve,…)

Even though these forms are irregular, do you see two different patterns?

Expresiones útiles: Para obtener más información

¿A qué hora?

¿Con qué frecuencia?

¿Con quién?

¿Cuándo?

¿Dónde?

¿Qué más?

Me gusta leer cómics con mi hermana.

Actividad 26

¡Firma aquí!

 Paso 1

Find at least five classmates who can answer **sí** to any of these questions. For each **sí** answer, ask that person at least one follow-up question to get more information. Keep careful records of how your classmates answer the questions; you will need the information in **Paso 2**.

1. ¿Asistes a muchos conciertos?

2. ¿Haces deporte todos los días?

3. ¿Sales a bailar?

4. ¿Comes en restaurantes elegantes?

5. ¿Cenas tarde?

6. ¿Lees cómics?

7. ¿Corres los fines de semana?

8. ¿Ves pelis (películas) en la computadora?

9. ¿Vas de compras con amigos?

10. ¿Visitas a tus parientes?

Paso 2

Sum up the information from **Paso 1**: Who are you most/least compatible with? Write at least two sentences to explain your conclusion. Present your conclusions orally to the class.

Modelo

Mark y yo asistimos a muchos conciertos, leemos cómics y hacemos mucho deporte. Somos compatibles.

Lauren cena con la familia todos los días, pero yo no ceno con mi familia. Lauren asiste a conciertos, pero no me gusta la música. No somos muy compatibles.

Actividad 27

Comparando familias

▶️ 🧭 Paso 1: Los blogueros con su familia

View and listen to Christian, María Laura, and Isaac talk about their family members, their homes, and the activities they do with their families. As you listen, list the family members mentioned and the activities they do together.

◯◯ 📧 🧭 Paso 2: Familias similares

Listen to the videos again, and identify the family that is most similar to yours or to a famous family of your choosing. What activities do they share? Write a short email to one of the video bloggers and tell about your family or the famous family you selected.

CHRISTIAN MARÍA LAURA ISAAC

Fecha:
De:
Para:
Asunto:

Expresiones útiles: ¿Con qué frecuencia?

a veces
sometimes

dos veces
(twice)

frecuentemente
often

nunca
never

siempre
always

todos los días
every day

una vez (por semana)
once (a week)

🧭 Mi progreso comunicativo

I can understand basic descriptions of families and the activities they do together.

Actividad 28

📖 Una encuesta nacional

Surveys of how Spanish families spend time together have shown the following results. What do you think is true for most families that you know or families in your community? Reorder the list and add any items that you think necessary to reflect what you think is true for your region or country.

Ver películas en casa	64%
Cenar juntos	48%
Leer juntos	45%
Hacer manualidades (pintamos, coloreamos, trabajamos con arcilla, etc.)	35%
Comer con los abuelos o parientes los fines de semana	34%
Salir con amigos o parientes	31%
Jugar a deportes (tenis, básquet, natación, etc.)	30%
Asistir a conciertos de música clásica	8%

Reflexión intercultural

✏️ ✺ Using what you have learned, compare your family's activities to those of Spanish families. Be careful to contrast the verb forms to be clear about who does what.

Modelo

....

Muchas familias españolas ven películas juntos, pero en mi familia no vemos películas con frecuencia.

Vacaciones en familia

Ubicado en la base de las importantes Montañas Rocallosas, Denver es una de las ciudades jóvenes más excitantes para explorar. Recorra el centro por el área peatonal de una milla de largo bordeada por tiendas, cafés al aire libre, restaurantes y centros nocturnos. Escuche un concierto bajo las estrellas en el Anfiteatro Red Rocks. Vea la obra maestra arquitectónica de Daniel Libeskind en el Museo de Arte de Denver. Descubra, en los restaurantes del vecindario, la innovadora cocina de Colorado, que va de fusión latina y platillos del suroeste a filetes de búfalo. Si se trata de compras, deportes y vida nocturna, **la vibrante ciudad**, capital de Colorado, lo tiene todo.

"Es difícil encontrar un lugar más bello que Denver, Colorado."
Global Traveler Magazine

VISITDENVER.COM

📖 Paso 1: ¿Qué podemos hacer en Denver?

You are helping to plan a family trip to Denver, Colorado. Skim the travel ad, and tell which of the activities are suggested in the text.

- acampar en las montañas
- comer al aire libre *(outdoors)*
- dar un paseo
- escuchar música
- esquiar
- explorar la arquitectura

- hacer deporte
- ir de compras
- sacar *(take)* fotos
- salir de noche
- visitar los museos

💬 Paso 2: Recomendaciones para la familia

What activities would different members of a family like to do in Denver? Use the models to describe your family, or a famous family of your choosing, and tell about their preferences.

Modelo

Mi madre es muy activa. Le gustaría hacer deporte.
Mi hermana Lupe es intelectual. Le gustaría visitar los museos.
Mi hermano come mucho. Le gustaría ir a restaurantes.

Síntesis de gramática

Los adjetivos

Adjectives (words that describe nouns) must change their form in Spanish to agree with the gender and number of the noun they refer to. **Primas** is feminine plural, so **dominicanas** shows a feminine (**a**) and plural (**s**) ending. This rule holds whether the noun and adjective are next to each other in the sentence or further apart:

<u>Las primas</u> <u>dominicanas</u> viven en Santo Domingo.
The Dominican cousins live in Santo Domingo.

<u>Las primas</u> de Sebastián son <u>dominicanas</u>.
Sebastian's cousins are Dominican.

Adjectives change their endings in three different ways. When you learn a new adjective, you should also learn which of the three groups it belongs to.

1. Group 1 adjectives have four different forms: **-o, -a, -os, -as**. The masculine singular ends in **-o**, and in this book, these adjectives are indicated in lists with **/a**.

   Tengo dos primos dominican<u>os</u> y una prima cuban<u>a</u>.
   I have two Colombian cousins and one Cuban cousin.

2. Group 2 adjectives only have two forms, singular and plural; they do not distinguish masculine and feminine. For the plural form, add **-s** to a final vowel and **-es** to a final consonant:

   Mi casa es <u>colonial</u>, y hay muchos edificios <u>coloniales</u> en el barrio.
   My house is colonial style, and there are many colonial buildings in the neighborhood.

3. Group 3 adjectives end in a consonant. To form the feminine and plural forms, add **-a, -es, as**.

   Mis tíos son español<u>es</u>, pero sus esposas son frances<u>as</u>.
   My uncles are Spanish, but their wives are French.

There are two other things you should notice about adjectives:

1. Unlike in English, descriptive adjectives in Spanish are usually placed after the noun:

   mi primo <u>chileno</u>   tus abuelos <u>españoles</u>
   my Chilean cousin   *your Spanish grandparents*

However, some common adjectives can also go before the noun. In the case of **bueno** and **malo**, the masculine singular form loses its final **-o** to give **buen**, **mal**:

un **buen** barrio	una **mala** casa
un barrio **bueno**	una casa **mala**

2. In sentences in which one adjective describes both masculine and feminine nouns, the adjective must be in the masculine plural form:

Tengo dos pri<u>mos</u> y tres sobri<u>nas</u> argenti<u>nos</u>.
I have two Argentine cousins and three Argentine nieces.

Los verbos (presente del indicativo)

So far you have seen the complete conjugations of all regular verbs (**-ar, -er, -ir**) in the present tense:

preparar		**comer**		**vivir**	
preparo	preparamos	como	comemos	vivo	vivimos
preparas	*preparáis*	comes	*coméis*	vives	*vivís*
prepara	preparan	come	comen	vive	viven

Irregular verbs deviate from these patterns, sometimes only in the first person singular (**yo**). But even very irregular verbs (**estar, ir**) have recognizable patterns that will help you remember the forms.

dar		**estar**		**hacer**	
doy	damos	estoy	estamos	hago	hacemos
das	*dais*	estás	*estáis*	haces	*hacéis*
da	dan	está	están	hace	hacen

ir		**salir**		**ver**	
voy	vamos	salgo	salimos	veo	vemos
vas	*vais*	sales	*salís*	ves	*veis*
va	van	sale	salen	ve	ven

Remember that the **vosotros/as** form is used only in Spain and is a strong marker of Spanish identity. Note also that if the verb form is only one syllable, a written accent mark is not used. The forms for **vos** (singular, used instead of **tú** in Argentina, Uruguay, Paraguay, Central America) are **das, estás, hacés, vas, salís, ves**.

Vocabulario

I can ask and tell about family members, pets, and their personal characteristics (Así se dice 1)

Esta es mi familia	*This is my family*
¿Quiénes son?	*Who are they?*

el/la abuelo/a	*grandfather/grandmother*
el apellido	*surname*
el/la bebé	*baby*
el/la bisabuelo/a	*great-grandfather/mother*
el/la esposo/a	*husband/wife*
el gato	*cat*
el/la hijo/a	*son/daughter*
el/la hermano/a	*brother/sister*
la madre	*mother*
la mascota	*pet*
el/la nieto/a	*grandson/granddaughter*
el nombre	*(given) name*
el padre	*father*
los padres	*the parents*
el perro	*dog*
el/la primo/a	*cousin*
el/la sobrino/a	*nephew/niece*
el/la tío/a	*uncle/aunt*

¿Cómo son?	*What are they like?*

Características físicas

alto/a	*tall*
amable	*nice; kind*
delgado/a	*thin*
gordo/a	*fat*
grande	*big*
joven	*young*
pequeño/a	*small*
viejo/a	*old*

Otras características

alegre	*happy*
callado/a	*quiet*
divertido/a	*fun*
educado/a	*polite*
gracioso/a	*funny; comical*
honesto/a	*honest*
impaciente	*impatient*
mayor (que)	*older (than)*
menor (que)	*younger (than)*
ordenado/a	*organized*
serio/a	*serious*
simpático/a	*friendly*
soltero/a	*unmarried; single*
talentoso/a	*talented*

Expresiones útiles

La descripción física

Es guapo/a	*He is handsome/She is pretty*	**Tiene los ojos…**	*He/she has… eyes*
Es moreno/a	*He/She is dark complected*	**azul**	*blue*
Tiene el pelo rubio	*He/she has blond hair*	**castaño/a**	*brown*
Tiene el pelo oscuro	*He/she has dark hair*	**de color café**	*brown*
Es rubio/a	*He/she is blond(e)*	**negro/a**	*black*
Es pelirrojo/a	*He/she is a red-head*	**verde**	*green*

I can talk about where I live (Así se dice 2)

Mi casa, mi hogar

el apartamento	apartment
el baño	bathroom
la casa	the house
la cocina	kitchen
el comedor	dining room
el dormitorio	bedroom
el garaje	garage
el jardín	garden; yard
el patio	patio
el piso	floor; flat; apartment (Spain)
la sala	living room
la terraza	terrace

¿Dónde está la casa?

a la derecha (de)	to the right (of)
a la izquierda (de)	to the left (of)
al fondo (de)	in the back (of)
al lado (de)	beside
detrás (de)	behind
en medio (de)	in the middle (of)
en una avenida	on a main street
en el barrio	in the neighborhood
en el campo	in the country
en la ciudad	in the city
en una calle tranquila	on a quiet street
en el pueblo	in the town

Obligaciones y excusas

Tengo que + infinitive	I have to (verb)
Lo siento.	I'm sorry.
No puedo.	I can't.

I can talk about activities that I do with my family and friends (Así se dice 3)

¿Qué te gustaría hacer?	What would you like to do?
andar en bicicleta	to ride a bicycle
ayudar	to help
cenar	to eat dinner; supper
comer juntos	to eat together
dar un paseo	to go for a walk/ride
explorar la ciudad/el campo	to explore the city/the country
hacer ejercicio	to get exercise
jugar deportes	to play sports
ir al cine	to go to the movies
salir con amigos	to go out with friends
ver la televisión/una película	to watch television/a movie

¿Con qué frecuencia? How often?

siempre	always
todos los días	every day
frecuentemente	frequently; often
a veces	sometimes
una vez (por semana)	once (a week)
dos veces	twice
nunca	never

Expresiones útiles: Cómo llegar a una solución común

Yo prefiero…	I prefer…
Mi propia habitación	My own room
Para mí es importante…	For me… is important.
¿Qué tal si tenemos…?	What if we have…?
¡No seas tonto/a!	Don't be silly!
De acuerdo.	Agreed.
Susana tiene razón.	Susana is right.

En camino

Mi progreso comunicativo

I can talk about family members and pets.

Actividad 30

Conversaciones entre amigos

 Paso 1

Choose five family members from the table below and fill in the grid with the information requested.

Miembro de la familia	Nombre y apellido	Edad	Descripción física	Descripción de personalidad
La madre/el padre				
El hermano/ la hermana				
El abuelo/la abuela				
El primo/la prima				
El tío/la tía				
La mascota				

 Paso 2

Using the information in **Paso 1,** present the family to a **compañero/a de clase**. Use complete sentences.

Actividad 31

Y tu casa, ¿cómo es?

Paso 1

How many questions can you write to inquire about a family's house and the activities taking place at home? Use as many interrogative words as you can to elicit details: **¿Qué? ¿Cómo? ¿Dónde? ¿Cuándo? ¿Cuántos/Cuántas?**

 Paso 2

Take turns with a **compañero/a de clase** asking the questions you have written. Answer his/her questions as fully as you can.

Actividad 32

Nuestras actividades nos definen como familia

▶ ✦ **Paso 1**

Watch and listen to Melissa talk about typical activities that families do in Colombia. List the items she mentions in the appropriate columns.

Mi progreso comunicativo

I can identify and interpret familiar words when I hear a person talk about his or her family.

	Lugares típicos	Actividades que hago allí
Melissa de Colombia		
Yo		

◯◯ ✦ **Paso 2**

Using the graphic organizer in Explorer, share information about places and activities in your community. Then compare family activities in both communities following the model below.

Modelo

En Colombia las familias van a _____ para hacer ejercicio, pero en mi comunidad las familias _____.

En Colombia las familias van a _____ para ver películas. En mi comunidad a las familias les gusta

_____.

Mi progreso comunicativo

I can write phrases and simple sentences to compare and contrast family activities.

Explora

Essential Question: How is my family similar to and different from some families in the Spanish-speaking world?

Overview

Family is one of the most important components of our life. In this segment you will explore the work of a poet from Spain and an artist from the U.S. to discover their perspectives on how family unites generations. You'll also hear from some Spanish families who are reaching out to share their home and promote language learning and cultural understanding through a family-based intercultural exchange.

La familia une las generaciones

Ana Serna Vara, de España, es escritora de libros para niños. Este poema se encuentra en su libro *Los superabuelos y sus nietos,* 1994.

Actividad 33

Poema: *Manuela mi abuela*

📖 Paso 1: Nuestros abuelos

Before reading the poem, answer the following questions. They will help you understand the poem more in depth.

1. ¿Cuáles son las características típicas de los abuelos y las abuelas?

2. ¿Tienes otras personas mayores en tu vida *(life)*— parientes o vecinos *(neighbors)* que sean como tus abuelos?

3. ¿Te gusta pasar tiempo con tus abuelos o personas mayores?

4. ¿Haces actividades con tu abuela o abuelo o personas mayores?

5. ¿Qué te gusta más sobre *(about)* la relación con tu abuela o con una persona mayor?

Paso 2: Escucha el poema

Listen to the poem, and follow along in the text. You don't need to understand all the words at this point; just get a general idea of how this girl feels about her grandmother. Also, focus on the sounds of the words at the end of each line. Does the poem have rhyme?

Manuela mi abuela

Esta es mi abuela,
se llama Manuela,
tiene el pelo blanco
y un **moño** muy alto. *bun*

No es alta ni baja,
ni gorda ni flaca,
viste traje oscuro *wears dark clothes*
y nos trae muchos **duros**. *nickles (coins)*

Su **piel** es muy **blanca**, *skin | white*
sus **ojos** muy **grises**, *eyes | gray*
lleva unos **pendientes** *earrings*
igual que las **mises**. *señoritas*

Se pone colonia, *she wears cologne*
se peina su pelo, *she combs her hair*
le gusta la leche *loves milk*
y los caramelos. *and sweets*

Tiene muchos **nietos**, *grandchildren*
a todos **quiere** igual, *love*
siempre nos **pide** fotos *asks*
para **poderlas mirar**. *can see them*

¡Me encanta mi abuela! *I love*
A ella le gusta escuchar,
te **consuela** y te **defiende**. *consoles | defends*
¡Es una abuela ideal!

Esta es mi abuela,
se llama Manuela,
tiene el pelo blanco,
y un moño muy alto.

ANA SERNA VARA

Vara, A.S. (1993). "Manuela mi abuela", *Poesía de ayer y de hoy para chicos y grandes*, Susaeta Ediciones, S.A.

📖 ✦ Paso 3: Encuentra los detalles

Read the questions below, and make sure you understand their meaning. Then read the poem, and find the answers to the questions. When you have finished, share your answers with the class.

1. ¿Qué sabes *(know)* de la abuela Manuela?

2. ¿Qué hace la abuela?

3. ¿Qué tipo *(kind)* de relación tiene con sus nietos?

4. ¿En qué estrofas *(stanzas)* se describen características físicas de la abuela?

5. ¿En qué estrofas se describe la personalidad de la abuela?

Mi progreso comunicativo

I can identify key words, the theme and some details in a poem about the family.

📝 Paso 4: Soy poeta también

Write a three stanza poem like *Manuela mi abuela* telling about a relative that you admire or respect.

Stanza 1: Introduce the person and describe what he or she looks like.

Stanza 2: Use 4 adjectives to describe what he or she is like.

Stanza 3: Tell what the person likes to do, and say how much you like this person.

Miguel, mi tío

Este es mi tío
Se llama Miguel
Tiene el pelo negro
Y ojos **color miel.**

honey color

Es muy divertido
Y no es impaciente
Es muy creativo
Y serio también.

¡Me encanta mi tío!
Le gusta bailar
Le gusta escuchar
¡Es un tío ideal!

TEXAS

MÉXICO   Kingsville

Carmen Lomas Garza es de Kingsville, Texas.

Pintura y texto

The following painting and text appeared in *En mi familia,* by Carmen Lomas Garza, 1996.

Actividad 34

Baile en El Jardín de Carmen Lomas Garza

🔍 Paso 1: Lluvia de vocabulario

Working with a partner, look at the painting and list all the words in Spanish that can help you talk about the work. Include names of objects and people you see, as well as descriptions.

🔍 📖 Paso 2: Observaciones

Look at the painting and write **sí** or **no** to indicate if each statement accurately describes the scene or not.

1. Estas personas están en casa de unos parientes.

2. Es de día.

3. Hay un conjunto musical que toca música alegre.

4. Los jóvenes y los viejos no bailan juntos.

5. Los bebés también bailan.

6. Para la artista, las fiestas familiares representan una tortura.

🔍 📖 Paso 3: ¿Qué dice el texto?

First, read the questions below. Then, look for the answers in the artist's text and painting.

1. ¿Qué día es?

2. ¿Dónde están las personas?

3. ¿Qué hacen?

4. ¿Cuántas personas tocan instrumentos en el conjunto?

5. ¿Qué instrumentos se mencionan en el texto?

6. ¿Por qué son importantes el padre y el abuelo de la artista?

7. ¿Las fiestas familiares son positivas o negativas para la artista? ¿Cómo lo sabes?

A esta niña le gusta bailar con su padre.

Baile en *El Jardín*

Ésta es una noche de sábado en *El Jardín*, en un restaurante familiar de mi pueblo natal (*hometown*). Es verano y hace tanto calor que la gente (*people*) baila afuera. Un conjunto toca con tambora (*drum*), acordeón, guitarra y bajo. Ésta es la música con la que crecí (*grew up*). Todos bailan formando un gran círculo: las parejas jóvenes, las parejas más grandes, y los viejitos (*old people*) bailan con adolescentes o criaturas (*young children*). Hasta los bebés se ponen a bailar.

Yo aprendí (*I learned*) a bailar con mi padre y mi abuelo. De ahí nació (*was born*) mi amor por el baile. Para mí, el baile representa fiesta, celebración. Aquí está la música, los hermosos vestidos, y todos los miembros de la familia bailan juntos. Es como (*like*) el cielo. Es la gloria.

Las familias unen las culturas

Gráfico

This graph was prepared with information published on the web by the Institute of International Education (IIE).

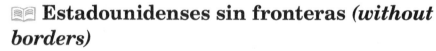

Actividad 35

📖 Estadounidenses sin fronteras (*without borders*)

The chart on page 187 provides information about students from the U.S. studying abroad during the decade from 2004 to 2014. Use the data presented to answer the following questions.

1. Write out in sentences two facts that are represented in the chart.

2. Which of the following are accurate inferences based on the data in the chart?

    a. Hay una explosión de interés en Costa Rica como destino para los estudios.

    b. Menos estudiantes van a México porque hay mucha violencia en el país.

    c. Los estudiantes que antes iban (*before went*) a México ahora van a Chile.

    d. México y España todavía (*still*) son los destinos más populares para los estudiantes norteamericanos.

3. Write a quick personal reaction to the information presented.

4. Write three additional questions about study abroad that you could research to explain the changes in popularity.

Estudiantes norteamericanos en los países hispanohablantes más populares

País	2004	2014	% cambio (change)
España	20.080	26.949	+34%
México	9.293	4.445	-52%
Costa Rica	4.510	8.578	+90%
Chile	2.135	3.333	+56%
TOTAL	36.018	43.305	+20,2%

Total global: 304.467 estudiantes de EE. UU. estudiando en el extranjero en 2013–2014.

Source: www.iie.org.

Actividad 36

Vivir o estudiar en el extranjero *(abroad)*

📖 Paso 1: Ventajas y retos

From your perspective as a student, what are the **ventajas** *(benefits)* and **retos** *(challenges)* of living with a family while studying or working abroad? Choose the three factors in each column that are most significant for you.

Mi progreso comunicativo

I can identify key details from charts and graphs and make inferences about cultural perspectives.

Ventajas posibles	Retos posibles
Puedo aprender otro idioma.	Puedo sufrir el choque cultural.
Aprendo mucho de otra cultura.	No me gusta estar lejos de mi familia.
Hago conexiones con otra familia.	Cuesta mucho dinero.
Es una buena preparación profesional.	El sistema educativo es muy diferente.
Es muy divertido.	No tengo amigos ni vida social.
Hago amistades *(friendship)* con jóvenes de otro país.	Las comidas no me gustan.
Es una buena experiencia intercultural.	Mi español no es suficiente.
Aprendo mucho sobre mí mismo/a *(myself)*.	No me gusta la familia con quien vivo.
Descubro nuevos intereses.	

🌐 Paso 2: Mi casa es tu casa

Now consider the perspective of a family who receives exchange students, and answer the following questions.

1. Has your family, or a family you know, ever hosted a student from another country or culture? What do you know about that experience?

2. Which of the following values or motivations do you think are the most important for **una familia anfitriona** *(host family)* who receives foreign students into their home? Add any others that you can think of.

   a. Valoran el aprendizaje *(learning)* de otras lenguas.

   b. Le gustan las experiencias interculturales.

   c. Es una manera fácil de ganar *(earn)* dinero.

   d. Los intercambios permiten una amistad duradera *(long-lasting)* entre dos culturas.

   e. Tiene mucho orgullo *(pride)* en su cultura local.

   f. ¿Qué más?

◎ Paso 3: Comparando perspectivas

Now read the **Enfoque cultural** on **Intercambios familiares,** and tell which of the ideas in **Paso 2** represent the perspective of Spanish families who host students.

Enfoque cultural

Perspectiva cultural: Intercambios familiares

Muchas familias españolas valoran las oportunidades de aprender otros idiomas y otras culturas. Algunas familias viajan durante *(during)* las vacaciones a otros países para una experiencia intercultural. Otras familias les dan a los hijos la experiencia de estudiar o vivir en otro país, o son anfitriones *(hosts)* de un joven extranjero en su hogar. La familia anfitriona comparte *(shares)* con el estudiante su cultura y su idioma. El estudiante se convierte *(becomes)* en un miembro más de la familia, y se forman relaciones para toda la vida *(lifetime)*, una conexión entre dos familias, dos pueblos y dos países.

🔗  Conexiones

Would you like to host an exchange student from a Spanish-speaking country in your home? What would you learn from the experience? What would the student learn?

Actividad 37

Un intercambio para ti

You are going to read blogs posted on the website of the organization *quieroaprenderidiomas.com*, a group that helps match people interested in hosting and participating in family exchanges.

Paso 1: Antes de leer

Have you ever considered living with another family? Try to visualize the idea, and answer the following questions with a partner.

1. What are some of the advantages and challenges of such an experience?

2. How could you go about finding a family?

3. What are the characteristics that you would look for when choosing a host family?

Paso 2: Buscando intercambios

Read the information posted by Lucía and José Antonio on the site *quieroaprenderidiomas.com*, and find the information that helps you answer the following questions for each blog post:

1. ¿Quién escribe la información, un/a adolescente o los padres?

2. ¿Por qué esta persona quiere hacer un intercambio?

3. ¿Qué ofrece la familia? ¿Por qué es interesante vivir con ellos?

Look at pictures and captions before you start to read!

Estrategias
Fotos y texto

It's amazing how much written Spanish you can understand, if you use your reading strategies! Look at the pictures and captions that accompany a written piece to guess what the text will say before you start to read. Then, as you dive into the text, you can use what you already know about the topic to help decipher the meaning of what you are reading.

Nombre: Lucía	
Edad: 14 años	
De: Toledo, Castilla-La Mancha	
Intercambio: Reino Unido, Irlanda e Estados Unidos	
Publicado: 21/2/2016	

Hola soy una chica española de 14 años, (en verano cumpliré 15), soy simpática y alegre, me encanta estudiar y explicar matemáticas y ciencias. Estudio inglés desde hace tres años, y busco alguien que esté interesado en practicar inglés y español conmigo, o en pasar unos días en España.

Vivo en la ciudad de Toledo con mis padres, mis hermanos y mi mascota, donde podemos montar en bicicleta, ir a la piscina y pasear por caminos naturales del campo. Toledo está situado a 75 km de Madrid y podemos ir a visitar la capital y todos sus monumentos. Es fácil llegar al aeropuerto internacional de Madrid, y hay trenes y autobuses a Toledo a todas horas. Si te gusta mi oferta, solo tienes que mandarme un e-mail.

Nombre: Jose Antonio	
De: Granada, España	
Intercambio: Jóvenes de habla inglesa	
Fecha para intercambio: Desde 1/8/16 al 31/8/16	
Publicado: 28/2/2016	

Hola, me llamo Jose Antonio y soy profesor de Educación Física. Tengo dos hijos de 8 y 12 años de edad. Me gustaría enseñar español a la vez que aprender inglés. Con este objetivo me gustaría compartir mi casa con algún chico de habla inglesa de entre 12 y 15 años de edad que desee estar en nuestras vacaciones en la playa con nosotros a partir del 15 de julio hasta el 30 de agosto. Mi intención es acercar el inglés a mis hijos.

Serían unas buenas vacaciones con paseos en kayak, partidos de fútbol, pescar, pasear, montar en bici, jugar a la Play Station, excursiones etc… Ojalá esta estancia pudiera ser recíproca otro año con otra familia para que pudiera acoger a mi hijo de 12 años.

📖 ✦ Paso 3: Reconoce la palabra

Find in the blog entries the Spanish phrases that best express the meaning of the following English words.

1. **Lucía:** friendly, explain, to practice, English, interested, natural, is situated, airport, international

2. **José Antonio:** learn English, objective, intention, good vacation, excursions, stay, reciprocal

✎ Paso 4: ¿Con qué familia vas?

Considering the information in the two posts, choose one of the two families, and justify your decision with information from the text.

Modelo

Voy a vivir con la familia de _____ porque tienen…

me gusta…

con ellos puedo (*I can*)…

Reflexión intercultural

✦ List the summer vacation activities mentioned in these blogs, then list six things young people in your community do on vacation. How similar or different are they? Discuss with your classmates in the discussion forum in Explorer.

Mi progreso comunicativo

I can understand and identify key ideas in a Spanish blog post.

Mi progreso intercultural

I can identify key details and cultural practices from authentic reading materials.

En mi comunidad

¿De dónde vienen tus familiares, de cerca o de lejos?

¿De dónde es tu familia?

📖 **Paso 1: Raíces familiares**

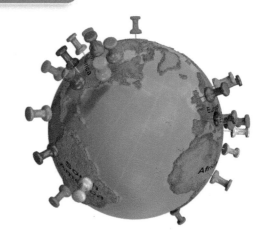

Can you trace your **raíces** *(roots)*? Do you know where your *abuelos* come from? How far back can you trace your family history?

Read the following narrative by Marina, our blogger from Spain, in which she talks about her family roots. Find on the map below the correct location for each of the relatives she mentions.

- abuelos maternos
- abuelos paternos
- tres tíos y ocho primos
- tres tíos y cuatro primos
- dos primos adoptados
- una tía y un primo
- su hermano

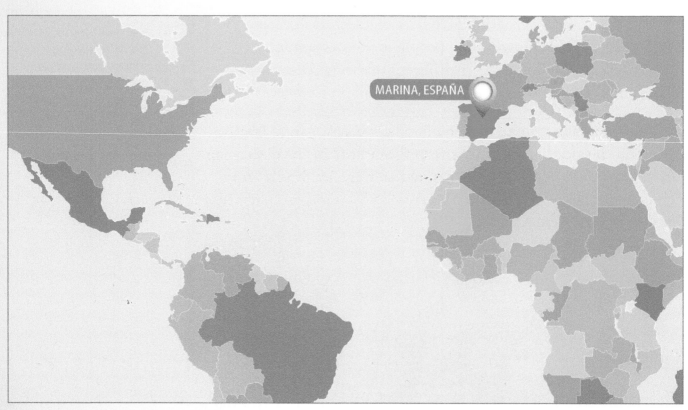

MARINA, ESPAÑA

"Mi familia es muy interesante. Mi madre es de la República Dominicana, en el Caribe, y mi padre es del País Vasco, en el norte de España. Entonces mis abuelos maternos viven en la República Dominicana y mis abuelos paternos viven en España. Aunque mi familia inmediata es pequeña, mi familia extendida es muy grande. En República Dominicana tengo tres tíos y ocho primos. En España tengo tres tíos y cuatro primos, dos son niños de Burkina Faso adoptados por mi tía. También tengo familia en México porque una hermana de mi papá vive allí con su hijo. Y ¿recordáis a mis hermanos? Mi hermano vive en Suecia, y mi hermana estudia en Holanda. ¡Somos una familia muy internacional!"

Marina y su familia caminan por la muralla (city wall) de Ávila, España, un monumento histórico en la ciudad.

Paso 2: ¿De dónde venimos?

Entrevista a un/a compañero/a con las siguientes preguntas, y apunta las respuestas.

1. ¿Quiénes son tus antepasados (ancestors)?

2. ¿De dónde son originalmente?

3. ¿Por qué países o estados pasaron (did they pass through)?

4. ¿Adónde llegaron (did they arrive) finalmente?

5. ¿Qué lenguas hablan?

Reflexión intercultural

What common ground can you find between Marina's family story and the story of your classmates' families? In the discussion forum in Explorer, identify two aspects of Marina's family story. Then explain how each aspect compares to the experience of some families in your community.

Mi progreso intercultural

I can identify common elements in family history across cultures.

Vive entre culturas

Familia nueva, cultura nueva

Essential Questions:

- What places and activities bring us together as a family?

- How is my family similar to and different from families in the Spanish-speaking world?

You have another opportunity to participate in an **intercambio** through the website *quieroaprenderidomas.com*. The following assessments are based on the ad posted by Yael Marañes.

Interpretive Assessment

📖 ✣ Mi familia de intercambio

Yael is a girl from Spain who wants to improve her English by participating in an exchange program with an English-speaking family. Look at the photographs of her and her family and read her post in the blog *quieroaprenderidiomas.com*.

YAEL

Interpersonal Assessment

  ### Una conversación con Yael

You have decided to participate in the summer exchange with Yael. Both of you have arranged to Skype at 4:00 p.m. your local time (Spain is six hours ahead of Eastern time in the U.S.). Yael has lots of questions about your family or an imaginary family you create.

Listen to Yael's questions and record your answers in your Explorer course.

Presentational Assessment

Mi familia: Un álbum de fotos

You have decided to participate in the summer exchange with Yael. Create a digital album to share information and photographs about your own family and home to make her feel comfortable when she visits.

UNIDAD 4
La comida es cultura

Unit Goals

- Share preferences, opinions and habits about food choices and food purchases.

- Interpret photographs, videos, ads, blogs and menus to understand food traditions.

- Create and present a series of menu items based on your food preferences and food traditions from a Spanish-speaking country.

- Recognize how traditions relating to meals and food reflect identity and how sharing in the food of another culture opens doors to intercultural communication.

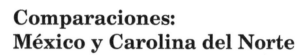

Essential Questions

What are some iconic foods from the Spanish-speaking world?

How do food products and food practices shape our cultural identity?

How can exploring new foods lead me to new intercultural experiences?

CHRISTIAN GARITA CARVALLO, NUESTRO VIDEO BLOGUERO DE MÉXICO

The foods we prepare, eat, and share say a lot about who we are. In this unit, you will learn to talk with Spanish speakers about what foods you like, and how to make food purchases in Spanish. You will explore how foods bring us together as we get to experience new cultures through food.

Comparaciones
◈ México y Carolina del Norte

Población

México
122 millones

79% urbana

21% rural

Carolina del Norte (Estados Unidos)

Hernando de Soto, explorador español, busca oro en Carolina del Norte

Carolina del Norte se une a los EE. UU. como estado 12

Andrew Jackson (de Carolina del Norte) elegido Presidente de los EE. UU.

James Polk (de Carolina del Norte) elegido Presidente de los EE. UU.

Primer vuelo de los hermanos Wright en Kitty Hawk, NC

	1325	1540	1789	1821	1828	1845	1903

México

Los aztecas fundan la ciudad de Tenochtitlán (hoy la Ciudad de México)

Independencia de España

México pierde la mitad de su territorio en la guerra con EE. UU.

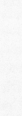

Carolina del Norte
10 millones

66% urbana

34% rural

MÉXICO

CAROLINA
DEL NORTE

State College, primera universidad para americanos nativos

La población hispana en Carolina del Norte aumenta 400%—el mayor crecimiento en EE. UU.—con la mayoría de los inmigrantes de México

Arqueólogos encuentran evidencia de la "Colonia perdida" de Roanoke, primer asentamiento británico en Norteamérica (1590)

Duke University gana el campeonato nacional de básquetbol (NCAA) por 5ª vez

1910–29	1943	1992	1990–2000	2012	2014	2015

La Revolución Mexicana

Publicación y estreno de *Como agua para chocolate*, novela y película con la comida mexicana como protagonista

En los Juegos Olímpicos, México gana la medalla de oro en fútbol

Inicio de nueva actividad volcánica del Popocatépetl, cerca de la Ciudad de México

Actividad 1

Productos de México y de Carolina del Norte

Paso 1

Observa las imágenes. ¿Puedes identificar las que muestran productos de México? ¿Y de los Estados Unidos? ¿Qué semejanzas y diferencias puedes notar?

Paso 2

¿Estas fotos reflejan tus experiencias con la comida? Indica dos o tres fotos de comida que te gusta, o que te gustaría probar *(to taste)*.

Comunica

Essential Question: What are some iconic foods from the Spanish-speaking world?

El comal es un utensilio importante en la cocina mexicana.

Soy Christian Garita Carvallo, el bloguero de Torreón (Coahuila), México.

El queso fresco

Video blog
Soy Christian

Actividad 2

Un plato emblemático de México

▶ ✦ **Paso 1: ¿Cómo se preparan los chiles rellenos?**

Christian va a hablar de la preparación de un platillo icónico mexicano: **los chiles rellenos** (*stuffed*). Mira el video sin sonido (*without sound*). Luego, trabajando con un/a compañero/a de clase, contesten a estas preguntas sobre el tema.

1. ¿Qué son los chiles? ¿Son los chiles poblanos grandes o pequeños?

2. ¿Has probado (*have you tasted*) este platillo? ¿Es picante (*spicy*) o no?

3. Miren las fotos en esta página. ¿Qué ingredientes usa Christian para hacer los chiles rellenos?

📖 🔤 ✴ **Paso 2: Para entender la preparación**

Christian hace las siguientes acciones en la preparación de los chiles. ¿Qué significa cada verbo?

_____ 1. lavar   a. to roast

_____ 2. pelar   b. to cut

_____ 3. asar   c. to wash

_____ 4. cortar   d. to put

_____ 5. meter/poner   e. to peel

🎥 📖 ✴ **Paso 3: El orden correcto**

¿Cómo se preparan los chiles? Primero, estudia esta lista de acciones. Luego, escucha y mira el video, y pon en orden las acciones, de 1 a 7.

_____ asar los chiles usando fuego *(stove burner, fire)*

_____ cortar los chiles y meter el queso *(cheese)*

_____ lavar los chiles

_____ meter los chiles en huevo *(egg)*

_____ meter los chiles en una bolsa *(bag)*

_____ pelar los chiles

_____ poner los chiles en una sartén *(frying pan)* y cocinarlos *(cook them)*

Vendedor de chiles: Mercado de la Merced, México, D. F.

Reflexión intercultural

✴ What dish is emblematic of your community's identity? How is it similar or different from the **chiles rellenos** prepared by Christian? Do you know how to prepare it? Share your observations in class and in Explorer.

Mi progreso intercultural

I can recognize some similarities and differences between foods in Mexico and in my community

El chile poblano

Además se dice

Más verduras

la ensalada	salad
las espinacas	spinach
el pepino	cucumber

Más frutas

el melón	cantaloupe
la sandía	watermelon

Las bebidas

el agua	water
el batido	shake; smoothie
el jugo	juice

Acciones en el mercado

beber	to drink
comprar	to buy
pedir	to ask for
probar (o → ue)	to try
tomar	to take; drink
vender	to sell

Así se dice 1

✦ En el mercado de La Merced (México, D. F.)

Actividad 3

  **Los colores del mercado**

¿Conoces las frutas y verduras por su color? Escribe por lo menos diez (10) frutas y verduras en la tabla según el color.

frutas y verduras...	
rojas	
amarillas	
anaranjadas	
verdes	

Actividad 4

¡Póngame dos, por favor!

  Paso 1: ¿Fruta o verdura?

Escucha los pedidos *(orders)* de varias personas en el mercado. ¿Piden fruta o verdura?

  Paso 2: ¿Cuánto cuesta?

Escucha otra vez los pedidos, mirando los precios en la página anterior. ¿Cuánto cuesta cada pedido en pesos mexicanos?

Enfoque cultural

Práctica cultural: El kilo

En casi todos los países del mundo, se usa el sistema decimal o métrico. La unidad de peso *(weight)* en los mercados es el **kilogramo**. El prefijo **kilo** significa "mil", así que *(so)* un kilogramo son 1.000 gramos, aproximadamente 2,2 libras *(lb or pounds)*. Si quieres comprar una libra de uvas, por ejemplo, tienes que pedir *(ask for)* **medio kilo**, que son 500g.

 Conexiones

Where have you encountered the metric system in your school, in your community, and/or in your travels outside the U.S.?

Además se dice

Más colores

azul	blue
blanco/a	white
morado/a	purple
negro/a	black
rosado/a	pink

Mi progreso comunicativo

I can identify basic foods and describe their color.

Bolsas de naranjas: 1 kilo c/u (cada una)

Actividad 5

🔤 🧭 La intrusa

Escoge *(Choose)* el alimento que no está en la misma categoría que los otros (por ejemplo, todas frutas excepto..., todas verduras excepto...)

1. a. la manzana   b. la piña   c. la lechuga   d. la uva

2. a. el limón   b. el pepino   c. la naranja   d. el plátano

3. a. la piña   b. el agua   c. el mango   d. la papaya

4. a. el melón   b. la sandía   c. la cebolla   d. la naranja

5. a. el agua   b. el batido   c. el jugo   d. el plátano

6. a. la lechuga   b. el pepino   c. la fresa   d. las espinacas

Actividad 6

La escamocha: Un coctel de frutas

🎬 🧭 Paso 1: Los ingredientes de la escamocha

Esta lista contiene ingredientes posibles para la escamocha. Lee esta lista de ingredientes posibles, y comprueba el significado de las palabras. Luego, mira y escucha la receta *(recipe)*, e indica qué ingredientes están en esta versión de la escamocha. ¡OJO! Two ingredients were not used.

cerezas *(cherries)*

el jarabe de granadina *(pomegranate syrup)*

piña

jugo *(juice)* de naranja

azúcar *(sugar)*

mango

uvas rojas

manzana

pera

melón

papaya

plátano

fresas

sal *(salt)*

limones

uvas verdes

naranja

[A/Z] Paso 2: Para mi escamocha necesito...

Vas a hacer tu propia *(own)* versión de la escamocha. ¿Qué ingredientes necesitas? Escribe una lista de por lo menos seis (6) frutas que tienes que comprar.

Paso 3: Comprando ingredientes

Vas al Mercado de La Merced para comprar los ingredientes para tu escamocha. Actúa la situación con un/a compañero/a de clase. Una persona compra, y la otra vende. Luego, cambien los papeles *(switch roles)* y repitan la situación.

Modelo

Cliente:	Greet the vendor.
Vendedor/a:	Greet the customer; ask how you can help.
Cliente:	Ask if vendor has your ingredients, and how much they cost.
Vendedor/a:	Respond with prices.
Cliente:	Ask vendor for specific quantities of the ingredients you need.
Vendedor/a:	Hand over the ingredients, and thank the customer.
Cliente:	Thank the vendor, and say good bye.

Mi progreso comunicativo

I can specify the quantity of foods for purchase.

Expresiones útiles: En el mercado

¿Qué va a llevar?
What can I get for you?

Quiero...
I'd like...

Póngame por favor...
Give me...

un kilo (de)
a kilo (of)

medio kilo (de)
half a kilo (of)

un cuarto de kilo (de)
fourth of a kilo (of)

cien gramos
100 grams

una docena (de)
a dozen

¿Cuánto es?
How much is it?

Son 30 pesos.
It'll be 30 pesos.

Aquí lo tiene.
Here you go / Here it is.

Actividad 7

Mi ensalada mixta

Ⓐⓩ Paso 1

Quieres preparar una ensalada especial para tu familia.
Escribe una lista de cinco ingredientes que quieres usar.

💬 Paso 2

Trabajando con un/a compañero/a, actúa la situación en el
mercado en que compras los ingredientes para tu ensalada.

Actividad 8

🎧 ✷ Ve al mercado

La mamá de Sofía necesita ingredientes para preparar una
comida especial en casa. Escucha sus instrucciones e indica la
letra de la imagen de cada ingrediente que Sofía debe comprar.

1. _____   2. _____   3. _____   4. _____

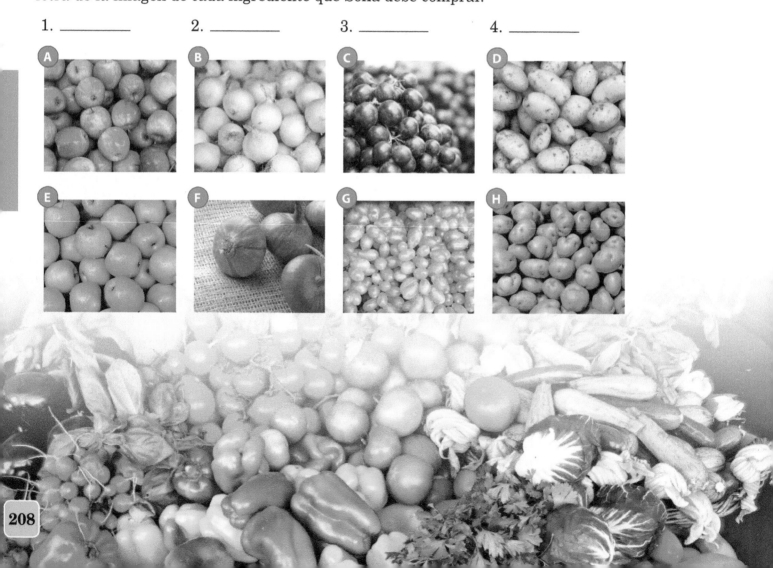

Actividad 9

📖 ¿Qué fruta o verdura es?

Lee la descripción de la fruta o verdura, y escribe el nombre.

1. Es una fruta amarilla que se usa para hacer limonada.

2. Es una verdura de muchas hojas *(leaves)* que se pone en una ensalada con tomate.

3. Es una fruta roja, verde o amarilla que se usa para hacer sidra.

4. Es una fruta tropical que se cultiva en Hawái.

5. Es una fruta pequeña de color verde o rojo. Se usa esta fruta para hacer vino.

6. Es una verdura verde por fuera *(outside)* y blanca por dentro; se usa típicamente en las ensaladas.

7. Es una fruta anaranjada que se cultiva en La Florida, California, España y otros lugares tropicales.

Enfoque cultural

Producto cultural: Las aguas frescas

Las aguas frescas son bebidas refrescantes y saludables que son populares en México y en partes de los Estados Unidos. Típicamente se venden en los mercados y en las calles *(streets)*. Los sabores *(flavors)* más populares son el agua de jamaica, de sandía, de limón, de melón, de piña, de tamarindo y de horchata (de arroz).

🔄 🌐 Conexiones

Are drinks prepared with fresh fruits sold in your community? Do you have a favorite? Which flavors would you like to try?

jamaica *(hibiscus flower and dried blossoms)*

Observa 1

¿Qué quieren ustedes?

¿Qué observas?

 In the dialog, notice the verbs in bold; they all mean "want." Look carefully at the spelling of the forms and see if you notice any patterns. Discuss your observations with a **compañero/compañera de clase**, view the Observa 1 resources in your *EntreCulturas 1* Explorer course, and check the **Síntesis de gramática** at the end of this section of the unit.

Actividad 10

 ✷ **En el mercado**

Clara y Jazmín hablan en el Mercado de la Merced, en la
Ciudad de México. Primero lee las siguientes oraciones, y
después de escuchar la conversación, decide si son ciertas (C)
o falsas (F).

1. Las chicas quieren comprar fruta.

2. Las dos chicas quieren comer algo en el mercado.

3. Hay tres sabores de aguas frescas.

4. Las chicas quieren comprar dos aguas frescas de sandía.

5. Las aguas cuestan veinte pesos.

Actividad 11

 ¿Quién habla?

¿Quién dice estas oraciones en el mercado probablemente—
el vendedor de frutas y verduras o una cliente con dos hijos?

1. Prefiero las manzanas verdes, por favor.

2. Papá quiere mucha fruta para el postre.

3. ¿Qué tipo de chiles quiere usted?

4. Quiero comprar un kilo de tomates.

5. ¿No quieres comer nada, mijo?

6. Recomiendo los mangos, señora; están muy buenos hoy.

7. Mi hijo quiere un agua fresca. ¿Qué sabores hay?

8. ¿Prefiere Ud. la lechuga verde o roja? Cada una cuesta
   6 pesos.

Detalle gramatical

**Otros verbos con
e → ie:**

Many verbs have the same
e → ie stem change
as **querer**. Here are two
more that are useful when
talking about food:

preferir *to prefer*
pref**ie**ro	pref**e**rimos
pref**ie**res	*pref**e**rís*
pref**ie**re	pref**ie**ren

recome**ndar**
to recommend
recom**ie**ndo
recom**ie**ndas
recom**ie**nda
recom**e**ndamos
*recom**e**ndáis*
recom**ie**ndan

En el restaurante

Estas oraciones incompletas se oyeron *(were overheard)* en un restaurante en Querétaro, México. ¿Qué palabra completa cada oración?

1. Yo _____ comer una hamburguesa.
   a. quieres b. quiero c quieren

2. ¿_____ Ud. agua o limonada?
   a. Prefiere b. Prefieren c. Prefieres

3. El mesero *(waiter)* _____ las aguas frescas.
   a. recomiendan b. recomiendas c. recomienda

4. Nosotros _____ el postre *(dessert)* con uvas verdes.
   a. preferimos b. prefieren c. prefieres

5. Mis hijas son vegetarianas; solo _____ comer verduras.
   a. quieres b. quieren c. quieren

6. Yo _____ tomar café con leche.
   a. prefiere b. prefieres c. prefiero

7. Todos los meseros _____ los tacos de carne.
   a. recomendamos b. recomiendo c. recomiendan

Enfoque cultural

Práctica cultural: El tianguis

México es famoso por sus mercados al aire libre *(open-air)*, o **tianguis**. Allí podemos encontrar todo tipo de productos: comida, ropa *(clothes)*, zapatos, artículos para la casa e incluso autos usados. Una característica importante del tianguis es que los precios no son fijos; uno puede regatear *(bargain)*.

 Conexiones

Are there open-air markets in your community? What do you buy there? In what types of businesses in your community is it possible to bargain for a better price? In what type of businesses are prices fixed?

Actividad 13

💬 ¿Qué prefieres?

Quieres planear un día especial para tu compañero/a de clase. Hazle estas preguntas para saber qué le gusta.

1. ¿Qué prefieres por la mañana: café, té o jugo de frutas?

2. ¿Qué almuerzas típicamente: una ensalada o una hamburguesa?

3. ¿Qué comida internacional prefieres: comida mexicana, tailandesa o italiana?

4. ¿Qué prefieres beber: jugo de naranja, jugo de manzana o solo agua?

5. ¿Puedes comer gluten, productos lácteos *(dairy)* y nueces *(nuts)*, o tienes alergias?

Actividad 14

💬 ¿Qué quieres?

Work with a compañero/a to create questions and answers based on the following pairs of words.

Modelo

naranja/manzana

Estudiante A: ¿Quieres una naranja o una manzana?

Estudiante B: Prefiero una manzana.

1. agua/jugo
2. piña/mango
3. manzana/plátano
4. fresas/uvas
5. ensalada/hamburguesa
6. comer algo *(something)*/beber algo

Detalle gramatical: Los verbos con cambio de raíz o → ue

Just as some verbs change their final root vowel **-e-** to **-ie-**, other verbs change their root-final **-o-** to **-ue-**, in the same four forms **(yo, tú, usted/él/ella, ustedes/ellos/ellas)**. Useful verbs of this type include **almorzar** *(eat lunch)*, **costar** *(cost)*, **poder** *(be able, can)* and **probar** *(try)*.

almo**rzar**

alm**ue**rzo	almorzamos
alm**ue**rzas	*almorzáis*
alm**ue**rza	alm**ue**rzan

po**der**

p**ue**do	podemos
p**ue**des	*podéis*
p**ue**de	p**ue**den

Mi progreso comunicativo

I can ask and answer questions about preferences for food and drink.

Así se dice 2

✦ ¿Qué quieres comer?

Araceli Argüelles Cabral nació en Durango, México.
Ahora vive en Durham, Carolina del Norte.

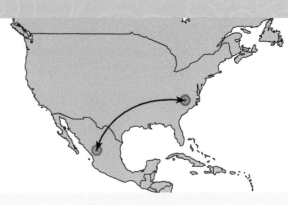

En mi casa en Durham, Carolina del Norte, EE. UU.

El desayuno	El lonche	La cena

7:00 am

Como **huevos fritos, pan tostado, y jamón.** Tomo **jugo** de naranja.

12:00 pm

Me gusta comer una **hamburguesa** y **papas** fritas, y de beber **un refresco.**

6:00 pm

Ceno un **sándwich de queso** y **sopa** de tomate, y bebo un **té helado** con limón.

En casa de mi abuela, Durango, México

El desayuno	La comida	La cena

9:00 am

Me encantan los **huevos** rancheros con **frijoles,** o simplemente un pan dulce y un **café con leche.**

2:00 pm

Como **pollo** con **mole** poblano, **arroz** y **frijoles** negros y **tortillas** de maíz. Tomo agua.

8:00 pm

No soy **vegetariana,** pero solo ceno una **ensalada** con lechuga, jitomate y **aguacate,** y tomo un **agua fresca.** Mi favorita es de jamaica.

Actividad 15

📖 ¿Qué categoría de comida es?

Escribe por lo menos dos (2) ejemplos de cada tipo de comida.

1. productos lácteos (*dairy*)
2. bebidas
3. carnes
4. verduras
5. platillos calientes (*hot*)

Actividad 16

Mis platos típicos

A2 ✤ **Paso 1**

Describe lo que te gusta comer y beber en un día típico.

	El desayuno	El almuerzo/ el lonche/ la comida	La cena
Típicamente como…			
En general, bebo…			

💬 **Paso 2**

Explícale a un/a compañero/a tus gustos.

Modelo

Para la cena me gusta comer pizza y me gusta beber agua.

Actividad 17

🎧 ✤ ¿Quién come qué?

A Daniel le gusta la carne, pero Javier es vegetariano.
Escucha las oraciones y decide quién dice cada una.

1. _____ 2. _____ 3. _____ 4. _____

Actividad 18

🎧 ✤ ¿El desayuno o no?

Escucha estos pedidos (*orders*) en un restaurante de Raleigh, Carolina del Norte. Decide si la comida es el desayuno o no.

1. _____ 2. _____ 3. _____ 4. _____ 5. _____ 6. _____

Además se dice

el bistec
steak

la carne
meat

los espaguetis
spaghetti

el helado (de vainilla, chocolate)
(chocolate, vanilla) ice cream

el pay de manzana
apple pie (Méx.)

el pastel
cake, pastry

el postre
dessert

algo
something

fuerte
strong, heavy

ligero/a
light

light
low-calorie

sin gluten
gluten-free

Mi progreso comunicativo

I can talk about what I eat at different meals, and what time I eat them.

María Lupe Arroyo Holguín
(15 años, Tlaxcala, México)
prepara tamales con su madre
y sus tías.

Observa 2
¿Qué comidas te gustan?

A Tía Julia

Me gustan los frijoles,
Me gusta el arroz,
Me gusta, en la cocina,
El canto de tu voz.

Me gustan las Posadas,
Qué bonita estación,
Me gustan los tamales
Con toda su tradición.

Me gusta ver tus manos
en la masa trabajar,
Me gusta como en la cocina
¡me enseñas a amar!

Gracias, Tía Julia, por enseñarme esta
tradición familiar. ¡Me gusta pasar las
Navidades contigo!

María Lupe

¿Qué observas?

🎧 ✦ In the poem, notice the expression **me gusta(n)** and the words around it. Can you figure out when the writer uses **gusta** vs. **gustan**? Which word tells who likes the different foods and activities? Discuss your observations with a **compañero/compañera de clase**. View the Observa 2 resources in Explorer and check the **Síntesis de gramática** at the end of this section of the unit.

Actividad 19

 Las comidas que me gustan

Decide si las ideas son ciertas (C) o falsas (F) para ti y luego compártelas con un/a compañero/a.

1. Me gustan los tamales.

2. Me gusta la pizza.

3. Me gustan las hamburguesas.

4. Me gusta el helado.

5. Me gusta la fruta.

6. Me gustan las verduras.

7. Me gusta la mayonesa.

8. Me gustan las cebollas.

9. Me gusta el sushi.

10. Me gustan los huevos.

Actividad 20

 ¿Dónde comemos hoy?

Escucha los gustos de los amigos, y recomienda un restaurante para cada persona.

Taquería Jalisco (comida mexicana)

Café Madeleine (comida francesa)

Hank's BBQ (comida sureña de EE. UU.)

Luigi (comida italiana)

Sakura (comida japonesa)

Además se dice

Cómo expresar tu opinión

To express a full range of opinions about foods, you can use expressions similar to **gustar**:

 Me **encanta** la pizza.
Me **encantan** los espaguetis.

 No me **gusta para nada** la mayonesa.
No me **gustan para nada** los brócolis.

Otras expresiones

 ¡Qué rico!
Yum! Delicious!

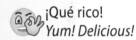

 ¡Qué asco!
How disgusting! Gross!

 Me da igual.
It's all the same to me.

México produce aguacate para el consumo nacional y para la exportación.

Actividad 21

Un nuevo menú en la cafetería

 Paso 1

La cafetería quiere incluir estas comidas en el menú regular.
¿Cuál es tu opinión? Escribe ocho oraciones expresando tus
ideas sobre estas posibilidades.

Me encanta(n)…		**Me gusta(n)…**			**No me gusta(n) para nada…**	
las hamburguesas	las uvas	la leche	el jugo de naranja	los huevos	las fresas	los batidos
los plátanos	el pay de manzana	las naranjas	el pollo	los refrescos	el té helado	
el café	las manzanas	el arroz blanco	el helado	el yogur	el bistec	los frijoles

Paso 2

Ahora entrevista a un/a compañero/a para saber sus preferencias.
El objetivo es llegar a un acuerdo *(come to agreement)* en una
lista de ocho (8) recomendaciones para la cafetería.

Modelo

Estudiante A:	¿Te gustan las hamburguesas?
Estudiante B:	No, no me gustan para nada. Soy vegetariano.
Estudiante A:	Bien. Eliminamos *(we'll eliminate)* las hamburguesas.

Actividad 22

¡Prepara la comida para todos!

 ⊕ **Paso 1**

A Valentina le gusta cocinar y mimar *(spoil)* a toda su familia. ¡Sabe los gustos de todos sus parientes! Completa estas descripciones con **le** o **les**.

1. A mi hermano _____ encantan los batidos con yogur y fresas.

2. A mi primo José _____ encantan las enchiladas con salsa roja.

3. A mis padres _____ gustan los platos simples, como frijoles con arroz.

4. A mis abuelos _____ encanta mi pastel de tres leches. Es perfecto para las fiestas.

5. A mis primas Elena y Gabriela _____ gusta comer tacos vegetarianos.

6. A mi perra Luna ¡_____ gusta todo lo que no comemos los humanos!

✎ ⊕ **Paso 2**

Usando las oraciones de **Paso 1** como modelo, escribe oraciones que expresan los gustos de tu familia.

El pastel de tres leches contiene leche condensada, leche evaporada y nata *(cream)*.

Detalle gramatical

¿A quién le gusta?

The verb **gustar** uses a sentence structure that is different from other verbs you have studied. Use the following set of pronouns to say whose preferences are being expressed:

Me gusta(n) *I like*

Te gusta(n) *you like*

Le gusta(n) *he/she likes*

Nos gusta(n) *we like*

Les gusta(n) *they like*

For the different varieties of regional and formal address ("you"):

Usted: **Le** gusta(n)

Ustedes: **Les** gusta(n)

Vosotros: **Os** gusta(n)

Vos: **Te** gusta(n)

Verbs like **gustar** also use this pattern:

Te encantan los chiles, ¿no?
You love chili peppers, right?

No **les** gusta para nada el cilantro.
They hate cilantro.

Actividad 23

 ### ¿Gustos similares o diferentes?

Lucas y Javier son gemelos *(twins)* de Monterrey, Nuevo León, México, y hablan de sus preferencias de comida. Lee las siguientes descripciones. Luego, escucha la entrevista, e indica si las descripciones son ciertas (C) o falsas (F).

1. A Lucas y a Javier les gusta el mismo desayuno.

2. Los dos son vegetarianos.

3. Les gustan los platos que prepara su madre.

4. Con las enchiladas, comen frijoles, arroz y tortillas.

5. A todos en la familia les encanta el postre que hace la madre.

Actividad 24

 ### Tu poema original

Usando el poema de María Lupe como modelo (p. 216), escribe un poema original para expresar una conexión entre las comidas que te gustan y una(s) persona(s) importante(s). La rima no es necesaria; puedes usar verso libre.

Reflexión intercultural

 Which foods for each meal of the day do you associate with your family? With your community? Are these foods associated with any particular culture? Of these foods, which is your favorite and why? Share your observations in class and on the discussion forum in Explorer.

 **Mi progreso intercultural**

I can identify some foods typically enjoyed in some Spanish-speaking communities at different meals and at different times of day.

Enfoque cultural

Práctica cultural: El horario de comidas

El horario de las comidas diarias varía de región en región. En México el **desayuno** (por ejemplo, pan y café) es a las 8:00 o el **almuerzo**, similar al *brunch*, a las 10:00. La **comida** principal *(main meal)* es a las 2:00 de la tarde. La **cena** es una comida ligera *(light)* a las 8.00 de la noche.

En España, los españoles típicamente desayunan café con leche, y una **tostada** con aceite de oliva o mermelada, o un **croissant**, entre las 8:00 y las 10:00. Como en México, la comida principal es a las 2:00 o las 3:00. Una diferencia notable es la cena: es más tarde en España, entre las 9:00 y las 11:00 de la noche.

En los dos lugares, muchas personas **meriendan** *(have a snack)* entre la comida y la cena. La **merienda** normalmente es algo dulce (pastel con café o té, o para los niños un chocolate caliente).

Conexiones

What are the most common meal times in your community? Do you typically eat at those times? How do your meal times compare with those in Mexico and Spain? Investigate meal times in other Spanish-speaking countries, and compare to the information you already know.

El chocolate con churros es una merienda popular en España.

Así se dice 3

✦ ¡Me encanta comer en la calle!

Taquerías en Petatlán, Guerrero, México

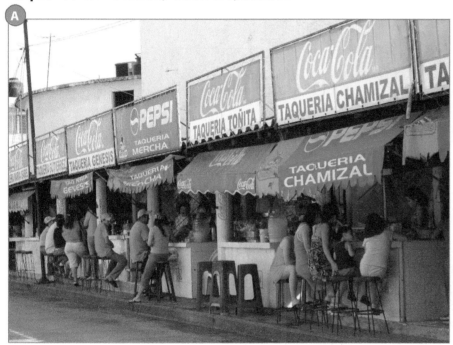

Las **taquerías** son **puestos** de tacos en la calle. Podemos comer allí, o **pedir tacos para llevar.**

El señor **prepara** tacos de **carne asada** con tortillas de maíz.

Los tacos de **carnitas** (carne de cerdo) **se sirven** con cebollas, cilantro y limón.

También hay **tacos** de pescado.

Los tacos se sirven con **salsas** rojas y verdes.

También **se sirven quesadillas,** con tortillas de **harina**, no de maíz.

Actividad 25

🎧 ✦ ¿Qué se vende en la calle?

Identifica las imágenes que se describen en el audio. Escucha bien las descripciones y escribe la letra de la imagen correcta.

1. _____ 2. _____ 3. _____ 4. _____ 5. _____ 6. _____ 7. _____ 8. _____

Actividad 26

▶ ✦ Los tacos de Juan

Vas a ver un reportaje sobre los tacos en la ciudad de Guanajuato, México. Primero, lee las categorías de información en la tabla, y al escuchar, escribe toda la información que puedas sobre *Los Tacos de Juan*.

Los saludos y despedidas	Las horas que se compran los tacos	Los ingredientes	Las salsas y acompañamientos

Actividad 27

💬 En la Taquería Toñita

Quieres pedir tacos en la Taquería Toñita para tus amigos; son para llevar. Primero, pregúntales a tus compañeros qué tacos quieren. Luego toma el papel del cliente, y actúa el diálogo con Toñita en su puesto.

Detalle gramatical

Los verbos e ⟶ i

Some -**ir** verbs have a stem change from -**e**- to -**i**-, in the same four forms we saw with **e** ⟶ **ie** and **o** ⟶ **ue**:

pedir *to ask for, order*

pido	pedimos
pides	*pedís*
pide	piden

servir *to serve*

sirvo	servimos
sirves	*servís*
sirve	sirven

Mi progreso comunicativo

I can order street food from a vendor.

Expresiones útiles: Comprando tacos en la calle

¡Tengo hambre!
I'm hungry!

¡Tengo sed!
I'm thirsty!

Tengo ganas de comer unos tacos de camarón.
I feel like like eating some shrimp tacos.

¿Qué le pongo?
What can I serve you?

Quiero tres tacos de pescado, por favor.
I want three fish tacos, please

¿Sirven aguas frescas?
Do you serve aguas frescas?

¿Con qué salsa?
With which salsa?

¿Para aquí o para llevar?
For here or to go?

Detalle gramatical

Los demostrativos

Demonstratives are "pointing" words, like *this* and *that* in English. In Spanish, they must agree with the gender and number of the noun they refer to. **Este/esta/estos/estas** refer to something relatively close to the speaker, and not close to the listener.

This (singular)
Este taco está buenísimo.
Esta ensalada me gusta mucho.

These (plural)
Estos tacos están buenísimos.
Estas ensaladas me gustan mucho.

La sopa azteca es una sopa tradicional de México. Se prepara con pollo, aguacate, tomates, cebolla y tortillas de maíz. También se llama sopa de tortilla.

Observa 3

¿Cómo está la comida?

¡Cuidado! El café está **caliente.**

¡Ay! Esta torta está **demasiado picante.** Necesito tomar un agua fresca.

¡Tengo sed! Ahhh, el agua **está fría.**

¡Ñam ñam! El flan **está muy dulce.** Se prepara con mucho **azúcar.**

Este sancocho (La sopa de pollo) **está muy salado,** tiene **demasiada** sal.

Estos taquitos **están sabrosos.**

¿Qué observas?

In the above, sentences, notice the expressions in bold. What do they all have in common? What do they all describe? What verb is used in each one? Discuss your observations with a **compañero/a de clase**. View the Observa 3 resources in Explorer, and check the **Síntesis de gramática** at the end of this section of the unit.

Actividad 28

¿Probable o improbable?

Escucha las descripciones de los platos, e indica **P** si son probables o **I** si son improbables.

1. _____ 2. _____ 3. _____ 4. _____ 5. _____

6. _____ 7. _____ 8. _____ 9 _____ 10. _____

Actividad 29

📖 ✦ ¿Qué tal está?

Completa las oraciones con la respuesta más lógica.

1. ¡Cuidado, señor! El café con leche está muy dulce/caliente/picante.

2. ¡Qué horrible! No puedo comer estos tacos. Están demasiado (*too*) dulces/salados/sabrosos.

3. Mamá, el arroz con leche tiene mucho azúcar. Para mi está demasiado picante/caliente/dulce.

4. ¡Qué explosión en la boca! Estos chiles están muy calientes/picantes/dulces.

5. Mesero (*waiter*), prefiero la sopa muy caliente. Pero esta sopa está dulce/sabrosa/fría.

Actividad 30

💬 Los críticos hablan

Tu compañero/a y tú son críticos que escriben reseñas (*reviews*) de restaurantes. Uno (*Estudiante A*) es positivo, y el otro (*Estudiante B*) es muy severo. Túrnense para expresar una reacción positiva y negativa a las siguientes comidas mexicanas del restaurante Achiote.

Modelo

la sopa de tomate

Estudiante A:	La sopa de tomate está deliciosa. ¡Me encanta!
Estudiante B:	La sopa de tomate está muy salada. No me gusta para nada.

1. el flan
2. el pollo con mole
3. los huevos rancheros

4. los tacos de bistec
5. la sopa azteca
6. los tacos de pescado

✦ Estrategias

Elaboration and detail

Prepositional phrases can help you elaborate and add important details when you communicate. The most commonly used prepositions in Spanish are *con, en, de* and *a*.

To specify **with** whom you do something use **con** + *una persona*.
To refer to yourself use **conmigo**.

Voy al restaurante **con** mis padres.
¿Quieres cenar **conmigo**? (*with me*)

To specify location, use **en** + *un lugar*.

La taquería en la calle Hidalgo es muy popular.

To specify what something is made of, use **de** + *comida*.

¿Quieres un sándwich **de** jamón y queso?

To specify the time of actions, use **a** + *la/las*.

Desayuno churros y chocolate **a** las ocho.

Mi progreso comunicativo

I can state personal reactions to the tastes of food.

Actividad 31

El desayuno en Cozumel, México

Cozumel, México

DESAYUNOS

Casa mission restaurant

7:30 AM
12:00 AM

HUEVOS AL GUSTO
Rancheros
A la Mexicana
Con Jamón
Divorciados
Motuleños

ENCHILADAS
Rojas
Verdes

CHILAQUILES
Rojos
Verdes

QUESADILLAS

CLUB SÁNDWICH

TACOS DORADOS

HOT CAKES

TOSTADAS
A LA FRANCESA

COCKTEL
DE FRUTAS

$65
Incluye: Café ilimitado y un vaso
de Jugo de Naranja

EXTRAS
Aguas $18
Horchata y Jamaica
Refrescos $20
Coca-Cola, Coca-cola Light,
Mirinda, 7up
Jugo de naranja $18
Agua Embotellada $18
Café Ilimitado $25
Ingrediente Extra $25

Free WiFi
Cablemas
User: damian.miranda@gmail.com
Password: Batallas5

📍 55 Av. entre Av. Juárez y 1a sur.
🌐 www.missioncoz.com

🐦 LaMissionCZM
f CasaMissionCzm
☎ 87 2 16 41

📖 **Paso 1: ¿Qué se sirve aquí?**

Estudia el menú y contesta a estas preguntas.

1. Los precios, ¿están en pesos o dólares, probablemente?

2. ¿Qué platos del menú se asocian con la comida mexicana? ¿Qué platos son internacionales?

3. ¿Qué platos te gustaría probar?

Mi progreso comunicativo

I can interpret a simple menu and order foods I would like to sample.

🗨️ Paso 2: Me gustaría probar...

Estás en Cozumel, México; son las 10:00 de la mañana y tienes mucha hambre. Decides desayunar en el restaurante Casa Misión en el centro de la ciudad.

Trabajando con un/a compañero/a, actúen la situación entre cliente y mesero *(waiter)*.

Mesero/a:	Greet the customer.
Cliente:	Respond. Ask what the waiter recommends.
Mesero/a:	Respond.
Cliente:	Say what you want to eat.
Mesero/a:	Ask if the customer wants something to drink.
Cliente:	Respond with your drink order.

(after the meal)

Mesero/a:	Ask if the customer likes the dish.
Cliente:	Respond affirmatively, and say it is delicious.

Enfoque cultural

Práctica cultural: Cómo pagamos

En México, el lugar de la compra determina cómo pagamos. En los puestos de la calle, en los tianguis y en muchas tiendas, se paga en efectivo.

En restaurantes o tiendas nacionales usamos la tarjeta de crédito o pagamos en efectivo.

 Conexiones

How do you pay when shopping in your community? Are there places of business that only accept cash?

Pagamos en efectivo en el tianguis.

Pagamos con tarjeta de crédito en ciertas tiendas.

Síntesis de gramática
Los verbos con cambios de raíz

So far you have learned to conjugate regular verbs by changing the endings added to **la raíz** *(verb stem or root)*. Some verbs have additional changes: the verb has a different stem in four of the six present-tense forms. Study closely the verb **querer** below; the last **-e-** of the stem (**quer-**) becomes the diphthong **-ie-** when the word stress falls on it.

Compare the conjugation of **querer**, with stem changes, to that of **beber**, which keeps the same vowel throughout:

querer		*beber*	
quiero	queremos	bebo	bebemos
quieres	queréis	bebes	bebéis
quiere	quieren	bebe	beben

Likewise, some verbs whose last stem vowel is **-o-** change it to **-ue-** in the same four forms as above:

probar		*tomar*	
pruebo	probamos	tomo	tomamos
pruebas	probáis	tomas	tomáis
prueba	prueban	toma	toman

Some students use the term "boot" verb to help remember which forms have **-ie-** or **-ue-**; the conjugation chart resembles the shape of a boot. You will have to memorize which verbs change their stems in the present tense when you learn the verb. In *EntreCulturas,* we indicate that a verb has a stem change by highlighting the corresponding vowel red font and listing it after the infinitive, e.g., **costar (o → ue)**.

In varieties of Spanish that use **vos**, the corresponding verbs have the stress on the ending, so the stem stays **-e-** or **-o-**: **vos querés, vos probás.**

Los verbos como *gustar*

You already know how to express likes and dislikes with **(no) me gusta**. This expression is different from the action verbs you have learned so far; you have seen that the verb ending tells who does an action, with an optional subject pronoun:

(Yo) desayun<u>o</u> a las 7:00.

Gustar works differently; literally, **me gusta** means "it is pleasing to me," so the thing you like ("it") is the subject of the verb, and **me** expresses to whom it is pleasing. We use a different set of pronouns **(me, te, le, nos, os, les)** before the verb, and only the third-person forms, singular **gusta** or plural **gustan**, depending on how many things we are talking about. The literal translation shows the same singular/plural options in English *(is/are pleasing)*:

Me gusta la pizza *(Pizza is pleasing to me, or I like pizza).*
Me gustan las papas fritas *(French fries are pleasing to me, or I like French fries).*

Other expressions that use this construction also have to do with experiences, rather than actions: **dar igual, encantar, molestar** *(to bother).* You will encounter many more of these verbs in your study of Spanish, and mastering the details of this structure can be a long process. Just be patient, and pay attention to the examples you come across.

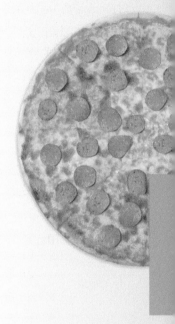

Estar con los adjetivos

The Spanish verbs **ser** and **estar** can both be translated into English as "to be," but they do not mean the same thing. When used with adjectives to describe, **ser** indicates a trait that is normal or expected (e.g., **el hielo es frío,** *ice is cold*). **Estar** with an adjective, on the other hand, expresses a trait that is out of the norm, exceptional, or when there is no normal state. For example, milk is good for you in general, but a particular glass you are trying may be especially satisfying:

La leche <u>es</u> buena para la salud.   *Milk is good for your health.*

¡Esta leche <u>está</u> buena!   *This milk is (tastes) delicious!*

Therefore, **estar** with an adjective is very useful when describing your reactions to foods that you are eating or have eaten:

El arroz con leche de mi abuela <u>está</u> muy rico.
My grandmother's rice pudding is delicious.

¡Caramba! Esta sopa <u>está</u> fría.   *Darn it! This soup is (got) cold.*

Arroz con leche

Vocabulario

I can purchase food in a market, supermarket or store

I can specify quantity of foods for purchase and describe color (Así se dice 1)

Las frutas	**Fruit**
la fresa	strawberry
la manzana	apple
el melón	melon
la naranja	orange
la papaya	papaya
la piña	pineapple
el plátano	banana (Méx., Esp.); plantain (L.A.)
la sandía	watermelon
la uva	grape

Las verduras	**Vegetables**
la lechuga	lettuce
el pepino	cucumber
las espinacas	spinach

Otros alimentos	**Other foods**
la cebolla	onion
el chile poblano	poblano chili
la ensalada	salad
la papa	potato

Las bebidas	**Beverages**
el agua (f.)	water
el agua fresca	fruit-flavored water
el batido	smoothie; shake
el jugo	juice

Los colores	**Colors**
anaranjado/a	orange
amarillo/a	yellow
azul	blue
blanco/a	white
morado/a	purple
negro/a	black
rojo	red
rosado/a	pink
verde	green

Los verbos	**Verbs**
beber	to drink
comprar	to buy
pedir (e → i)	to ask for; to order
pensar (e → ie)	to think
preferir (e → ie)	to prefer
probar (o → ue)	to try
querer (e → ie)	to want
recomendar (e → ie)	to recommend
vender	to sell

Expresiones útiles

En el mercado

¿Qué va a llevar?	What can I get for you?	una docena (de)	a dozen
Quiero…	I'd like…	¿Cuánto es?	How much is it?
Póngame por favor…	Please give me…	Son 30 pesos.	It'll be 30 pesos.
un kilo (de)	a kilo (of)	Aquí lo tiene.	Here you go/Here it is.
medio kilo (de)	half a kilo (of)		
un cuarto de kilo (de)	fourth of a kilo (of)		
cien gramos	100 grams		

I can list several foods I typically eat for breakfast, lunch, dinner, and snacks (Así se dice 2)

Las comidas diarias	Daily meals
el almuerzo	lunch
la cena	dinner
la comida	midday meal
el desayuno	breakfast

La comida	Food
el aguacate	avocado
el arroz	rice
el bistec	steak
la carne	meat
los frijoles	beans
la hamburguesa	hamburger
el helado de vainilla	vanilla ice cream
los huevos fritos/ rancheros	fried/ranchero-style eggs
el jamón	ham
el pan dulce	sweet bread
el pastel	cake; pastry
la tostada	toast
las papas fritas	French fries
el pollo con mole	chicken with mole sauce
el sándwich de queso	cheese sandwich
la sopa azteca	tortilla soup
la sopa de tomate	tomato soup
la tortilla de maíz	corn tortilla
el pay de manzana (Mex.)	apple pie
el postre	dessert
el yogur con frutas	yogurt with fruit

Más bebidas	More beverages
el café con leche	coffee with milk
el refresco	soft drink
el té helado	iced tea

I can express likes and dislikes with regards to food items (Así se dice 2)

¡Qué rico!	Yum! Delicious!
¡Qué asco!	How disgusting! Gross!

I can order food from a menu or menu board (Así se dice 3)

La comida callejera	Street food
el puesto	stand
la quesadilla	quesadilla
la salsa	salsa, sauce
los tacos de carne asada	beef tacos
los tacos de carnitas	pork tacos
los tacos de pescado	fish tacos
la tortilla de harina	flour tortilla
la taquería	taco stand

I can ask questions about and share reactions to food (Así se dice 3)

¿Cómo está la comida?	How's the food?
bueno/a	good; tasty
caliente	hot
delicioso/a	delicious
dulce	sweet
este/esta	this
estos/estas	these
fresco/a	fresh
frío/a	cold
picante	spicy
rico/a	delicious
sabroso/a	tasty, delicious
salado/a	salty

Las expresiones con tener	
tener ganas de + inf.	to feel like + -ing
tener hambre	to be hungry
tener sed	to be thirsty

En el restaurante	
el azúcar	sugar
cocinar	to cook
el flan	egg custard
pagar	to pay
en efectivo	in cash
con tarjeta de crédito	by credit card
llevar	to carry; take out
preparar	to prepare
la sal	salt
servir (e → i)	to serve

**Marina Ferrara Hernández,
nuestra bloguera de España**

En camino

La comida española

Marina, our video blogger from Spain, describes her eating schedule and talks about a very famous dish from Spain.

▶ ✦ Paso 1: Detalles del video blog

Marina is going to mention the information below. Make sure you understand the categories, then watch and listen to the blog and jot down the information requested.

Hora del desayuno	
Hora de la comida	
Hora de la cena	
Ingredientes de la tortilla española	
Frutas y comidas favoritas de Marina	

💬 ✦ Paso 2: ¿Qué es la tortilla?

A tortilla in Spain is different from a tortilla in Mexico. Based on the information in this chapter, describe the difference. Which would you you prefer to eat? Compare your preference with a classmate.

Mi progreso comunicativo

I can talk about similarities and differences in foods across cultures.

✉ ✦ Un email a la Ciudad de México

You ate a delicious dish in a Mexican restaurant in your city. Write an email to a friend in Mexico City in which you describe the dish following the guidelines below.

- Greet your friend.

- Name and describe the dish, and express your personal reaction to it.

- Ask at least one question about his/her favorite food in Mexico.

- Say goodbye.

Mi progreso comunicativo

I can produce brief written descriptions of foods from the target culture.

Actividad 34

En la Taquería Chamizal

You are in Mexico City with a friend and you both are hungry. You are going to order tacos from Taquería Chamizal. Use the menu board below.

Taquería Chamizal

TACOS
$6.00 c/u

DE CANASTA
(chorizo, papa, chicharrón, mole verde)
SUADERO (carne de res)
POLLO
PASTOR (carne de cerdo)
CARNITAS (carne de cerdo)
PESCADO

AGUAS FRESCAS
$15.00 c/u

PIÑA
GUAYABA
PAPAYA
SANDÍA
MELÓN
JAMAICA

REFRESCOS FRÍOS
$10.00 c/u

¡BUEN PROVECHO!

📖 💬 **Paso 1: ¿Qué vamos a comer?**

With a classmate decide what you are going to order from the menu above. Each person has to defend his choice by describing the options using **gustar, encantar, estar** + adjective.

💬 **Paso 2: ¡Quiero dos tacos, por favor!**

You and your classmate order tacos and drinks from another classmate who works in the taco stand.

Mi progreso comunicativo

I can order foods from a basic menu or menu board.

Explora

Essential Questions:

- How do food products and food practices shape our cultural identity?

- How can exploring new foods lead me to new intercultural identities?

Overview

Enjoying food with friends, family, and others around us nourishes us physically and makes us a community. Learning about and sharing food from other cultures can create intercultural connections.

La comida expresa nuestras raíces   235

Explore traditional dishes from Costa Rica and Paraguay as well as a short history of BBQ in the Americas to learn how **food is an expression of our roots** and our past.

Video blog	*El gallo pinto: un desayuno costarricense*
Video blog	*El vorí-vorí: una sopa paraguaya*
Lectura	*La barbacoa: una tradición con historia*

La comida nos une   239

Explore how immigrants are sharing their food traditions with their new communities in North Carolina.

Mapa	*Los latinos en los Estados Unidos*
Gráfico	*Población latina en Carolina del Norte*
Video	*La comunidad hispana en Carolina del Norte*
Artículo	*Una cadena de comida rápida mexicana en Carolina del Norte expande sus operaciones*

En mi comunidad   244

Festivales de comida: Celebraciones de identidad local.

La comida expresa nuestras raíces

Actividad 35

Un desayuno tico

🔍 **Paso 1: El desayuno de Isaac, de Costa Rica**

Mira la foto, y escribe una lista de los alimentos que reconoces.

▶️ ✺ **Paso 2: Los alimentos**

Escucha a Isaac hablar de su desayuno, que incluye **el gallo pinto,** un plato tradicional de Costa Rica. ¿Qué alimentos de esta lista menciona?

- ❏ arroz
- ❏ café (con leche)
- ❏ cereal
- ❏ ceviche
- ❏ frijoles
- ❏ guacamole

- ❏ huevo frito
- ❏ jugo de naranja
- ❏ natilla *(sour cream)*
- ❏ plátano maduro *(ripe plantain)*
- ❏ tomate
- ❏ tortillas

Un desayuno típico costarricense le da energía a Isaac antes de ir al colegio.

⊚ 📝 **Paso 3: Compara**

Compara tu desayuno con el desayuno de Isaac. Usa un diagrama de Venn.

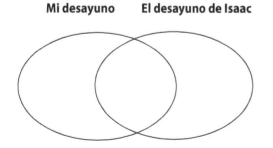

Mi desayuno   El desayuno de Isaac

Expresiones útiles

es caliente

es diferente

es frío

es más grande que

es más nutritivo que

es similar

El gallo pinto es la combinación de frijoles y arroz.

¡Los platos típicos paraguayos le encantan a María Laura!

El vorí - vorí

La mandioca o yuca acompaña muchas comidas paraguayas.

Actividad 36

El vorí - vorí: una sopa paraguaya

Paso 1: Mis hábitos de comer

Contesta a estas preguntas por escrito *(in written form)*. Luego, compara tus respuestas con otro estudiante.

1. ¿A qué hora desayunas típicamente? ¿A qué hora almuerzas? ¿A qué hora cenas?

2. **Meriendas** *(do you snack)* ocasionalmente? ¿Qué te gusta merendar? ¿A qué hora?

3. ¿Tu familia tiene una **huerta** *(vegetable garden)*?

4. ¿Qué verduras te gustan? ¿Cuál es tu opinión de las **arvejas** *(peas)*?

5. ¿Comes estas raíces *(root vegetables)* en tu casa?
   batata *(sweet potato)*
   mandioca *(yuca)*
   remolacha *(beet)*
   zanahoria *(carrot)*

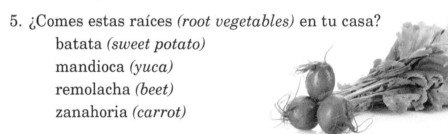

Paso 2: Los hábitos de María Laura

Lee las preguntas. Mira y escucha el video blog para encontrar las respuestas.

1. ¿Cuál es el horario de comidas de María Laura (desayuno, almuerzo, merienda, cena)?

2. ¿Cuáles son los ingredientes del vorí-vorí?

3. ¿Qué tipo de platos le gustan a María Laura?

4. ¿Qué alimentos no le gustan?

Paso 3: Compara

Compara el vorí - vorí, la sopa de María Laura, con una sopa típica en tu comunidad. ¿En qué son similares o diferentes?

Reflexión intercultural

⊕ Which foods that Isaac and María Laura mentioned would you like to try? Are there some foods that seem unappealing to you? Why?

Describe some of your food habits, preferences and favorite dishes, and those of some other people in your family and community. What aspects do you think would surprise Isaac and María Laura? Why?

Answer the questions in the forum in Explorer then read and comment on at least three of your classmates' answers.

 Mi progreso intercultural

I can recognize how my food habits and preferences reflect my culture, and compare that with those of young people in Spanish-speaking countries.

Actividad 37

La barbacoa: una tradición con historia

Paso 1

Observa y describe la imagen. Prepara una lista de comidas preparadas con esta técnica en tu comunidad.

Orígenes de la barbacoa: los indígenas powhatan (actual estado de Virginia) preparan pescado sobre una fogata. Publicado en 1590.

Paso 2

Lee el texto, y prepara tres ilustraciones para representar "La historia de la barbacoa".

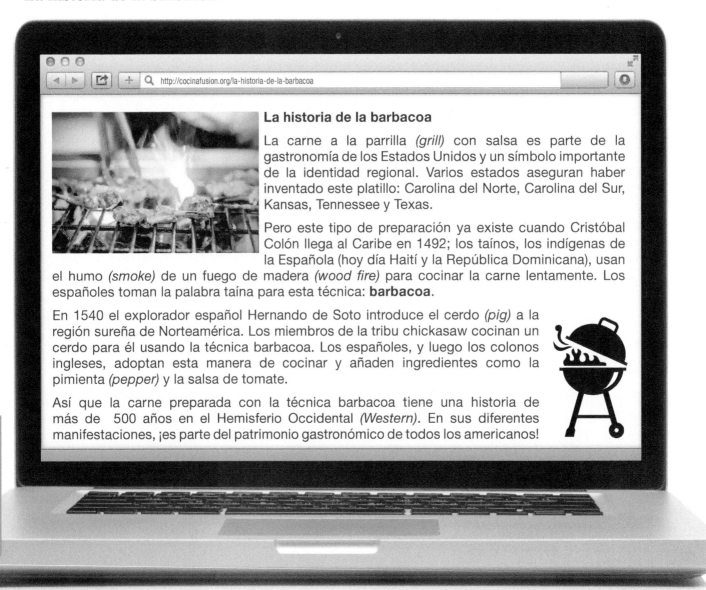

La historia de la barbacoa

La carne a la parrilla *(grill)* con salsa es parte de la gastronomía de los Estados Unidos y un símbolo importante de la identidad regional. Varios estados aseguran haber inventado este platillo: Carolina del Norte, Carolina del Sur, Kansas, Tennessee y Texas.

Pero este tipo de preparación ya existe cuando Cristóbal Colón llega al Caribe en 1492; los taínos, los indígenas de la Española (hoy día Haití y la República Dominicana), usan el humo *(smoke)* de un fuego de madera *(wood fire)* para cocinar la carne lentamente. Los españoles toman la palabra taína para esta técnica: **barbacoa**.

En 1540 el explorador español Hernando de Soto introduce el cerdo *(pig)* a la región sureña de Norteamérica. Los miembros de la tribu chickasaw cocinan un cerdo para él usando la técnica barbacoa. Los españoles, y luego los colonos ingleses, adoptan esta manera de cocinar y añaden ingredientes como la pimienta *(pepper)* y la salsa de tomate.

Así que la carne preparada con la técnica barbacoa tiene una historia de más de 500 años en el Hemisferio Occidental *(Western)*. En sus diferentes manifestaciones, ¡es parte del patrimonio gastronómico de todos los americanos!

Paso 3

¿Qué platos típicos son importantes para la identidad de tu comunidad?

Reflexión intercultural

Barbecued pork can be considered a "fusion" food, the result of contact between different cultures—indigenous American and European. Research the phenomenon of the so-called "Columbian exchange" to see what other combinations were brought together in this first wave of globalization.

Mi progreso intercultural

I can identify examples demonstrating how foods reflect interactions between cultures.

La comida nos une

En Carolina del Norte, la población de origen hispano está creciendo (*is growing*) mucho. Ahora se habla español, se escucha música latina y se comen platos de diferentes países latinoamericanos. Los cambios demográficos afectan a todos los aspectos de la comunidad, hasta (*even*) la comida.

Gráficos

La información en el mapa fue publicada en el sitio de web del *Council of State Governments* con datos del *Pew Hispanic Center*.

Los latinos en los Estados Unidos

SD +103%
NY
NJ
DE +96%
MD +106%
IL
KY +122%
CA
CO
NC +111%
AZ
NM
TN +134%
AR +114%
SC +148%
MS +106%
AL +145%
GA +96%
TX
FL

- 10 estados con mayor población latina
- 10 estados con mayor crecimiento latino (2000-2010)

Población latina en Carolina del Norte

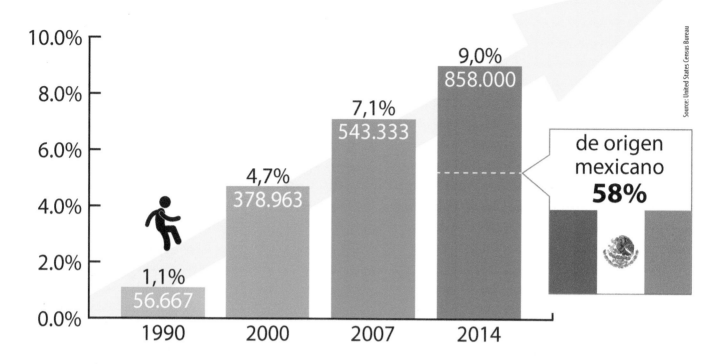

Actividad 38

¿Nuevos vecinos, nuevas costumbres?

🔍 **Paso 1: Los latinos en los EE. UU.**

En grupos de dos, estudien el mapa y el gráfico, y contesten a las siguientes preguntas.

1. ¿Dónde están las poblaciones latinas más grandes en Estados Unidos?

2. ¿Qué estados tienen el mayor crecimiento (*growth*) en la población latina?

3. ¿Qué grupo latino es el más grande en la Carolina del Norte?

Paso 2: Impacto latino

¿Cuáles son los impactos más probables de este crecimiento en las comunidades que lo experimentan? Piensen en estas categorías:

- las celebraciones
- la comida
- la educación
- la música
- los negocios (las tiendas y los mercados)
- la religión.

Paso 3: Busquemos en el mapa

Usen la función de mapas de su navegador de internet para buscar mapas y temas del **Paso 2** en las ciudades de Asheboro, Monroe, Sanford o Selma, Carolina del Norte. ¿Qué tipos de escuelas, negocios, iglesias, etc., encuentran? ¿Cómo se llaman? ¿Son muchos o pocos?

Paso 4: La comunidad hispana en Carolina del Norte

Ahora mira el video "La comunidad hispana en Carolina del Norte" y apunta ejemplos—productos y prácticas—de las categorías del **Paso 2**.

Reflexión intercultural

Which aspects of the Hispanic communities in North Carolina would you like to experience? What opportunities are there in your community to have an intercultural experience? How can a growing Hispanic population affect a community in the U.S. in a positive way? Share your observations with your classmates in Explorer.

Mi progreso intercultural

I can identify opportunities to create intercultural experiences.

Actividad 39

Una cadena *(chain)* de comida rápida

A2 Paso 1: Anticipación: Para mí es importante

Indica qué es importante para ti cuando escoges *(choose)* un restaurante de comida rápida. Pon en orden de preferencia los criterios siguientes (de 1 a 4, 1 es el más importante). Comparte tus respuestas con un/a compañero/a.

_____ la ubicación (está cerca de tu casa, por ejemplo)

_____ el precio

_____ el ambiente *(atmosphere)*

_____ la calidad de comida

Paso 2: Al leer

Lee el artículo a la derecha y contesta a las preguntas siguientes.

1. ¿Qué platillos puedes pedir en este restaurante?

2. ¿Cuál es el origen del nombre del restaurante?

3. ¿Cómo se llaman los fundadores *(founders)* de la cadena? ¿Dónde encuentran la inspiración para las comidas que sirven?

4. ¿Cuáles son tres aspectos positivos de la cadena mencionados en el artículo?

5. Con la información del artículo, ¿qué puedes inferir de la importancia de la comida mexicana en la Carolina del Norte?

Paso 3: Quiero comer en Salsarita's

Lee el mensaje siguiente de un amigo y escribe una respuesta. Explica por qué quieres comer en Salsarita's esta noche *(tonight)*.

> Hola, amigo,
> ¿Quieres cenar conmigo en Salsarita's esta noche? Voy con mis padres y ellos te invitan *(it's their treat)*. Mis padres dicen *(say)* que la comida en Salsarita's es deliciosa. Vamos a las 7:00. Escríbeme pronto.

EE. UU.- Una cadena de comida rápida mexicana en Carolina del Norte expande sus operaciones

Los tradicionales burritos, tacos, nachos, quesadillas, enchiladas, ensaladas, chips mexicanos al estilo "Cantina Fresca" han convertido a Salsarita's en una de las cadenas de restaurantes de comida rápida de mayor crecimiento del país.

Paul Mangiamele, el director ejecutivo, explica que el nombre Salsarita's provino de "Salsa, que denota baile, y Rita, bebidas, como la Margarita".

Salsarita's fue fundada[1] en Charlotte, la ciudad más poblada de Carolina del Norte, en el año 2000 por Bruce Willette y Thang Nguyen, con bastante experiencia en administrar diversas cadenas de restaurantes.

"Viajaron por varias zonas de México en búsqueda de[2] los sabores y colores propios de la comida mexicana para crear recetas[3] únicas, que se han ido combinando para ofrecer opciones diferentes", apuntó Mangiamele.

La franquicia[4] de comida ofrece una variedad de platillos: el mismo cliente puede seleccionar sus ingredientes, el tipo de carne, fríjoles, arroz, salsa o tortilla que contendrá su burrito, quesadilla, o que desea en su pizza, ensalada, al igual que la cantidad.

Esa filosofía de "mi casa es tu casa" de ofrecer comida fresca, nutritiva, en un ambiente acogedor[5], divertido, colorido, festivo, con excelente atención al cliente, es lo que ha permitido que la cadena continúe aumentando[6] su presencia a nivel nacional.

1 was founded 2 in search of
3 recipes 4 franchise
5 welcoming 6 increasing

En mi comunidad

Festivales de comida: Celebraciones de identidad local

Actividad 40

Cada lugar con su festival

📖 **Paso 1: Anuncios de festival**

Estos dos pósters son para festivales de platos icónicos: la barbacoa de Carolina del Norte y los tamales mexicanos. ¿Qué información tienen en común los dos anuncios? Identifica los siguientes elementos:

1. el nombre del festival

2. la fecha

3. el horario

4. el lugar

5. el precio de entrada

6. el entretenimiento (*entertainment*)

🔍 📖 💬 **Paso 2: Iconos comestibles**

Trabajando con un/a compañero/a, contesten a estas preguntas basándose en los anuncios.

1. ¿Qué símbolos de identidad local o regional hay en las imágenes de los anuncios?

2. ¿Qué tipos de actividades se hacen en estos festivales probablemente?

3. ¿Te gusta participar en este tipo de festivales? ¿Por qué sí o no?

México bate récord con la línea de tacos de cochinita pibil más grande del mundo

EFE, www.efeamerica.com (2015). Retrieved from http://tinyurl.com/z9sfy5p.

La línea de tacos más grande del mundo: la cochinita pibil, típica de Yucatán

La ciudad de Guadalajara, en el occidente de México, rompió hoy el récord de la línea tacos de cochinita pibil más grande del mundo, con una hilera de 2.757 metros de longitud.

Con una fila continua de 44.000 tacos preparados con 36.145 kilos de tortillas, una tonelada de carne y 300 litros de salsa, la capital del estado de Jalisco superó la marca anterior de 1.990 metros impuesta en Estados Unidos, de acuerdo con Pedro Evia, uno de los *chefs* participantes.

Un notario público certificó el largo de la línea, así como la cantidad de ingredientes empleados, con la finalidad de certificar el logro ante la organización del **Récord Guinness**.

La elaboración de los tacos se llevó a cabo como parte de las actividades del festival gastronómico **Come,** que se realiza anualmente en esta ciudad y este año tiene como invitado al estado de Yucatán, en el sureste de México.

Las manos de 200 *chefs* prepararon durante seis días la cochinita pibil, un platillo típico de Yucatán a base de carne de cerdo con una salsa de jugo de naranja agria, achiote, canela, chile y otras especias.

Luego de la ceremonia de certificación, los tacos fueron repartidos entre unas cinco mil personas, coronados con un poco de cebolla morada y chile habanero para resaltar su sabor.

🗒 Paso 3: Publicidad para un festival

¿Existen festivales de comida en tu comunidad? Escribe una lista de festivales o de comidas típicas populares para inventar un festival.

🎤 🗒 ✎ ✦ Paso 4: Un festival en tu comunidad

Crea un póster y/o un anuncio audio en español para anunciar a la comunidad hispanohablante el festival de una comida o un plato icónico del lugar donde vives. Incluye los siguientes aspectos:

- comida típica o icónica
- música
- actividades culturales
- la temporada adecuada del año
- otras imágenes o símbolos que comuniquen la identidad de la comunidad o región.

Comparte tu anuncio con la clase en la guía digital.

Vive entre culturas

Aquí se vende comida hispana

Essential Question: What are some iconic foods from the Spanish-speaking world that I think I would like, given my existing food preferences?

Un *food truck* para mi colegio

The Director of Food Services in your school district has decided to go global and expand food choices for students. She has proposed the idea of an international food truck from which students can purchase their lunch and is asking students for input. You and two classmates have decided to design and promote a food truck that will feature items from at least two Spanish-speaking countries that you have studied or researched.

Interpretive Assessment

📖 ⊕ El *food truck* que vende tacos en la República Dominicana

Before you design your food truck, read about a food truck in the Dominican Republic that sells traditional food from Mexico. Look at the images and map, and discuss them with your teacher before you do the assessments in Explorer based on this reading.

Interpersonal Assessment

 ⊕ **¿Vamos a Don Camarón?**

The Don Camarón food truck is located today on Calle Juan Bosch in Punta Cana, República Dominicana. Following the instructions in Explorer, write a text message to a friend inviting him/her to get something to eat from Don Camarón.

Presentational Assessment

 ⊕ **Visita nuestro *food truck* internacional!**

You and two **compañeros de clase** are going to design and promote a food truck for your school. Carefully read the guidelines in Explorer.

Los cocineros de Don Camarón llevan máscaras de la lucha libre mexicana para promocionar su camión.

UNIDAD 5
La vida es un carnaval

Bailarines de música folclórica de la República Dominicana

Unit Goals

- Express preferences for leisure activities.

- Make simple social plans.

- Interpret print and audiovisual material about the Dominican celebration of Carnaval.

- Recognize the mutual influences between the Dominican Republic and the U.S., including sports and music.

⊕ Essential Questions

What leisure activities help to define my community and me?

How do popular celebrations reflect history and culture?

How do leisure activities create bridges between cultures?

CONOCE A PAOLA PABLINO HERNÁNDEZ, DE LA REPÚBLICA DOMINICANA

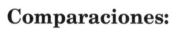

"Variety is the spice of life." Learn about Dominican teens and the typical activities they do for fun, during the week and on weekends—playing sports, going to movies, or just getting together with friends. In this unit, you will meet Paola from Dominican Republic, who will tell you about her favorite activities in her video blog.

Comparaciones:
La República Dominicana y Nueva York 250

Discover how La República Dominicana and New York are similar and different by exploring a timeline with information and images of special events that define their culture, relations, traditions, folklore, and history.

Comunica: La vida es un carnaval 253

Learn to ask and answer questions about traditions, special events, and daily activities you do with friends and family when you visit places.

Síntesis de gramática y vocabulario 282

Review the language needed to make plans for leisure activities with friends (**ir + a +** infinitive), use questions words (**¿cómo?, ¿dónde?,** etc.) to get more information about activities and events and express your reaction to different situations (**estar** + adjective). Use affirmative and negative words (**algo, nada,** etc.) when talking about leisure activities, and tell about what you did last weekend (**yo** form of preterit).

Explora 288

Read promotional ads and interpret videos of typical life in Dominican Republic to gain insights into the daily life of people of the country. Reflect on how traditions and customs help define a society and its values.

Vive entre culturas 300

Your class is planning a trip to Santo Domingo, Dominican Republic. In preparation, you research the country and the typical activities that young people your age do, like **el carnaval dominicano**.

Comparaciones
✦ La República Dominicana y Nueva York

Nueva York
(Estados
Unidos)

Algunos
grupos
indígenas
de Nueva
York son los
delaware, erie,
iroqueses,
mohawk,
oneida y
seneca.

Nueva York es
el estado 11
de los trece
originales

George
Washington
elegido primer
Presidente de
EE. UU.

Abolición de
la esclavitud
en el estado
de Nueva York

	Antes de 1492	1492	1496	1788	1789	1827	1844, 1865
La República Dominicana	Los indígenas taínos habitan la isla de Quisqueya o Haití	Colón llega a la isla en su primer viaje; le pone el nombre de La Española (Hispaniola)	Fundación de Santo Domingo				Primera y segunda independencia

Nueva York
8.5 millones

88% urbana

12% rural

NUEVA YORK

LA REPÚBLICA
DOMINICANA

Juegos
Olímpicos de
invierno en
Lake Placid,
Nueva York

Los Yankees de Nueva
York ganan la Serie
Mundial de béisbol

Huracán Sandy

Cae la tormenta
de nieve más
grande de la
historia: 70 cm

1930–61	1932	1977, 1978, 1996, 1998, 1999, 2000	2012	2013	2016

Dictadura
del General
Trujillo

Huracán Sandy

La República
Dominicana
gana el World
Baseball
Classic

Actividad 1

Productos de la República Dominicana y del estado de Nueva York

🔍 ⊘ Observa las imágenes. ¿Puedes identificar las que representan la República Dominicana? ¿Y los Estados Unidos? ¿Puedes identificar algunas conexiones entre los dos lugares?

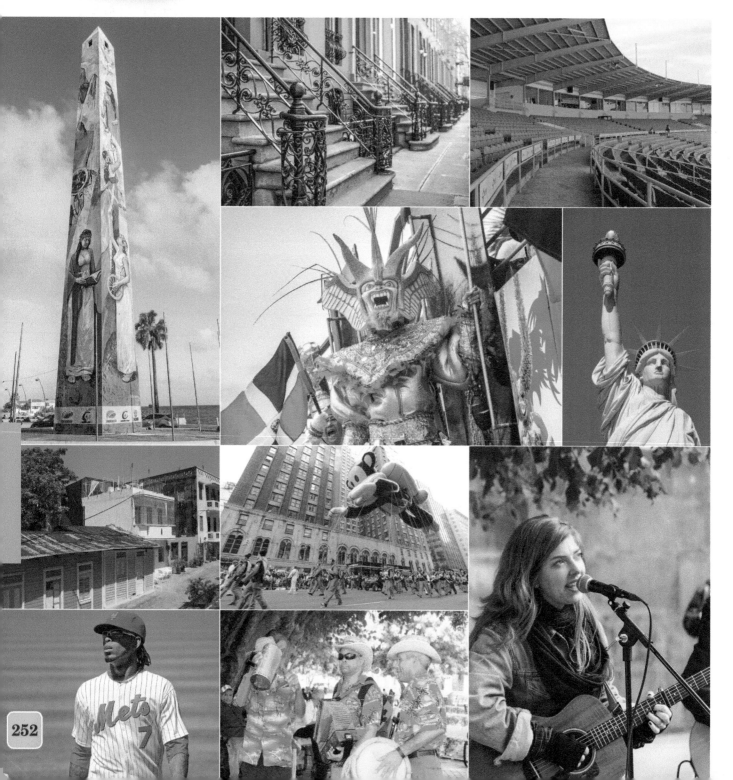

Comunica

Essential Question: What leisure activities help to define my community and me?

Las semillas (*seeds*) del cacao, un producto importante de la República Dominicana, es el origen del chocolate.

Check your progress to show what you have learned, and to discover areas where you may need some more practice to reach your learning goals.

Iglesia de San Estaneslao, ubicada en La Villa de Altos de Chavón, República Dominicana

Santo Domingo

Paola Pablino Hernández

Las personas de Higuey, República Dominicana, van de compras al centro del pueblo.

Puedes montar a caballo en la playa cerca de Las Galeras.

Video blog
Hola, soy Paola

Actividad 2

"Durante mi tiempo libre…"

Vas a escuchar a Paola, de la República Dominicana, hablar de sus actividades durante su tiempo libre, específicamente durante la semana y durante el fin de semana.

🅰🇿 ⊕ Paso 1: Mis actividades

Antes de ver el blog, habla con un/a compañero/a sobre tus actividades. ¿Haces cosas diferentes entre semana (during the week) y en el fin de semana? Escriban una lista de por lo menos seis actividades que ustedes hacen entre semana y seis actividades que hacen en el fin de semana.

> asistir a conciertos, dar un paseo, hacer tareas domésticas, jugar al fútbol, hacer la tarea, hacer camping, asistir a las clases, mirar películas

▶ ⊕ Paso 2: Las actividades de Paola

Mira y escucha el blog de Paola. ¿Cuáles actividades de la lista NO menciona?

- ❏ andar en bicicleta
- ❏ bailar
- ❏ tocar la guitarra
- ❏ ir de compras
- ❏ jugar al fútbol
- ❏ cantar
- ❏ tomar fotografías
- ❏ descansar
- ❏ pintar

▶ ⊕ Paso 3: ¿Cuándo lo hace?

Mira y escucha otra vez y anota las actividades de Paola en tres columnas: *Entre semana / Fin de semana / Días feriados (holidays)*. Compara tus listas con las de un/a compañero/a.

entre semana	el fin de semana

◯◯ ▱ ✳ **Paso 4: ¿Similar o diferente?**

Compara tus actividades con las actividades de Paola. Sigue el modelo.

Modelo

· ·

Durante mi tiempo libre…

Paola toma fotos, pero yo no tomo fotos.

Entre semana/En el fin de semana…

Paola hace la tarea, y yo también.

Vista de la playa Macao en Bavaro, República Dominicana

Enfoque cultural

Práctica cultural: El español caribeño

The Spanish of the Caribbean (República Dominicana, Puerto Rico, Cuba, Venezuela) has features that distinguish it from other varieties of the language, and speakers recognize them as important for the identity of the region:

Pronunciation of "s" at the end of a syllable: The [s] sound at the end of a syllable may be pronounced like [h], or not pronounced at all. **¿Cómo estás?** may sound like **¿Cómo etá?**

No inversion in questions: The order of words in questions is the same as in statements. Instead of **¿Dónde estás tú?**, you may hear **¿Dónde tú etá?**

Replace final -r with -l: The [r] at the end of a syllable may be pronounced as [l]: **hablal** instead of **hablar, depolte** for **deporte, pol favol** for **por favor**.

Of course, **caribeños** learn 'standard' Spanish in school and spell words the same as in other countries. The same person may vary his/her pronunciation according to the situation; these regional features emphasize a shared Caribbean identity in informal settings.

✺ ✳ **Conexiones**

What expressions or typical accents identify people from your region or community?

Así se dice 1

✦ ¿Qué haces los sábados?

Los sábados…

Voy a las **fiestas de cumpleaños** de mis parientes y amigos.

Voy al **centro comercial** con mis amigos.

Juego pelota (béisbol) con mi vecino *(neighbor)*.

Juego al dominó con mis tíos en la plaza.

Voy al **museo** de las Casas Reales.

Voy al **Parque** Colón para caminar.

Actividad 3

🎧 ✦ ¿Qué planes tienen?

Observa las fotos en **Así se dice 1,** y después escucha a las personas hablar de sus planes. Escribe la letra de la imagen que corresponde a la actividad que describen.

Parque Colón, Santo Domingo

1. _____ 2. _____ 3. _____ 4. _____ 5. _____ 6. _____

Actividad 4

¿Qué hacen estas personas?

A2 ⊕ **Paso 1**

Mira las fotos y di qué hacen estas personas los fines de semana.

Modelo

Dan un paseo en la playa.

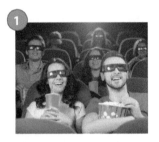

🎤 **Paso 2**

Ahora, di qué actividades de las fotos tú también haces, y las cosas que no haces.

Modelo

Yo también doy un paseo en la playa.
Me gusta hacer esquí acuático.

No doy un paseo en la playa.
No me gusta jugar al dominó.

Además se dice

Otras actividades

andar en bicicleta
ride a bicycle

andar en patineta
skateboard

asistir al carnaval
go to Carnival

dormir (o → ue)
una siesta
take a nap

escalar montañas
climb mountains

hacer esquí acuático
water ski

hacer máscaras
make masks

ir a un desfile
go to a parade

ir a una fiesta
go to a party

ir a la piscina/playa
go to the pool/beach

ir al cine
go to the movies

jugar (u → ue) al dominó
play dominoes

jugar (u → ue) al ajedrez
play chess

tocar en una banda
play in a band

tomar el sol
sunbathe

ver programas deportivos
watch sports on TV

Mi progreso comunicativo

I can state likes or dislikes and preferences relating to leisure activities.

Expresiones útiles: ¿Cuándo?

entre semana
during the (work) week

los fines de semana
on the weekends

el lunes
on Monday

los lunes
on Mondays

el domingo
on Sunday

los domingos
on Sundays

En la playa de Punta Cana, puedes nadar, tomar el sol, hacer kayak y otras actividades.

Actividad 5

ᴬᶻ Cada actividad en su lugar

¿Qué actividades (verbos) puedes hacer en los siguientes lugares? Nombra todas las actividades que se te ocurran.

1. el parque
2. la plaza
3. el museo
4. el campo deportivo
5. la casa
6. el centro comercial

Actividad 6

ᴬᶻ ⊕ ¿Cuándo lo haces?

¿Qué actividades haces sólo en momentos específicos de la semana? Clasifica tus actividades en estas categorías:

Cosas que sólo hago entre semana	Cosas que hago en cualquier día (*any day*)	Cosas que sólo hago los fines de semana

Actividad 7

 **¿Qué haces tú los fines de semana?**

Convierte estos verbos en preguntas para tus compañeros de clase. Luego, encuentra una persona que pueda contestar "sí" a diez (10) actividades.

andar en patineta	jugar al dominó
asistir a un concierto de música rap	leer un libro interesante
dar un paseo en el parque	montar en bicicleta
escalar montañas	tocar en una banda
hacer esquí acuático	tomar el sol en la playa
ir a una fiesta	ver una película con amigos
ir de compras en el centro comercial	

Modelo

Estudiante A:	¿Escalas montañas?
Estudiante B:	¡Sí, escalo montañas! / No, no escalo montañas.

El Limón

Detalle gramatical: El verbo *jugar*

The verb **jugar** is the only verb in Spanish that has a stem-change from **u ⟶ ue** in the present tense.

j**ue**go	j**u**gamos
j**ue**gas	*j**u**gáis*
j**ue**ga	j**ue**gan

Mi progreso comunicativo

I can ask and answer questions in a conversation about leisure activities that I like to do everyday or during the weekends.

Observa 1

¿Qué vas a hacer en las vacaciones?

Hola, María Dolores:

¡Saludos desde D. R.! Por fin estoy de vacaciones de verano, y **voy a estar** muy ocupada. Mis padres, mi hermano y yo **vamos a ir a la playa** por cuatro días. Después ellos **van a viajar** a Santo Domingo por asuntos de trabajo por tres semanas. Yo tengo que cuidar a mi hermano (con mis abuelos, por supuesto). Él **va a practicar pelota** y yo tengo que llevarlo a las prácticas. Y tú, ¿**vas a venir** a la República Dominicana por lo menos por una semana? ¡Me muero por verte!

Muchos besos, Pao

María Dolores
 Heins-Carmona
2112 Weimer Circle
Bronx, NY 10451
USA

¿Qué observas?

Look at the words in bold that Paola used in her postcard to talk about her plans in July. What expression does she use to talk about activities in the future? Did you observe a pattern in the construction of the sentences? Discuss your observations with your classmates and teacher. Review the **Observa 1** resources for this unit in your *EntreCulturas 1* Explorer course, and check the **Síntesis de gramática** at the end of this section of the unit.

Actividad 8

📖 ¿Planes lógicos?

En estas oraciones, Paola nos habla de otras actividades. ¿Son lógicas o no? Si no, cámbialas para darles más sentido.

1. "Me gusta el agua. Voy a nadar en la playa".

2. "A mi hermano le gusta comer mucho. Va a tomar el sol".

3. "Mi abuelo es súper activo. Va a caminar todos los días".

4. "Soy una persona intelectual. Voy a leer un libro de historia".

5. "Me gusta mucho la música. Voy a tocar en mi banda".

6. "Me gusta ir de compras. Voy a comer en un restaurante".

7. "No me gustan los deportes. Voy a jugar a la pelota".

8. "Me encanta bailar y charlar con amigos. Voy a ir a una fiesta".

Playa salvaje (*wild*), Samana

Bailarinas folklóricas, Altos de Chavón

En Santo Domingo, a la gente le gusta tomar algo con los amigos en las plazas de la ciudad.

Actividad 9

 ◈ **El lugar perfecto**

¿Cuál es el lugar perfecto para hacer estas actividades durante el próximo fin de semana? Combina elementos de las tres columnas para crear oraciones lógicas.

Yo	andar en patineta	en las montañas Adirondack de Nueva York
Mis padres	asistir al carnaval	en la biblioteca
Mi amigo/a y yo (nosotros)	escalar montañas	en casa
Mis hermanos	hacer esquí acuático	en casa de los amigos
Mis abuelos	ir a una fiesta	en la ciudad
Mis amigos	jugar al dominó	en el cine
	leer un libro	en la playa
	montar en bicicleta	en el parque
	tocar en la banda	en la sala de conciertos
	ver una película	

Modelo

. . . .

Mis padres **van a jugar** al dominó en el parque con mis abuelos.

Detalle gramatical:

El verbo *ir*

Recall the present tense forms of the verb **ir**:

voy	vas	va
vamos	*vais*	van

Actividad 10

 Todos somos voluntarios

Todos van al centro cultural de la ciudad este fin de semana para trabajar como voluntarios. ¿Qué va a hacer cada persona? Lee estas oraciones e indica una actividad probable.

Modelo

La profesora ayuda en el teatro.

Ella va a organizar los disfraces para el ballet folklórico.

1. Los estudiantes ayudan en el museo.
2. El padre de mi amigo Juan ayuda durante los conciertos.
3. Tú ayudas con los ancianos (*senior citizens*).
4. Marta ayuda durante las ceremonias.
5. Nosotros ayudamos en la cocina.
6. Yo ayudo con los niños.

Actividad 11

Un buen amigo siempre ayuda

Tu amigo/a no está bien hoy, y quieres proponer actividades para levantarle el ánimo (*cheer him/her up*). Un/a estudiante expresa cómo está, y el/la compañero/a sugiere una actividad.

Modelo

Estudiante A:	Estoy triste.
Estudiante B:	¿Por qué no vamos al cine? Vamos a ver una comedia.
Estudiante A:	¡Buena idea! ¡Vamos!

Mi progreso comunicativo

I can describe future plans and actions.

Expresiones útiles: ¿Cómo estás?

The verb **estar** is used with adjectives to describe a person's physical, mental, and emotional states or feelings.

estar aburrido/a *bored*

estar alegre/feliz/ contento/a *happy*

estar cansado/a *tired*

estar emocionado/a *excited*

estar enojado/a *angry*

estar genial *great, super*

estar interesado/a *interested*

estar nervioso/a *nervous*

estar ocupado/a *busy*

estar preocupado/a *worried*

estar triste *sad*

¡OJO! **Estar** is not used to describe sensations like hunger, thirst, hot, or cold; use **tener** + noun instead:

Tengo calor. *I'm hot.*

Tengo sed. *I'm thirsty.*

¿Tienes frío? *Are you cold?*

¿Tienes hambre? *Are you hungry?*

Así se dice 2

✦ ¿Quieres ir conmigo?

Yefry, un chico dominicano de 16 años, invita a dos amigos (Alex y Rafa) a una fiesta.

YefryDM — Alex04

> Hola, Alex, ¿k tal? ¿Qué haces mañana?

>> Hola, Yefry. Nada especial.

> ¿Quieres ir conmigo a una fiesta?

>> ¡Me encantaría! ¿De quién? ¿Dónde?

> Es en casa de Sofía.

>> Genial. ¿A qué hora?

> A las ocho.

>> Perfecto. ¿Cómo llegamos?

> ¿Por qué no vamos en metro? Paso por ti a las 7:45 y vamos juntos.

>> No, mejor vamos en guagua.

> ¡Chévere! Hasta mañana entonces.

YefryDM — Rafa2001

> ¡K lo K, Rafa! ¿Quieres ir conmigo a una fiesta mañana?

>> Hola, Yefry. No puedo mañana.

> ¿Qué pasa? ¿Qué vas a hacer?

>> Ya tengo planes, un evento familiar. Mis primos vienen de Nueva York.

> ¿Rosa y Migue? ¡Chévere!

>> Sí, vamos a pasarla bien, pero no puedo ir a la fiesta. Lo siento.

> No es para tanto. La próxima vez.

>> Sí, hasta la próxima.

Actividad 12

📖 Unas invitaciones

Lee las dos invitaciones en **Así se dice 2** y decide quién (Yefry, Alex o Rafa) hace la acción.

1. Acepta la invitación con mucho gusto.

2. Invita a dos amigos a una fiesta.

3. Prefiere ir en autobús.

4. Tiene que ver a sus primos.

5. No puede ir a la fiesta.

6. Quiere ir a la fiesta en metro.

7. Quiere saber la hora de la fiesta.

8. Explica dónde es la fiesta.

9. Tiene parientes en Nueva York.

10. No tiene planes para el fin de semana.

Actividad 13

📖 ¿Qué lo qué, amigos?

Lee los mensajes que Yefry les escribe a Rafa y a Alex. Contesta a las preguntas, y compara tus respuestas con las de un/a compañero/a. ¿Entendieron lo mismo?

1. ¿Qué quiere hacer Yefry?

2. ¿Cómo reaccionan Alex y Rafa al mensaje de Yefry?

3. ¿Cuáles son los planes (*plans*) de Rafa y de Alex?

4. ¿Qué palabra se usa en la República Dominicana en lugar de (*instead of*) "autobús"?

5. ¿Cómo reacciona Yefry a la respuesta de Rafa?

Check out the Learning Strategies video in Explorer for ideas to help you study vocabulary.

✦ Estrategias

Learning strategy: Study and practice

Remembering new words when you need them takes study and practice. Vary the way you practice new words: group words in different ways, make flashcards, draw pictures, and say the words aloud when you happen to be doing the action or using an object during your daily routines.

Altos de Chavón

Además se dice

Los elementos de una buena fiesta

¿Qué tipo de fiesta es?

el aniversario

la boda *wedding*

el cumpleaños

la fiesta de disfraces *costume party*

la fiesta sorpresa

la fiesta de graduación

¿Qué vamos a hacer?

cantar canciones *sing songs*

decorar con globos *decorate with balloons*

llegar tarde *arrive late*

llevar una máscara *wear a mask*

traer (g) flores *bring flowers*

traer (g) regalos *bring presents*

¿Qué llevo a la fiesta?

el disfraz *costume*

la ropa formal/informal

los pantalones cortos/largos

las sandalias

el traje *suit*

el vestido *dress*

¿Cómo llegamos? El transporte

tomar *to take*

la guagua (el autobús)

el metro

el taxi

Actividad 14

🔤 ✦ Muchas invitaciones

Estas oraciones vienen de diferentes invitaciones. ¿Qué oraciones a la derecha siguen lógicamente a las oraciones a la izquierda?

1. Ay, no puedo ir este sábado.
2. ¿A qué hora es la fiesta?
3. ¿Cómo llegamos?

4. ¿Dónde es la fiesta?
5. Mejor vamos en el metro, ¿no?
6. ¿Qué pasa? ¿Por qué no?
7. ¿Quieres ir conmigo a la fiesta?
8. Perfecto, hasta el sábado.

a. ¡Chévere!
b. Es a las 8:00 de la noche.
c. Es en el gimnasio de la escuela.

d. Lo siento, no puedo ir.
e. ¡Me encantaría!
f. No es para tanto.
g. ¿Por qué no vamos en guagua?
h. Ya tengo otros planes.

Actividad 15

🎧 ✦ ¿Invita, acepta o rechaza?

Escucha estas oraciones de diferentes invitaciones. ¿La persona <u>invita</u>, <u>acepta</u> o <u>rechaza</u> *(turns down)* una invitación?

1. _____   2. _____   3. _____

4. _____   5. _____   6. _____

La guagua (el autobús) es un transporte importante en la República Dominicana.

Actividad 16

A Z Preparaciones para la fiesta

La semana que viene *(next week)* quieres ir a una fiesta en casa de unos amigos. ¿Cómo va a ser? Completa estas oraciones para indicar lo necesario para una fiesta divertida.

Evento: Vamos a celebrar _____.

Lugar: La fiesta va a ser en _____.

Fecha: La fiesta va a ser el _____.

Comida: Vamos a comer _____, y vamos a beber _____.

Música: Vamos a escuchar _____.

Invitados: _____ van a ir.

Ambiente: La gente tiene que llevar ropa _____.

Actividades: En la fiesta, vamos a _____.

Actividad 17

? Padres preocupados

Quieres permiso para ir a una fiesta, pero tu padre/madre está preocupado/a; quiere saber más sobre el evento. En grupos de dos, actúen la situación en que una persona es el adolescente y la otra es el padre/la madre. Usen las **Expresiones útiles:** Las preguntas.

Expresiones útiles: Las preguntas

Question words **(las palabras interrogativas)** help you get more information about activities and events. Note that these words always carry a written accent mark. Also, remember to start a question with an inverted question mark.

¿A qué hora empieza la fiesta?

¿Por qué empieza tan tarde?

¿Cuánto tiempo va a durar?

¿Quién va a ir a la fiesta?

¿Qué vamos a comer en la fiesta?

¿Dónde es la fiesta?

¿Cuándo voy a recibir la invitación?

¿Cómo llegamos a la fiesta?

Actividad 18

💬 ✦ ¿Vamos juntos?

Escoge una de estas tres actividades de cultura dominicana en Nueva York, e invita a un/a compañero/a de clase a participar contigo. Prepárate para contestar a las preguntas de tu compañero/a sobre el evento.

Estudiante A: Invita y contesta a las preguntas de tu compañero/a.

Estudiante B: Escucha, pregunta sobre el evento y acepta la invitación.

Actividad 19

La invitación

Escribe una invitación para la fiesta de cumpleaños que vas a enviar (send) a los invitados. Decora tu invitación con imágenes apropiadas para el tema de la fiesta.

Modelo

Vamos a celebrar
La quinceañera
de
Mayanara Matas Rodríguez
29 de mayo
De las 7:00 pm a las 11:00 pm
Avenida Miraflores 32
Santo Domingo

*S.R.C.:
(877) 815-1530
O envía un correo a
mayanaram@amigos.com
Traje formal

*S.R.C. = se ruega contestación

Actividad 20

Excusas

Tus amigos te invitan a muchas actividades, pero estás muy ocupado/a y tienes que rechazar todas las invitaciones.

Paso 1: ¿Por qué no vas?

Con un/a compañero/a, escriban una lista de cinco excusas por las que una persona no puede aceptar una invitación. Sigan el modelo.

Modelo

Tengo que estudiar.

Paso 2: Una conversación difícil

Con un/a compañero/a, actúen la situación en que una persona invita y la otra explica por qué no puede participar.

Modelo

Estudiante A:	¿Quieres ir conmigo al partido de fútbol el viernes?
Estudiante B:	Lo siento, Marta, no puedo. Tengo que cenar con mi familia.

Mi progreso comunicativo

I can turn down invitations politely.

Observa 2

¡Vamos a la fiesta en metro!

Metro de Santo Domingo

Normas de uso del Metro de Santo Domingo

Siempre seguir las instrucciones del personal del Metro.

Siempre llevar el comprobante[1] de pago (tíquet, tarjeta o bono).

Nunca pasar la línea de seguridad del andén[2] mientras el tren esté en movimiento.

No molestar[3] a **nadie** en los andenes o vagones del tren.

No llevar **ningún**[4] objeto peligroso o prohibido.

No fumar[5] en los trenes ni en las estaciones.

Nunca entrar en la cabina del conductor.

No viajar con animales a excepción de perros lazarillos.

1 proof; 2 platform; 3 bother; 4 (not) any; 5 smoke

Descargue la App para su Smartphone

¿Qué observas?

📹🧭 Study the bold expressions in this list of rules for using the Metro in Santo Domingo. Which words tell you what **not** to do? Where can they appear in the sentence with respect to the verb—before, after, or both? Discuss your observations with your classmates and teacher. Review the **Observa 2** resources for this unit in Explorer, and check the **Síntesis de gramática** at the end of this section of the unit.

Expresiones útiles para las reglas (afirmativas y negativas)

todo el mundo	alguien	nadie
everybody	*somebody*	*nobody*
todo	algo	nada
everything	*something*	*nothing*
siempre	a veces	nunca
always	*sometimes*	*never*

Estación Juan Pablo Duarte en el Metro de Santo Domingo

Actividad 21

📖 ¿Puedo ir en metro?

Quiero ir en metro a diferentes lugares de Santo Domingo, pero ¿es posible en las siguientes circunstancias? Cita la norma que permite o prohíbe cada caso.

1. Quiero llevar a mi perra Linda a casa de mis abuelos.

2. Me gustaría llevar fuegos artificiales al Parque Mirador del Norte.

3. Mi tío Alberto es conductor, y quiero saludarlo en el tren.

4. Tengo una Tarjeta Viajero mensual *(monthly)*, pero no la llevo conmigo, está en casa.

5. Quiero vender *souvenirs* de los Tigres del Licey en las estaciones del metro.

Niños en Las Gasleras, la República Dominicana juegan pelota con sus vecinos

Enfoque cultural

Práctica cultural:
El béisbol en la República Dominicana

El béisbol, o la pelota, es el deporte oficial de la República Dominicana. Este deporte llega al país a finales del siglo XIX convirtiéndose en uno de los pasatiempos más populares de la época. Hoy en día los dominicanos cuentan con unos de los beisbolistas más populares del mundo. Peloteros dominicanos profesionales juegan fuera del país con ligas profesionales en los Estados Unidos, Japón, Canadá y otros países donde este deporte es de gran demanda popular. Se dice que la República Dominicana es el mayor exportador de jugadores de béisbol. Hasta el momento hay 76 jugadores en la historia de la Liga Mayor de Béisbol que nacieron *(were born)* en San Pedro de Marcoris.

Los tres equipos de beisbol más populares entre los dominicanos

Tigres del Licey   Leones del Escogido   Águilas Cibaeñas

🌐 Conexiones

In your opinion, which sport is the most important for the national identity of the U.S.? And in Canada? In other countries that you know?

La Romana, ciudad turística en la zona oriental de la República Dominicana

Santo Domingo

Mi progreso comunicativo

I can describe social norms and rules for events and celebrations in my community.

Actividad 22

🅐🆉 ✦ El invitado perfecto

Un buen invitado sigue las reglas de cortesía. Escoge *(choose)* la expresión que complete el comportamiento cortés de un/a invitado/a a una fiesta.

1. *Cuando recibo una invitación, incluso si no puedo asistir:*
   - ❑ **Siempre** respondo.
   - ❑ **A veces** respondo.
   - ❑ **Nunca** respondo a la invitación.

2. *Ropa para la fiesta:*
   - ❑ Es importante llevar **algo** apropiado.
   - ❑ Es importante **no** llevar **nada** apropiado.

3. *Puntualidad:*
   Llegar unos minutos tarde, para que el anfitrión *(host)* termine las preparaciones…
   - ❑ **siempre** está bien.
   - ❑ **a veces** está bien.
   - ❑ **nunca** está bien.

4. *Interacción con las personas que no conozco en la fiesta:*
   - ❑ Trato de hablar con **todo el mundo.**
   - ❑ Trato de hablar con **alguien.**
   - ❑ **No** trato de hablar con **nadie.**

5. *Comida / bebida:*
   Cuando el anfitrión *(host)* ofrece de comer y de beber…
   - ❑ quiero pedir **todo** especial.
   - ❑ quiero pedir **algo** especial.
   - ❑ **no** quiero pedir **nada** especial.

6. *Salida:*
   Ser la última persona en salir de la fiesta
   - ❑ **siempre** es bueno.
   - ❑ **a veces** es bueno.
   - ❑ **nunca** es bueno.

Actividad 23

✎ Reglas para el evento

Escribe una lista de normas para una actividad o un evento en tu escuela, usando **siempre/nunca, algo/nada, todo el mundo/alguien/nadie.**

Actividad 24

Planes para el sábado

📖 ✴️ **Paso 1: Una invitación**

Elena y Samuel hablan sobre los planes para el fin de semana. Completa el diálogo de una manera lógica con **nunca, siempre, nadie, también, algo, alguien**.

Elena: ¿Qué lo qué, Samuel? ¿Vas a hacer ___ este fin de semana?

Samuel: ¡Hola, Elena! No voy a hacer ___ el sábado, pero sí tengo ___ el domingo.

Elena: Ay, ¡___ estás ocupado los domingos! ___ tienes tiempo para mí.

Samuel: Bueno, ya sabes. Mis abuelos ___ nos invitan a comer.

Elena: Entonces, ¿qué tal el sábado?

Samuel: Pues puedo conseguir boletos para un partido de pelota—los Tigres del Licey juegan en el Estadio Quisqueya.

Elena: ¡Me encantaría! ___ voy a partidos de béisbol. Sería ___ diferente para mí. ¡Qué idea más buena!

💬 **Paso 2: Tus planes**

Actúa el diálogo anterior con un/a compañero/a de clase, cambiando los detalles para tu situación personal.

Actividad 25

💬 **Los planes del finde**

Conversa con un/a compañero/a sobre los planes del fin de semana. Usa las siguientes sugerencias para guiar tu conversación.

1. Por lo general, ¿tienes planes los fines de semana? ¿Qué haces?

2. ¿Sales más con amigos o con la familia?

3. ¿Cómo llegas a tu destino? ¿Tomas transporte público? ¿Caminas?

Esta plaza en Santo Domingo es un lugar de encuentro con los amigos.

Siempre encontramos algo interesante en las calles de Santo Domingo.

✴️ **Mi progreso comunicativo**

I can make simple social plans.

Así se dice 3

✦ Fiestas y festivales

Programa de desfiles y celebraciones
Nueva York 2017

Celebramos la cultura dominicana en el

Desfile Nacional Dominicano

Domingo, el 13 de agosto de 2017

Brindamos el **Año Nuevo** en Times Square

Viernes, el 1 de enero de 2017

Aplaudimos los fuegos artificiales el

Día de la Independencia

Lunes, el 4 de julio de 2017

Apreciamos las carrozas **el Día de Acción de Gracias**

Jueves, el 23 de noviembre de 2017

¿Qué hacemos en los días feriados?

ir a un concierto
ir a la iglesia/al templo/a la mezquita
ir al zoo
ir a un museo
preparar comidas especiales
sacar fotos
ver las carrozas del desfile
ver los fuegos artificiales

Actividad 26

¿Cómo son estas celebraciones?

[A|z] **Paso 1: ¿En qué momento del día?**

¿Cuál es mejor momento del día para celebrar estas ocasiones? Contesta con *por la mañana, por la tarde* o *por la noche*.

1. Los fuegos artificiales del Día de la Independencia.

2. La comida del Día de Acción de Gracias.

3. La fiesta de Año Nuevo.

4. La fiesta de graduación del octavo (8°) grado.

5. La fiesta sorpresa de mis 16 años.

6. El desfile del Día de Acción de Gracias en Nueva York.

7. La boda de una tía.

8. La fiesta de disfraces el 31 de octubre.

[A|z] **Paso 2: ¿Qué tono tiene la fiesta?**

Clasifica el tono de las celebraciones en el **Paso 1**; ¿son actividades *serias, divertidas* o *emocionantes* para ti?

A esta abuela le encanta preparar el pavo *turkey* para el Día de Acción de Gracias.

Actividad 27

💬 ¿Qué te gusta hacer?

Entrevista a un/a compañero/a de clase para saber qué actividades le gusta hacer en las celebraciones de la actividad anterior.

Modelo

Estudiante A: ¿Qué te gusta hacer en el Día de la Independencia?

Estudiante B: Me gusta ver los fuegos artificiales y comer perritos calientes en el parque.

Mi progreso comunicativo

I can describe my preferences for celebrating holidays.

Estos músicos participan en una fiesta local en un barrio de Santo Domingo.

Actividad 28

Aprende más sobre las fiestas

Paso 1: Las preguntas

Vas a entrevistar a un/a compañero/a de clase sobre la fiesta que más le gusta. Tienes la primera pregunta abajo. Escribe por lo menos cinco preguntas más sobre las fiestas, para preparar la entrevista.

Modelo

. . . .

¿Cuál es la celebración que más te gusta?

Paso 2: La entrevista

Ahora, en parejas, túrnense haciendo las preguntas preparadas sobre las fiestas.

Actividad 29

Las fiestas de tu comunidad

Prepara un póster publicitario para anunciar por lo menos tres fiestas o festivales en tu comunidad. Incluye los siguientes aspectos:

- el nombre de las fiestas
- la fecha de cada evento
- el lugar de los eventos o desfiles
- las actividades en las que el público puede participar
- la comida que el público puede probar o comprar.

Reflexión intercultural

What day-to-day leisure activities and what local celebrations could provide visitors to your community or region with opportunities to experience the local culture? Explain why each activity or celebration could help a visitor better understand your community.

Enfoque cultural

Práctica cultural: Cómo chatear en español

El lenguaje del chat en español es algo nuevo, y los jóvenes de todos los países hispanohablantes contribuyen con mucha creatividad a esta manera de comunicarse.

No hay reglas fijas, solo tendencias:

No se escriben las letras mudas (silent):
ola = hola, **aora** = ahora

Muchas vocales se omiten:
vms a l plicla = vamos a la película
tngo q ir = tengo que ir
cm smpr = como siempre

Las letras k y x sustituyen a otras letras:
x fv = por favor
xq = porque
amigx = amigos y amigas
xao = chao
bns noxs = buenas noches
ak = acá

Se usan símbolos en lugar de letras:
t veo + trde = te veo más tarde
to2 ls ds = todos los días
salu2 = saludos

Se usan emoticones similares a los del inglés:
:) = estoy contento
:(= estoy triste

 Conexiones

Send a message to a friend (text or online) and make plans for Saturday. Can you communicate using Spanish "chat"?

Reflexión intercultural

Write a list of five or six expressions and shortcuts used when texting in English. Are there "rules" or patterns like those described in the **Enfoque cultural** segment? Do you think text would be an easy way to communicate with Spanish speakers? Why or why not?

ola ruben

holaaaaa q pasa?

q tal

uf studiando cm 1 loco

:(trbjas tmbn?

si stoy medio muerto

i tu presentacion el lunes?

no, es para l 7. i tu?

currando cm smpr

ns vms x ai?

si, mñna n l cafe

vale. bns noxs

xao

Mi progreso intercultural

I can understand basic conventions for communicating in different media, like text messages.

Observa 3

¿Qué hiciste ayer?

Érika Durán Toribio, (16 años, Baní, R. D.) escribe sobre su sábado en su diario

Domingo, 14 de mayo

Querido diario:

¡Qué día más fabuloso! **Hice** muchísimas cosas. **Fui** a casa de mi amiga Susana y **pasé** la mañana con ella. **Hablé** un rato con su abuela, una persona súper interesante, y **comí** con su familia. Luego, **fui** al centro comercial y **compré** zapatillas de fútbol nuevas. **Salí** a jugar con Daniel y Rosalba un rato. ¡**Metí** tres goles, estuvo chévere! Después, **vi** una película en casa de Rosalba.

En fin, un día súper lleno, nada especial, pero hizo mucho sol, no **estudié** ni **trabajé**, y ¡la **pasé** bomba! ¡Me gustaría otro sábado así! Hasta mañana . . .

¿Qué observas?

Look at the actions (verbs) in bold, which tell what Érika did on Saturday. Can you guess the meaning of the actions? Think about the conjugation of each verb (**-ar**, **-er**, or **-ir**). Do you notice any patterns in how each conjugation shows the **yo** form in the past? Discuss the examples with your classmates and teacher, view the **Observa 3** resources for this unit in Explorer, and check the **Síntesis de gramática** at the end of this section of the unit.

Actividad 30

📖 ¿Qué evento fue?

Estas oraciones son de otras entradas del diario de Érika. Lee las descripciones de actividades, y adivina qué fiesta o evento fue probablemente. ¡Hay más de una respuesta posible!

1. "Abrí regalos".

2. "Vi fuegos artificiales".

3. "Llevé una máscara".

4. "Comí un pastel especial".

5. "Bailé mucho".

6. "Comí barbacoa".

7. "Vestí ropa elegante".

8. "Decoré el salón con globos".

9. "Rompí una piñata".

10. "Escuché bachata, merengue y salsa".

Otras actividades en el pasado

¿Qué hiciste?

¿Adónde fuiste?

Jugué videojuegos con mi hermano.

Visité el museo de historia natural.

Asistí a un concierto de música clásica.

Dormí una siesta de tres horas.

Detalle gramatical: El pretérito

To express completed past actions, Spanish uses the **pretérito**, which has distinct endings from the present tense. Note that **-er** and **-ir** verbs have the same endings in this tense.

tom**ar** —→ yo tom**é**
          tú tom**aste**

corr**er** —→ yo corr**í**
          tú corr**iste**

escrib**ir** —→ yo escrib**í**
          tú escrib**iste**

Some verbs are irregular, and the forms must be memorized:

hacer —→ yo **hice**
          tú **hiciste**

ir —→ yo **fui**
   tú **fuiste**

You will learn more about the past tenses in Spanish in books 2 and 3 of *EntreCulturas*.

Actividad 31

¿Qué hiciste tú la semana pasada?

Paso 1: ¿Qué hiciste?

Escoge tres preguntas para un/a compañero/a de clase, para saber qué hizo *(he/she did)* el fin de semana pasado.

¿Jugaste a un deporte?	¿Viste una buena película?
¿Jugaste un videojuego?	¿Viste un partido (de fútbol, baloncesto, béisbol, etc.)?
¿Montaste en bicicleta?	¿Hiciste la tarea de español?
¿Hablaste español con un amigo?	¿Saliste con amigos?
¿Tocaste un instrumento?	¿Fuiste de compras?
¿Escribiste muchos mensajes de texto?	¿Fuiste a una fiesta?

Paso 2: ¿Y tú también?

Ahora circula entre tus compañeros, y busca a tres personas diferentes que hayan hecho *(have done)* las mismas actividades que tú.

Modelo

Estudiante A: **¿Montaste** en bicicleta?

Estudiante B: Sí, **monté** en bicicleta.

Estudiante A: ¡Yo también!

Actividad 32

Mi último cumpleaños

¿Qué hiciste en tu último *(last)* cumpleaños? ¿Te gustó? ¿Cómo estuvo? Escribe por lo menos cinco actividades para describir la ocasión, y una reacción o evaluación de cada actividad. Usa las **expresiones útiles**.

Cinco cosas que hice	¿Cómo estuvo?

Actividad 33

Querido diario

Escribe una entrada en tu diario personal sobre los eventos y las actividades del mes pasado. ¿Qué cosas hiciste todos los días? ¿Hiciste algo excepcional? Incluye por lo menos una oración de evaluación o reacción para cada actividad.

Modelo

Martes, el 4 de marzo

Querido diario:

Fui a un concierto de la banda de mi escuela. Estuvo genial y me gustó mucho.

Mi progreso comunicativo

I can talk about what I did on a recent weekend, at a party, or an event.

Punta Cana

Síntesis de gramática

El futuro

You can describe future actions using the expression **ir + a +** infinitive, similar to *going to* in English:

Voy a jugar al dominó con mis tíos este fin de semana.	*I'm going to play dominoes with my uncles this weekend.*
Vamos a comer con los abuelos el domingo.	*We're going to eat with our grandparents on Sunday.*
¿**Vas a ver** la nueva película de Amandla Stenberg?	*Are you going to see Amanda Stenberg's new movie?*

Las expresiones negativas

Unlike English, a Spanish sentence can have multiple negative words in it. If a negative word is placed after the verb, **no** must go before the verb.

No hice **nada** el sábado por la noche.	*I didn't do anything Saturday night.*
No vi a **nadie** en el museo.	*I didn't see anyone in the museum yesterday.*
Nadie va a esa fiesta.	*Nobody is going to that party.*
No voy a conciertos **nunca**. **Nunca** voy a conciertos.	*I never go to concerts.*

It is helpful to learn these expressions with their affirmative counterparts, as in these mini-conversations:

—¿Quieres **algo**?	*Do you want something?*
—**No** quiero **nada**.	*I don't want anything.*
—¿**Alguien** va contigo?	*Is someone going with you?*
—**Nadie** va conmigo.	*Nobody is going with me.*
—Voy a la fiesta.	*I'm going to the party.*
—Yo **también**.	*Me too.*
—No voy a la fiesta.	*I'm not going to the party.*
—Yo **tampoco**.	*Me either.*

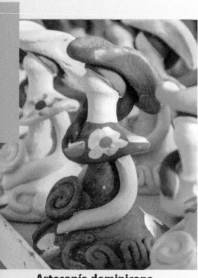

Artesanía dominicana

El pretérito (pasado)

To express a completed past action in Spanish, we use forms called the **pretérito**. The endings for the **yo** and **tú** forms of regular verbs are as follows. Make sure you pronounce them with a strong stress on the last syllable of the **yo** form.

-ar ⟶ **-é**

visitar ⟶ (yo) visit**é**

(tú) visit**aste**

-er ⟶ **-í**

beber ⟶ (yo) beb**í**

(tú) beb**iste**

-ir ⟶ **-í**

escribir ⟶ (yo) escrib**í**

(tú) escrib**iste**

Some verbs have irregular (unpredictable) forms. Note that unlike the regular verbs above, the stress is on the next-to-last syllable:

hacer ⟶ (yo) **hice**, (tú) **hiciste**

ir ⟶ (yo) **fui**, (tú) **fuiste**

"Fui de compras en Santo Domingo y compré algo bonito para mi madre."

Four additional details you should know about the preterit:

1. Verbs that end in **-car** and **-gar** have spelling changes in the **yo** form:

   jugar ⟶ ju**gué**, jugaste

   marcar ⟶ mar**qué**, marcaste

   practicar ⟶ practi**qué**, practicaste

   sacar ⟶ sa**qué**, sacaste

2. Verbs that have stem changes in the present tense keep the same stem as the infinitive:

   pr**o**bar ⟶ pr**o**bé *(present: pr**ue**bo)*

   recom**e**ndar ⟶ recom**e**ndé

   *(present: recom**ie**ndo)*

"Canté y toqué música con mis amigos en la playa de Bávaro."

3. Verbs of one syllable are not written with an accent mark:

   ir ⟶ fui

   ver ⟶ vi

4. Many speakers add a final **-s** to the tú form of the preterit when speaking informally (e.g., hablastes, comistes, fuistes), but the standard language forms end in the vowel **-e**.

You will learn the complete set of forms in books 2 and 3 of *EntreCulturas*.

Vocabulario

I can talk about leisure activities that I like to do. (Así se dice 1)

andar en bicicleta	ride a bike
andar en patineta	ride a skateboard
asistir al Carnaval	go to Carnival
la banda	(music) band
el centro comercial	shopping center
el cumpleaños	birthday
el cine	movie theater
el desfile	parade
el dominó	dominoes
la fiesta	party
dormir (o → ue) una siesta	take a nap
escalar montañas	climb mountains
hacer esquí acuático	water ski
el museo	museum
jugar (u → ue)	play (a game; sport)
la máscara	mask
el parque	park
la pelota	ball; baseball
la piscina	pool
la playa	beach
el programa deportivo	sports show
tocar	play (music)
ver	see; watch

Expresiones útiles: ¿Cuándo?

ayer	yesterday
entre semana	during the (work) week
el fin de semana	weekend
el lunes	on Monday
los lunes	on Mondays

Expresiones útiles: ¿Cómo estás?

estar aburrido/a	to be bored
estar alegre	to be happy
estar cansado/a	to be tired
estar emocionado/a	to be excited
estar enojado/a	to be angry
estar genial	to be great; super
estar interesado/a	to be interested
estar nervioso/a	to be nervous
estar ocupado/a	to be busy
estar preocupado/a	to be worried
estar triste	to be sad
tener calor	to be hot
tener frío	to be cold
tener hambre	to be hungry
tener sed	to be thirsty

I can accept and reject invitations to an event. (Así se dice 2)

¿A qué hora?	At what time?; When?
¿Cómo llegamos?	How will we get there?
conmigo	with me
contigo	with you
juntos/as	together
Lo siento.	I'm sorry.
Hasta el sábado.	See you on Saturday.
Hasta la próxima.	See you next time.
¡Me encantaría!	I would love to!
No es para tanto.	It's no big deal.
No puedo.	I can't.
la próxima vez	next time
¿Qué pasa?	What's going on?
Ya tengo planes.	I already have plans.

I can talk about the kinds of events that I like to participate in. (Además se dice)

el aniversario	anniversary
la boda	wedding
la canción	song
corto/a	short
decorar	to decorate
el disfraz	costume, disguise
la fiesta de disfraces	costume party
la fiesta sorpresa	surprise party
la flor	flower
el globo	balloon
la graduación	graduation
la guagua	bus (Caribbean)
el metro	subway
ir a pie	to go on foot
largo/a	long
llegar tarde	arrive late
llevar	carry; wear
los pantalones	pants
el regalo	gift
el taxi	taxi
la ropa	clothes
las sandalias	sandals
tomar	to take
el traje	suit
el traje de baño	swimsuit
traer (g)	bring
el vestido	dress

I can inquire about an event that I would like to participate in. (Expresiones útiles: Las preguntas)

¿A qué hora?	At what time?; When?
¿Cómo?	How?
¿Cuánto?	How much?
¿Dónde?	Where?
¿Por qué?	Why?
¿Quién?	Who?
¿Qué?	What?

Expresiones útiles para las reglas (afirmativas y negativas)

algo	something
alguien	someone
a veces	sometimes
nada	nothing
nadie	no one
nunca	never
siempre	always
todo	everything
todo el mundo	everybody

I can talk about different events and festivities that I like to attend. (Así se dice 3)

el Año Nuevo	New Year's
la carroza	parade float
el Día de Acción de Gracias	Thanksgiving
el Día de la Independencia	Independence Day
el desfile	parade
la foto	photo; picture
los fuegos artificiales	fireworks
la iglesia	church
la mezquita	mosque
el templo	temple

I can talk about positive and negative reactions to an event that I attended. (Expresiones útiles: ¿Cómo estuvo el evento?)

Estuvo aburrido.	It was boring.
¡Estuvo chévere!	It was great!
¡Estuvo fantástico!	It was fantastic!
¡Estuvo genial!	It was great!
Estuvo horrible.	It was horrible.
¡La pasé bomba!	I had a great time!
¡Me divertí mucho!	I had lots of fun!
No hice nada especial/ divertido.	I didn't do anything special/fun.
No me gustó nada.	I didn't like it at all.

Alejandra

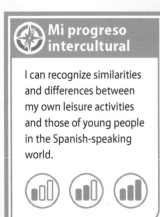

Isaac

En camino

Actividad 34

Los blogueros

Paso 1: Mis pasatiempos

Alejandra (de Quito, Ecuador) e Isaac (de Costa Rica) hablan sobre sus pasatiempos favoritos. Mira y escucha el video, y escribe la información que da cada uno. Puedes ver los videos más de una vez.

¿Qué hacen los blogueros para divertirse?

Alejandra	Isaac

Paso 2: ¿Qué tienen en común?

Después de ver y escuchar a Alejandra e Isaac, contesta a las preguntas.

1. ¿Qué actividades tienen Alejandra e Isaac en común?

2. ¿Quién baila salsa y quién baila los bailes tradicionales?

3. ¿Qué pasatiempos tienes tú en común con Alejandra? ¿Y con Isaac? ¿Con quién te identificas más?

Actividad 35

Las mejores fiestas del año

The principal has asked you to create a video blog in Spanish to inform new families about events related to school events and holidays. Select three important events and describe them with details: the name, date(s), and several activities typically associated with the celebration.

Modelo

. . . .

La graduación es muy importante en Brandon High School. Siempre es en junio. Tenemos una barbacoa, preparamos pasteles, decoramos los pasillos y los *seniors* tienen una fiesta el viernes antes de la ceremonia.

Actividad 36

  Un verano lleno de actividades

Describe at least five activities you did last summer. You can talk about activities like fun and leisure, work, study, sports and travel. For each activity, include a reaction.

Modelo

Trabajé todos los días en una heladería. Comí mucho helado, y ¡me gustó mucho!

Actividad 37

El próximo verano

 Paso 1

You want to make plans to enjoy a week this summer with a classmate, without interruptions from work, studies, or family travel. First to plan this week, write out a list of all your summer obligations and activities, with dates and times.

Modelo

En junio, voy a pasar tres semanas con mis abuelos.
Del 4 al 12 de julio, voy a trabajar en un campamento de verano.

Paso 2

Now, compare your calendar with your classmate's, explaining your activities. Find a time when you are both free.

Modelo

Estudiante A:	En junio, voy a pasar tres semanas con mis abuelos. ¿Qué tal la última semana de junio?
Estudiante B:	No puedo. Voy a estar en Tejas con mi familia.

Explora

Essential Question: How do leisure activities create bridges between cultures?

Overview

Entertainment and traditions are important components of our lifestyle and identity. As people move, these leisure activities can be a powerful way to maintain cultural traditions, and also to share traditions in new places. Carnaval celebrations, music, baseball, and dominoes provide those connections between the Dominican Republic and New York.

Partido de béisbol

Desfile Dominicano en Nueva York

Celebremos las tradiciones

Gráficos

These graphs were prepared with information from the Pew Research Center and the United States Census Bureau.

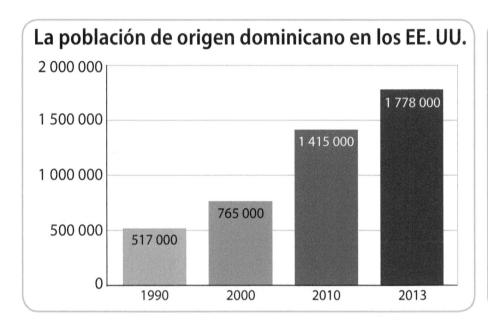

La población de origen dominicano en los EE. UU.

- 1990: 517 000
- 2000: 765 000
- 2010: 1 415 000
- 2013: 1 778 000

Los dominicanos en los EE. UU.

- Nueva York **47%**
- Otros estados **53%**

Actividad 38

📖 **Los dominicanos en Nueva York**

1. Observa los gráficos. ¿Qué nos indican de la distribución de personas de origen dominicano en los Estados Unidos?

2. ¿Por qué crees que crece *(is growing)* tan rápidamente la población dominicana en la ciudad de Nueva York?

Actividad 39

¡Vamos al carnaval en la República Dominicana!

🌐 🗨 **Paso 1: Desfiles en mi comunidad**

Con la clase, escribe una lista de las celebraciones más importantes de tu comunidad. ¿Cómo participan ustedes en las celebraciones? ¿Qué elementos contribuyen a hacer los eventos muy especiales?

📖 ✦ **Paso 2: Una invitación: Acércate a la República Dominicana**

Lee el anuncio publicado en un panfleto *(brochure)* de viajes. Busca la evidencia en el texto para indicar si las afirmaciones son ciertas o falsas.

1. La República Dominicana celebra el carnaval los doce meses del año.

2. Celebran el carnaval en todas las provincias de la República Dominicana.

3. Todos los carnavales tienen la misma popularidad.

4. Los carnavales son muy festivos y alegres.

Máscara de un diablo cojuelo en un desfile de carnaval en Santo Domingo

Descubre RD.com

Te invito a visitar la República Dominicana en el mes de febrero para que disfrutes de su hermoso carnaval, el cual se celebra durante todo este mes en varias de las provincias del país. Los carnavales más destacados y conocidos son los de la ciudad de Santo Domingo y La Vega. Descúbrenos y disfrutarás de un Carnaval lleno de cultura, color y alegría.

Muchos jóvenes dominicanos participan en los desfiles de carnaval.

🎥 ✦ **Paso 3: Observa la celebración**

El video *Febrero: mes del carnaval* fue publicado por AcércateRD en enero de 2016.

Escucha y mira el video, y escribe una lista de los elementos que observas en la celebración de carnaval.

 Paso 4: Compara

Con un/a compañero/a, prepara un diagrama de Venn comparando el desfile en el video con una celebración en tu comunidad.

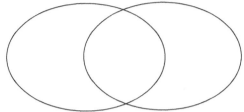

Paso 5: Comparte tu celebración

Para la celebración o evento que describiste en el **Paso 1**, escribe un anuncio similar al presentado por *Descubre RD.com*. En tu anuncio debes de incluir:

- el nombre del evento
- el motivo de la celebración
- las fechas del evento
- las actividades en la celebración
- las personas que participan
- por qué es un evento especial para la comunidad.

Enfoque cultural

Práctica cultural: Carnaval de la Vega, R. D.

El carnaval de La Vega es considerado como el mejor del país y del Caribe.

Todos los años atrae a miles de personas. En 1547 se establece la tradición del carnaval en La Vega y, en 1977, la Cámara de Diputados de la República Dominicana lo reconoce como Patrimonio Folklórico del país.

Durante la temporada de carnaval, hay actividades todos los domingos desde enero hasta marzo. La gente disfrazada de diablos cojuelos *(limping)* llevan ropas de colores muy llamativos y salen a la calle para participar en los desfiles, ver las carrozas y divertirse, pero sobre todo a disfrutar.

Conexiones

Which festivals or celebrations are important in your community? Do they make you feel like you are part of the community?

Actividad 40

El carnaval viaja a Nueva York, Estados Unidos

Paso 1: Visualización

1. Trabajando con un/a compañero/a, y escriban una lista de palabras en español para describir las fotos en estas páginas.

2. Compartan sus descripciones con otros compañeros.

Paso 2: Predicciones

Lee el titular (*headline*) del artículo. Con un/a compañero/a, contesta a las siguientes preguntas:

1. ¿De qué trata el artículo?

2. ¿Qué crees que significa la palabra *Parada*?

3. ¿Qué palabra aprendiste en esta unidad que significa lo mismo (*means the same*) que *Parada*?

GRAN CELEBRACIÓN EN NUEVA YORK: *PARADA DOMINICANA EN EL BRONX

Una vez más el tradicional desfile va a ocurrir a fines del mes de julio en el llamado condado de la salsa en el Bronx de Nueva York. Como de costumbre, las calles se van a vestir de los colores rojo, azul y blanco para conmemorar un año más el Desfile Dominicano en El Bronx.

El recorrido de la Gran Parada va a ser desde La avenida Este de Tremond hasta la calle 167 como en los 26 años de su celebración.

En los últimos años, muchas carrozas, comparsas, bandas, y orquestas musicales han participado y se espera que este año 20 o más carrozas participen. Es muy común ver a muchas celebridades participando en el desfile así como a muchas cadenas de televisión que estarán reportando y cubriendo el evento en vivo desde las calles del condado de la salsa. Los dominicanos residentes de la urbe neoyorquina y todas las personas que quieran participar en esta parada van a poder disfrutar de este evento por más de cuatro horas a partir de la 1:00 de la tarde. ¡Felicidades, dominicanos!

*La palabra *parada* es un regionalismo usado por los dominicanos en la ciudad de Nueva York para referirse a un desfile.

📖 **Paso 3: Búsqueda de detalles en el texto**

Estás interesado en asistir a este evento en el mes de julio.
Busca la siguiente información en el artículo. ¡OJO! Si el dato
no se incluye, contesta con **No hay datos en el anuncio.**

1. ¿Cómo se llama el evento?

2. ¿Cuándo es el evento?

3. ¿Por qué se llevan los colores rojo, azul y blanco?

4. ¿Dónde se celebra cada año?

5. ¿Cuántas carrozas van a participar este año?

📖 🔤 **Paso 4: Palabras clave**

Encuentra en el anuncio las palabras en español que
expresan lo siguiente:

1. in the county

2. as customary

3. reporting and covering

4. live

🌐 **Paso 5: Inferencias culturales**

Trabaja con un/a compañero/a y contesta a las siguientes
preguntas.

1. ¿Por qué crees que celebran este desfile en Nueva York?

2. ¿Qué otros grupos en la ciudad de Nueva York celebran
   sus tradiciones importantes?

3. ¿Qué aspectos del evento en el artículo son similares o
   diferentes a uno en tu comunidad?

Actividad 41

Tres grandes bachateros

 ⊕ Paso 1: Infórmate

Lee sobre tres artistas importantes de música bachata en los perfiles presentados y contesta a las preguntas.

1. ¿Cuántos años tiene cada artista?

2. ¿Cuáles tienen la misma nacionalidad?

3. ¿Qué tienen en común los tres? ¿Qué diferencias hay?

▶ ⊕ Paso 2: Investiga

Después de leer, busca en el internet un video musical de una canción reciente de cada uno de los tres cantantes. Comparte con la clase la canción que te gusta más.

Tres grandes de la bachata

NOMBRE: Geoffrey Royce Rojas de León

CONOCIDO COMO: Prince Royce

NACIÓ: 11 de mayo de 1989

NACIONALIDAD: Estadounidense

GÉNERO MUSICAL: Bachata, Pop latino

OCUPACIÓN: Cantante

INSTRUMENTO: Guitarra, voz

NOMBRE: Juan Luis Guerra Seijas

CONOCIDO COMO: Juan Luis Guerra

NACIÓ: 7 de junio de 1957

NACIONALIDAD: Dominicana

GÉNERO MUSICAL: Bachata, merengue, mambo, balada

OCUPACIÓN: compositor, cantante, productor, arreglista

INSTRUMENTO: Guitarra, voz

NOMBRE: Anthony Santos

CONOCIDO COMO: Romeo Santos

NACIÓ: 21 de julio de 1981

NACIONALIDAD: Estadounidense

GÉNERO MUSICAL: Bachata

OCUPACIÓN: Cantante

INSTRUMENTO: Voz

El béisbol y el dominó nos unen

Actividad 42

📖 Tres peloteros dominicanos en los Estados Unidos

Lee la información de los tres peloteros dominicanos. ¿Qué tienen en común? ¿En qué se diferencian?

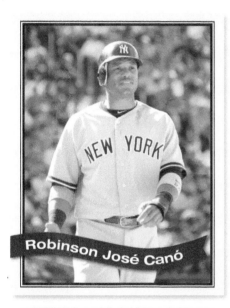

Robinson José Canó

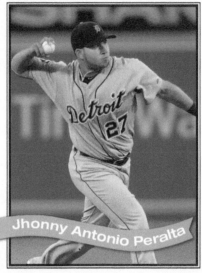

Jhonny Antonio Peralta

Yeixon José Ruiz

LUGAR DE NACIMIENTO: San Pedro de Macoris, República Dominicana
NACIÓ: 22 de octubre 1982
EQUIPO: Yankees/Mariners
POSICIÓN: Segunda base
PESO: 210 libras
ALTURA: 1.83 m

LUGAR DE NACIMIENTO: Santiago, República Dominicana
NACIÓ: 28 de mayo 1982
EQUIPO: Indians/Tigers/Cardinals
POSICIÓN: Interbase - Medio y Tercera base
PESO: 225 libras
ALTURA: 1.87 m

LUGAR DE NACIMIENTO: San José de Ocoa, República Dominicana
NACIÓ: 19 de mayo 1991
EQUIPO: St. Lucie Mets
POSICIÓN: Segunda base
PESO: 155 libras
ALTURA: 1.83 m

Actividad 43

El sueño (*dream*) de ser pelotero

💬 Paso 1: El deporte en mi vida

¿Qué importancia tienen los deportes en tu vida? Escribe una lista de razones para jugar un deporte, y compara tus ideas con las de la clase.

▶ ✣ Paso 2: El béisbol: ¿un sueño para el futuro?

Lee las siguientes preguntas, y luego ve y escucha el video para buscar las respuestas.

1. ¿Qué quieren los adolescentes en el video?

2. ¿Por qué ser pelotero es la meta *(goal)* de muchos dominicanos?

3. Según la narradora, ¿qué quieren algunos de los padres?

4. ¿Qué es más importante para estos jóvenes, estudiar o practicar el deporte?

Mi progreso intercultural

I can recognize ways sports can bridge cultural differences.

Reflexión intercultural

✣ What other sports include players of different nationalities? Have you played sports with people who speak other languages? Why do you think sporting events bring people of different backgrounds together so well? Share your observations in class and in Explorer.

Actividad 44

A jugar al dominó

▶ ✣ Paso 1: El dominó en Santo Domingo

Escucha y mira las noticias sobre un evento en Santo Domingo.

1. ¿Qué hacen las personas en el video?

2. ¿Dónde están las personas?

3. ¿Están contentos? ¿Cómo lo sabes?

El dominó es un elemento importante en la identidad de los dominicanos.

Enfoque cultural

Producto cultural: El dominó

De la mesa a la nación

El juego de dominó es un elemento muy importante para la identidad dominicana. Por las tardes, es típico ver a grupos de personas en las plazas jugando una partida de dominó. Además de ser una forma de entretenimiento que se practica entre grupos grandes o pequeños, el dominó es una disciplina que brinda elementos importantes como lo deportivo, lo cultural y lo educativo a la cultura de los dominicanos. En 2010 se declaró como **Deporte Nacional** por ser el juego más practicado en el país.

Conexiones

Is the game of dominoes popular in your home or community? In your opinion, is it a sport or a board game? Use the forum in your Explorer course to share your observations.

Paso 2: Mis juegos de mesa favoritos

Trabajando en grupo, contesten a las siguientes preguntas.

1. ¿Qué juegos de mesa les gusta jugar? Escriban una lista.

2. ¿Dónde, cuándo y con quién juegan?

3. ¿Los juegos de mesa son populares con personas de diferentes edades en su comunidad?

4. ¿Hay algún juego de mesa (ajedrez, bingo, dominó u otro) que se asocie con diferentes generaciones en tu comunidad?

El ajedrez es un pasatiempo popular en la República Dominicana.

Unos juegan y otros observan:
Camaguey, Cuba

En mi comunidad

¡Vamos a jugar!

Juegos de mesa en Vinales, Cuba

Actividad 45

¡Fiesta de dominó!

En esta actividad, la clase va a planear y participar en un evento para jugar al dominó con estudiantes de otras clases de español.

 **Paso 1: Planea el evento**

1. ¿A quiénes vamos a invitar?

2. ¿Cuándo vamos a jugar? Anota el día, la fecha y la hora del evento.

3. ¿Dónde vamos a jugar?

Paso 2: Prepara las invitaciones

Con la información de **Paso 1,** prepara carteles, volantes o invitaciones personalizadas. Visita otras clases de español. Habla con los estudiantes para invitarles al evento.

Paso 3: Las reglas del juego

1. Lee la lista de **expresiones útiles para el dominó**. ¿Cuáles comprendes?

2. Escucha y observa el video que explica como jugar al dominó. ¿Puedes identificar el significado de las otras palabras?

3. Prepara un visual para cada mesa con las reglas y frases necesarias para jugar.

Paso 4: Vamos a jugar

El día del evento, organiza cada mesa con estudiantes de diferentes clases. Usa español para enseñar a los invitados a jugar al dominó, y ¡diviértete!

Actividad 46

El juego nos conecta

Paso 1: Investigación

¿Qué oportunidades hay en tu comunidad para unir generaciones con el juego? Piensa en tu familia, en tu vecindario y en las organizaciones comunitarias. Prepara una lista de lugares con la clase.

Paso 2: Participación

Contacta con los lugares o las organizaciones del **Paso 1.** Si es posible, organiza un evento de dominó con un grupo de la lista.

En un parque en Miami, Florida, EE. UU.

Expresiones útiles para el dominó

el centro - *center*

el doble - *double tile*

el extremo - *end tile*

la ficha - *tile*

el jugador - *player*

jugar en parejas - *play with partners*

el punto - *point*

repartir - *deal*

el tapete de dominó - *table, board*

el vencedor - *winner*

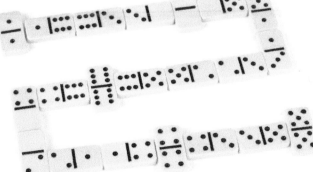

Niños, jóvenes y adultos observan el Diablo Cojuelo durante las celebraciones de carnaval.

Las bailarinas llevan trajes tradicionales durante el desfile de Carnaval en Santo Domingo, República Dominicana.

Las comparsas desfilan en el Carnaval del Caribe.

Vive entre culturas

Vamos a visitar Santo Domingo

Essential Question: How do celebrations reflect the history and culture of a place?

Carnaval, un evento espectacular

Your class is traveling to Santo Domingo in the República Dominicana. While in the city, you suggest that your classmates and friends go to the Carnaval, a celebration famous for its **desfiles,** and **comparsas, comidas.**

The following assessments are based on an article published by Redacción TTC en Eventos, 14 de febrero de 2015.

Interpretive Assessment

Carnavales dominicanos

📖 ✇ Paso 1: Preparación

Look at the photographs on this page, and read the captions. In groups of three, share your interpretations.

Los disfraces del Diablo Cojuelo dan color a la celebración de carnaval.

Paso 2: Ruta del carnaval dominicano

Read a map to discover where Carnaval is celebrated. Follow the directions in your Explorer course.

  Paso 3: Carnavales de República Dominicana

Read the article and answer the questions following the instructions in Explorer.

Ruta del carnaval dominicano

Interpersonal Assessment

  Conversación virtual: #MarzoRD

Imagine you are traveling to the Dominican Republic soon. Participate in a Text Chat with Paola, the blogger from the Dominican Republic, to help her prepare for your visit. Follow the instructions in Explorer.

Presentational Assessment

  Turistas en Santo Domingo

For your upcoming trip to República Dominicana with your class, you want to have a full and well-thought-out plan. Design an itinerary with places that you are going to visit and the activities that you are going to do in each place. Organize your thoughts by answering the questions **¿Cuándo?, ¿Dónde?, ¿Con quién?, ¿Por qué?,** etc. Collect pictures to represent what you plan to do, and make a short, narrated video or slideshow to send to Paola to share your plans for the trip. Record the video in the space provided in Explorer.

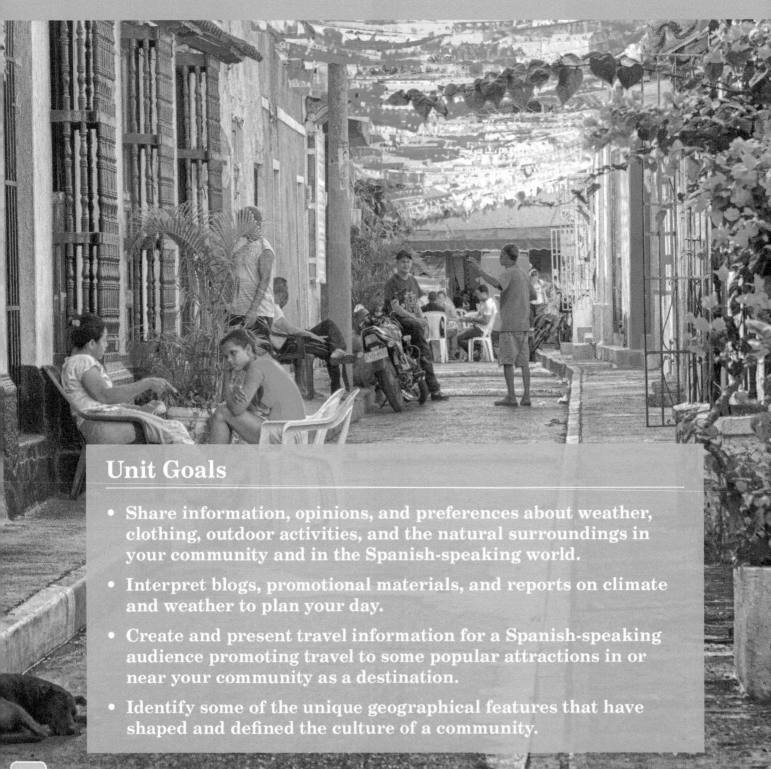

UNIDAD 6
El mundo en el que vivo

Unit Goals

- Share information, opinions, and preferences about weather, clothing, outdoor activities, and the natural surroundings in your community and in the Spanish-speaking world.

- Interpret blogs, promotional materials, and reports on climate and weather to plan your day.

- Create and present travel information for a Spanish-speaking audience promoting travel to some popular attractions in or near your community as a destination.

- Identify some of the unique geographical features that have shaped and defined the culture of a community.

CONOCE A MELISSA MONTERO VARGAS, NUESTRA VIDEO BLOGUERA DE COLOMBIA

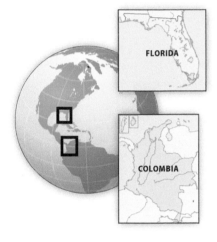

Essential Questions

How do the culture, climate, and the people around us affect how we live, work, and play?

What makes a place unique?

How do my surroundings shape my identity?

The natural world and the towns and cities we inhabit shape who we are. In this unit, you will learn to describe your surroundings and explore how the diverse natural and urban environments of Colombia shape life there.

303

Comparaciones
✦ Colombia y Florida

Colombia
46.7 millones

76% urbana

24% rural

Florida (Estados Unidos)

| Los indígenas timucua, apalachee y calusa habitan Florida | El explorador español Ponce de León llega a la península de Florida | Termina la Guerra de los Siete Años, y el control de Florida pasa por un tiempo de España a Inglaterra | | Florida se une a los EE. UU. como estado número 27 |

1500	**1513**	**1763**	**1819**	**1845**	**1830–63**	**1903**

Colombia

| | | | Simón Bolívar lucha por la independencia de la "Gran Colombia" (Colombia, Ecuador, Panamá, Venezuela) | | División de la "Gran Colombia" en tres naciones (Colombia, Ecuador, Venezuela) | Panamá se independiza de Colombia bajo presión de EE. UU. |

600–1600 EC : Los indígenas chibcha o muisca habitan el área de los Andes

Florida
20.2 millones

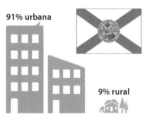

91% urbana

9% rural

FLORIDA

COLOMBIA

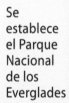
Se establece el Parque Nacional de los Everglades

Se abre *Walt Disney World* en Orlando

Huracán Andrew

1946	1948–57	1964	1971	1985	1992	2000	2016
	Guerra civil colombiana	Tayrona declarado Parque Nacional Natural		Erupción del volcán Nevado del Ruiz		Inicio del "Plan Colombia", esfuerzo con EE. UU. para combatir el narcotráfico	El Gobierno colombiano y dos grupos de insurgentes (FARC y ELN) negocian la paz, después de 50 años de conflicto

Actividad 1

🔍 Productos de Colombia y Florida

Observa las fotografías. ¿Puedes identificar los productos de Colombia? ¿Y los de Florida? ¿Tienen algo en común?

Comunica

Essential Question: How do the culture, climate and the people around us help shape how we work, live and play?

Check your progress to show what you have learned and to discover areas where you need more practice to reach your learning goals.

Video blog
Soy Melissa

Un jardín de rosas en el Jardín Botánico de Bogotá

Actividad 2

El tiempo en Bogotá

Melissa Montero Vargas, nuestra bloguera de Colombia, va a hablar del clima de su ciudad, Bogotá.

Paso 1: Para hablar del tiempo

Antes de ver el video blog, empareja las frases a la izquierda con la frase equivalente a la derecha.

_____ 1. clima   a. *in a matter of seconds*

_____ 2. soleado   b. *climate*

_____ 3. frío   c. *cold*

_____ 4. llueve   d. *storm*

_____ 5. tormenta   e. *sunny*

_____ 6. cambia   f. *it rains*

_____ 7. en cuestión de segundos   g. *it changes*

_____ 8. estaciones   h. *seasons*

Desierto de la Tatacoa, Colombia

▶ ✦ Paso 2: El clima de Bogotá

Lee las siguientes oraciones y confirma el significado. Luego, mira y escucha el video blog y decide si las oraciones son ciertas (C) o falsas (F).

1. Melissa está en el parque.

2. Ella quiere hablar del clima.

3. Es un día muy frío.

4. En Colombia hay cuatro estaciones.

5. Hace sol (*It is sunny*).

6. El calor en Bogotá no es muy fuerte.

7. Hay tormentas de nieve (*snow*) fuertes en Bogotá.

8. El clima en Bogotá cambia rápidamente.

El café se cosecha (*is picked*) a mano.

📖 💬 Paso 3: El clima de mi región

Contesta las siguientes preguntas, y luego comparte tus respuestas con un compañero/una compañera de clase.

1. ¿Te gusta el clima de tu región?

2. Melissa dice que hay dos estaciones en Bogotá. ¿Cuántas estaciones hay en tu región?

3. ¿Cuál es tu estación favorita?

4. ¿Qué haces en tu estación favorita?

5. ¿Qué haces cuando llueve?

6. ¿Prefieres un clima caliente o un clima frío?

7. Para ti, ¿qué lugar tiene un clima ideal?

Las playas caribeñas de Sapzurro y Capurganá son destinos turísticos remotos del extremo norte de Colombia, en la frontera con Panamá.

Así se dice 1

✦ Entornos para todos los gustos

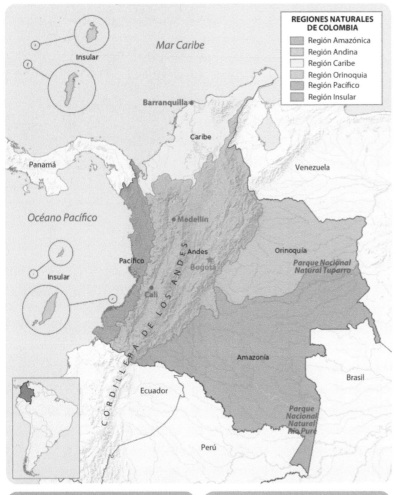

REGIONES NATURALES DE COLOMBIA

- Región Amazónica
- Región Andina
- Región Caribe
- Región Orinoquia
- Región Pacífico
- Región Insular

el desierto

El desierto de la Tatacoa

la selva tropical

La Amazonía (**zona del río** Amazonas)

los llanos

La Orinoquía (**zona del Río Orinoco**)

las montañas

La cordillera de los Andes

La Sierra Nevada de Santa Marta

los valles

El valle del Cauca

El valle del Magdalena

las costas

el **océano** Pacífico   el **mar** Caribe

Actividad 3

 A Z ✥ **La geografía de Colombia**

Completa estas descripciones con el término adecuado, según el mapa.

1. El Caribe es _____.

   a. un océano   b. un mar   c. un lago   d. un río

2. El Pacífico es _____.

   a. un océano   b. un mar   c. un lago   d. un río

3. La cordillera de los Andes va del norte _____.

   a. al centro   b. al este   c. al sur   d. al oeste

4. Perú está _____ de Colombia.

   a. al norte   b. al este   c. al sur   d. al oeste

5. La Amazonía es una zona _____.

   a. de lagos y montañas   b. de costas e islas   c. de llanos y valles   d. de ríos y selvas

La palma de cera (wax) es el árbol nacional de Colombia.

Actividad 4

🎧 ✥ **¿Es correcto?**

Escucha estas descripciones de Colombia. ¿Son correctas o incorrectas?

1. _____   2. _____   3. _____

4. _____   5. _____   6. _____

Además se dice: Más geografía y clima

aquí	*here*
allí	*there*
el agua	*water*
el glaciar	*glacier*
el hielo	*ice*
la isla	*island*
la lluvia	*rain*
la nieve	*snow*
la playa	*beach*

Vista panorámica de Cali, Colombia

Expresiones útiles: ¿Dónde está?

Barranquilla **está en** la costa.
Bogotá **está en el centro** del país.

El mar Caribe **está al norte** de Colombia.
Ecuador **está al sur** de Colombia.
Venezuela **está al este** de Colombia.
El océano Pacífico **está al oeste** del país.

Colombia **tiene fronteras con** cinco países (Brasil, Ecuador, Panamá, Perú, Venezuela).

Mi progreso comunicativo

I can identify geographical features and explain their location in relation to each other.

Además se dice: Descripciones

aislado /a	*isolated*
alto/a	*tall; high*
bonito/a	*pretty; beautiful*
enorme	*huge*
extenso/a	*extensive*
feo/a	*ugly*
grande	*big; large*
pequeño/a	*small*

Actividad 5

¿Dónde está?

Usando el mapa de **Así se dice 1,** escribe oraciones para describir la ubicación *(location)* relativa de estos lugares en Colombia.

Modelo

Bogotá, la capital del país ~ Medellín

→ Bogotá, la capital del país, **está al sur de** Medellín.

1. Cali ~ el océano Pacífico
2. La Sierra Nevada de Santa Marta ~ la costa del Caribe
3. El Parque Nacional Natural de Tuparro ~ Venezuela
4. Las islas colombianas ~ el continente de América del Sur
5. La región de la Amazonía ~ La Orinoquía

Actividad 6

¿Qué rasgos tiene tu país?

Paso 1: La geografía de tu país

¿Cuáles son los rasgos *(features)* geográficos más importantes de tu país? Trabajando con un/a compañero/a, dibujen *(draw)* en un mapa los rasgos más importantes, y escriban una oración para describir cada rasgo. Usen las expresiones de la lista.

Modelo

Los Grandes Lagos son enormes.

Las montañas de Colorado son muy altas y bonitas.

Paso 2: ¿Es similar o diferente?

¿Qué rasgos geográficos de Colombia son similares a los de tu país?

Modelo

Los llanos de Colombia son similares a las Grandes Llanuras *(the Great Plains)* de Estados Unidos.

Reflexión intercultural

What impact does geography have on the culture of a region?

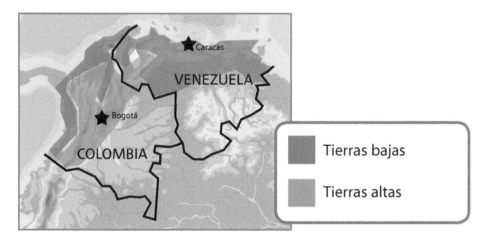

Llanos orientales en el Departamento del Meta

Mi progreso intercultural

I can recognize some ways geography impacts culture.

Enfoque cultural

Perspectiva cultural: Naciones y regiones culturales

We tend to think of nations or countries as the primary divisions of a continent, but geographical and cultural regions may have a bigger impact on people's identity and how they live. Colombia, for example, is actually a collection of very different environments. Each region has a distinct history, varied cultural practices, and even a different variety of Spanish.

National boundaries do not always match cultural boundaries. For example, the people in the lowland parts of Colombia, or **tierras bajas** (like the Caribbean coast), while proud Colombians, share many cultural practices and language features with Venezuelans from the coastal area. On the other side of the coin, Venezuelans from the highland areas of that country (**tierras altas**, the Andean region) sound more like highland Colombians than their compatriots from the capital, Caracas, which is in the lowland area.

 Conexiones

What are the cultural regions in your country? Do you identify strongly with the culture of your region? Consider examples of places where history, geography, and migration give people complex identities: Mexican-Americans in southern Texas, French speakers in Maine, Puerto Ricans in New York, etc.

Observa 1

¿Qué tiempo hace en Colombia?

Colombia está cerca de la **línea del ecuador,** por lo tanto, hay poca variación entre las **estaciones** del año.

En general, hay dos temporadas:

 una de **lluvia** (el "**invierno**"), de abril a noviembre,

 y otro período **seco** (el "**verano**"), de diciembre a marzo.

Prácticamente no existen **primavera** y **otoño**.

Pero, ¿por qué varían tanto **las temperaturas** en Colombia? ¿No es una zona tropical?

El factor más importante es **la altitud**:

 los pisos térmicos determinan las temperaturas, del **calor** de **los valles**

 al **frío** de **las sierras**.

¡Uno puede viajar muy pocos kilómetros y estar en un **clima** completamente distinto!

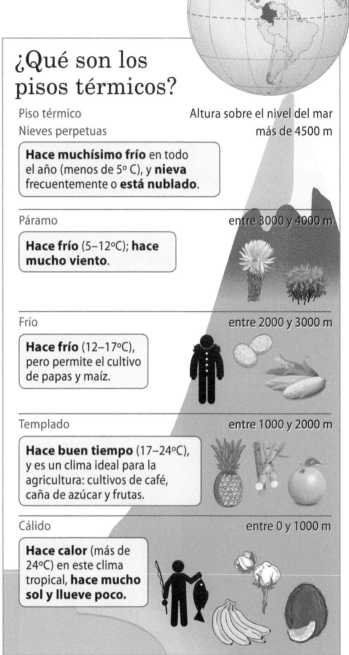

¿Qué son los pisos térmicos?

Piso térmico	Altura sobre el nivel del mar
Nieves perpetuas	más de 4500 m

Hace muchísimo frío en todo el año (menos de 5° C), y **nieva** frecuentemente o **está nublado**.

Páramo	entre 3000 y 4000 m

Hace frío (5–12°C); **hace mucho viento**.

Frío	entre 2000 y 3000 m

Hace frío (12–17°C), pero permite el cultivo de papas y maíz.

Templado	entre 1000 y 2000 m

Hace buen tiempo (17–24°C), y es un clima ideal para la agricultura: cultivos de café, caña de azúcar y frutas.

Cálido	entre 0 y 1000 m

Hace calor (más de 24°C) en este clima tropical, **hace mucho sol y llueve poco**.

¿Qué observas?

In the infographic, which expressions that describe weather use the phrase **hace...**? Which ones use another verb? Discuss your observations with a **compañero/ compañera de clase,** view the **Observa 1** resources online in *EntreCulturas 1* Explorer, and check the **Síntesis de gramática** at the end of this section of the unit.

La espeletia, o frailejón, sobrevive las duras condiciones del páramo colombiano

Actividad 7

🄰🄩 Actividades para todos los climas

¿Qué actividades puedes hacer en las siguientes condiciones? ¿Qué NO te gusta hacer?

1. Hace mucho calor; la temperatura está a 35°C.

2. Hace frío; la temperatura está a 3°C.

3. Hace mucho viento.

4. Está nublado.

5. Llueve.

Modelo

Si hace mucho calor, me gusta dormir una siesta. No me gusta hacer ejercicio.

Actividad 8

🄰🄩 ¿Cómo reaccionas al clima?

¿Cómo te afecta el tiempo? Combina expresiones de las tres columnas para expresar la relación entre el clima y tu humor *(mood)*.

Si hace calor		aburrido/a
Si hace frío		cansado/a
Si hace buen tiempo		contento/a
	me siento *(I feel)*	enojado/a
Si hace mal tiempo	estoy	fantástico/a
		preocupado/a
Si llueve		triste
Si nieva		¿...?

Detalle gramatical: Cómo identificar y describir

Remember that the verb **ser** is used with a noun to identify:

Bogotá **es** la **capital** de Colombia.
La Amazonía **es** una **región** de selvas y ríos.

To describe, use **ser** with adjectives, and/or expressions with **estar** and **hacer**:

Los desiertos siempre **son secos**.
Está muy **húmedo** en la Amazonía.
Hace calor allí también.

Climas variados

 Paso 1: La diversidad climática en EE. UU.

¿Qué tiempo asocias con los diferentes lugares? Empareja cada lugar con su geografía, y describe el clima típico.

Modelo

Kansas

Kansas tiene llanos; en el verano hace calor, y en el invierno hace mucho frío.

1. Alaska
2. Arizona
3. Colorado
4. Hawái
5. Florida

a. la selva tropical
b. la playa
c. las montañas
d. el desierto
e. la tundra

Enfoque cultural

Práctica cultural: La escala centígrada o Celsius

En Estados Unidos se usa la escala Fahrenheit para las temperaturas, pero en el resto del mundo encontramos grados Celsius. No es necesario aprender la fórmula para calcular los equivalentes. Es más fácil recordar algunos puntos de referencia importantes, como los del gráfico.

Conexiones

Using the reference points on the thermometer to the right, indicate an approximate temperature in degrees Celsius for each situation:

- a cold winter day in your community
- the temperature of a person with a slight fever
- a warm summer day in your community
- the temperature in the room you are in today.

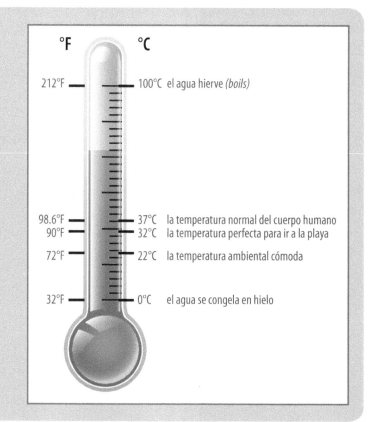

📝 🧭 Paso 2: La diversidad climática colombiana

¿Qué región colombiana se parece más a los lugares en el **Paso 1**? Usa el mapa de Colombia en la página 310 para encontrar la información y describir el clima de cada región.

Modelo

La Orinoquía es como Kansas; tiene llanos. Tiene dos estaciones: en el verano hace calor y no llueve, y en el invierno hace fresco y llueve más.

Actividad 10

En nuestra región

Un grupo de estudiantes colombianos viene a visitar la región donde ustedes viven durante seis meses. Tienen que saber qué tiempo hace allí para preparar el viaje.

🔤 ⏺ Paso 1: Preparamos la información

Trabajando en parejas, apunten *(jot down)* información sobre los siguientes aspectos de su región:

- una descripción básica de la geografía de la región

- si es posible, una región de Colombia con características similares

- los seis meses del año ideales para la visita

- el tiempo que los invitados pueden experimentar *(experience)* durante la visita

- sugerencias para actividades posibles en diferentes condiciones climáticas.

🧭 Paso 2: Publicamos la información

Escriban una guía *(guide)* con imágenes para los estudiantes colombianos que incluya la información del **Paso 1**. Usen las expresiones útiles de **Hablando de fenómenos generales**.

Expresiones útiles: Hablando de fenómenos generales

a veces
sometimes

en general
in general

frecuentemente
frequently, often

típicamente
typically

A veces la temperatura **varía** de 10 a 20 grados.

En general, las temperaturas en las montañas **bajan** *(go down)* mucho de noche.

En el desierto, la temperatura **frecuentemente sube** *(goes up)* a 42 grados.

Mi progreso comunicativo

I can describe the typical weather at different times of year in the region where I live.

Así se dice 2

✦ **Actividades turísticas para todos**

¿Qué tipo de turista eres?

La respuesta depende del entorno y las actividades que te gusten...

TURISMO DE SOL Y PLAYA
tomar el sol • nadar

TURISMO COMERCIAL
visitar mercados de artesanía • conocer zonas urbanas

TURISMO SOLIDARIO O RELIGIOSO
hacer un peregrinaje *(pilgrimage)*
colaborar en proyectos sociales

TURISMO RURAL
montar a caballo
trabajar en una granja *(farm)*

TURISMO DE MONTAÑA
esquiar
hacer senderismo *(hiking)*

TURISMO ARTÍSTICO-CULTURAL
visitar museos
probar la gastronomía local

ECOTURISMO
navegar en kayak o canoa
visitar la selva tropical

TURISMO DE SALUD
cuidar el cuerpo *(body)* y el espíritu
visitar un balneario o spa

Hemis / Alamy Stock Photo

Actividad 11

¿Qué hacen estas personas?

Escucha a estas personas describir sus viajes favoritos. ¿Qué tipo de turismo es?

1. _____ 2. _____ 3. _____

4. _____ 5. _____ 6. _____

Actividad 12

📖 ¿Qué categoría es?

Clasifica las actividades de **Además se dice** en las ocho categorías de turismo. ¡OJO! Una actividad puede estar en más de una categoría.

Actividad 13

¿Dónde lo haces?

Pregúntale a un/a compañero/a dónde le gusta hacer seis (6) de las actividades en **Así se dice 2** y **Además se dice**.

Modelo

caminar

Estudiante A: ¿Dónde te gusta caminar?

Estudiante B: Me gusta caminar *en el bosque.*

Lugares posibles:

en el campo   *en la playa*   *en un parque*   *en el bosque*

en las montañas *en la ciudad*   *en el zoo*   *¿...?*

Además se dice: Otras maneras de conocer el mundo

andar en bicicleta

apreciar las plantas y los animales

asistir a conciertos

caminar en el bosque *(forest)*

conocer *(meet)* a amigos nuevos

correr en la playa

dar un paseo en el campo

descubrir los parques nacionales

escalar *(climb)* montañas

hacer camping

hacer esquí acuático

hacer un tour con guía *(guide)*

ir de compras

pescar *(fish)*

visitar catedrales, iglesias, mezquitas *(mosques)* o templos

relajarse *(relax)*

sacar fotos *(take pictures)*

viajar *(travel)*

visitar el zoo

Una visita al Parque nacional de Tayrona, en la región caribeña de Colombia, puede incluir una salida en barco.

Piedra de Penol

Actividad 14

Comparando tipos de turismo

Trabajando en parejas, encuentren (*find*) imágenes en internet que ilustren dos tipos de turismo de **Así se dice 2,** con elementos de **Además se dice** en la página 319. Preparen una descripción del contraste entre los dos tipos de turismo.

Modelo

Turismo rural vs. turismo de montaña:

En turismo rural, montamos a caballo o trabajamos en una granja.

En turismo de montaña, caminamos en el bosque, escalamos montañas o hacemos camping.

Actividad 15

"Ocho preguntas": ¿Qué tipo de turista llevas por dentro?

Camina por la clase y entrevista a tus compañeros sobre el tipo de turista que quieren ser. Usen elementos de **Así se dice 2** y de **Además se dice** en la página 319.

1. ¿Te gusta el turismo solidario (*justice tourism*)? ¿Por qué sí? ¿Por qué no?

2. ¿Te parece interesante el turismo de montaña? ¿Por qué sí? ¿Por qué no?

3. ¿Qué hacen las personas en el turismo de salud?

4. ¿Te gustaría hacer ecoturismo? ¿Qué hace un ecoturista exactamente?

5. ¿Dónde se hace turismo de sol y playa en los EE. UU.?

6. ¿Cuál es un buen lugar para un turista artístico-cultural? ¿Por qué?

7. ¿Es turismo rural y turismo de montaña lo mismo? ¿Por qué sí? ¿Por qué no?

8. ¿Eres un/a turista comercial? ¿Qué actividades haces?

Actividad 16

✎ Turismo local

¿Qué tipos de turismo son posibles en tu comunidad y región? Prepara un póster con ideas para personas que quieren visitar el lugar donde vives. Incluye los siguientes aspectos:

- los tipos de turismo

- actividades posibles en cada categoría

- los meses del año recomendados para cada actividad.

El ecoturismo es una opción popular en las islas de coral del Caribe. Aquí, los turistas aprenden a identificar los animales acuáticos.

Los turistas pueden apreciar las esculturas de Fernando Botero en la Plaza de Botero de Medellín.

El Parque Nacional Natural Tayrona es un destino perfecto para los turistas de sol y playa. Allí pueden nadar, navegar en kayak o tomar el sol.

Observa 2

¿Qué estás haciendo en esta foto?

Michelle Rodríguez, Miami FL,
EE. UU., 17 años

Fotos de mi viaje a Colombia

Pasé una semana en la costa del Caribe.

Aquí, mi amigo Erik **está navegando** en kayak.

Estamos jugando vóleibol en la playa.

En esta foto, **estamos visitando** la parte histórica de Cartagena.

Aquí, **están vendiendo** arepas en la calle. ¡Qué ricas!

Aquí **estoy asistiendo** a un concierto de música regional al aire libre en Barranquilla.

Estoy escribiendo mi primera postal de Colombia. Es para mis padres, por supuesto.

Pasé otra semana en el valle del Cauca.

Estoy leyendo el itinerario del viaje. ¡Hay tantas cosas que ver en Colombia! Dos semanas no son suficientes.

Aquí, **estoy aprendiendo** sobre el café, en una plantación del valle del Cauca. (Este señor no se llama Juan Valdés.)

Estoy hablando con mi novio en Miami. ¡Lo extrañé mucho durante el viaje!

¿Qué observas?

🎧 🧭 In these photo narrations, observe the two-word verbs in bold that Michelle uses to tell what she is doing in each scene. What is the first verb in every case? What do the second verbs have in common? Discuss your observations with a **compañero/compañera de clase,** view the **Observa 2** resources in Explorer, and check the **Síntesis de gramática** at the end of this section of the unit.

Actividad 17

🎧 ✷ ¿Qué foto es?

Escucha y escribe la letra de la foto que corresponde a cada frase.

1. _____   2. _____   3. _____   4. _____

5. _____   6. _____   7. _____

Actividad 18

📖 🔤 ¿Dónde están?

Lee las siguientes acciones, y di dónde está la persona, probablemente.

1. "Estoy leyendo un libro de referencia para aprender de la historia del café en Colombia".

2. "Estoy viendo una nueva película cómica".

3. "¡Mira! Esas personas están vendiendo máscaras para el desfile".

4. "Estoy hablando con mis padres sobre mi viaje de verano".

5. "Estoy jugando básquetbol".

6. "Estamos andando en patineta".

7. "Estoy preparando estos platillos para la cena de esta noche".

8. "Estoy escuchando al profesor de español".

El café es importante en la economía de Colombia, y es un importante símbolo nacional.

Actividad 19

 **¿Qué están haciendo?**

¿Dónde están estas personas ahora mismo *(right now)*? ¿Qué están haciendo probablemente?

1. yo

2. mis padres

3. mi profesor/a de español

4. mi mejor amigo/a

5. mis vecinos *(neighbors)*

6. mi gato o perro

Modelo

Mi mejor amigo, Jacob, está en otra escuela ahora. Está estudiando matemáticas.

Mi progreso comunicativo

I can share information about a variety of activities by describing what is happening.

Actividad 20

Fotos de las vacaciones

Trae a clase cinco fotos de tu familia, tus amigos u otras personas que muestran las actividades que más les gustan. Explícales a tus compañeros de clase lo siguiente:

• ¿Quién es cada persona en las fotos?

• ¿Qué está haciendo cada persona?

Modelo

Son mis primos. Están esquiando en Bariloche, Argentina.

Actividad 21

✦ Cambios importantes en Colombia

Colombia ha tenido (*has had*) una historia difícil durante los últimos 50 años, pero las cosas están cambiando para mejor. Usando estos fragmentos y el presente progresivo, escribe oraciones completas que describen los cambios recientes.

1. el Gobierno | combatir | el tráfico de drogas

2. la seguridad (*safety*) | aumentar

3. el Gobierno | desarrollar | la infraestructura para el turismo

4. la economía | mejorar mucho

5. los restaurantes | ofrecer | una buena experiencia gastronómica

6. los artistas | crear | obras de importancia mundial

Parque Nacional del Café, Quidío, Colombia

Actividad 22

Cambios en mi comunidad

 Paso 1: ¿Qué está cambiando?

¿Qué está cambiando en tu comunidad? Trabajando con un/a compañero/a, investiguen las siguientes categorías:

- la educación

- la infraestructura (parques, carreteras, negocios, restaurantes, etc.)

- la demografía (la población, los grupos étnicos o culturales, etc.)

- la cultura popular

Museo del Oro, Bogotá, Colombia

 Paso 2: Presentamos nuestra investigación

Presenten las ideas a la clase. Si es posible, incluyan fotos para representar cada cambio.

Modelo

Están construyendo más escuelas en nuestro estado.

Así se dice 3

◈ ¿Qué ropa llevo?

QUÉ ROPA LLEVAR

Al hacer la maleta, ropa para cada temperatura

PUNTA GALLINAS

SAN GIL

PARQUE NACIONAL
NATURAL LOS NEVADOS

LETICIA

Destino de playa

40°C

Punta Gallinas

Tomar el sol y conocer la cultura de los indígenas wayúu

Es mejor usar ropa **ligera** blanca o de colores claros.

Puedes llevar **sandalias.**

Es importante **proteger** la cabeza con un **sombrero** o **gorra.**

Puedes llevar el **traje de baño** en la **mochila**, por si las moscas.

Destino templado

20°C

San Gil (Santander)

Hacer kayak o visitar una plantación de café

Basta una **camisa** o **blusa** ligera, con una **chaqueta** o **sudadera.**

Tienes que cubrirte las piernas con **pantalones** largos o **bluejeans.**

Usa **zapatos** abiertos o cerrados.

Destino de verano

30°C

Leticia (Amazonía)

Visitar el Parque Ecológico Mundo Amazónico

Tienes que llevar ropa ligera: **camiseta** con **pantalones cortos.**

Hay que usar **gafas de sol** y repelente de insectos.

Es mejor llevar un **paraguas** o **impermeable** para las inevitables lluvias.

Destino de nieve

0°C

Parque Nacional Natural Los Nevados

Hacer senderismo y ciclomontañismo

Tienes que vestir por capas: **ropa interior, suéter, abrigo.**

Es importante **cubrir**te el cuello con una **bufanda.**

Hay que llevar **calcetines** de lana y **botas** en los pies.

Adapted from www.despegar.com.ar.

Actividad 23

🔤 La protección adecuada

¿Qué ropa o accesorios necesitas para las siguientes situaciones? Consulta la infografía de **Así se dice 3** para encontrar lo que necesitas. Incluye todas las posibilidades que se te ocurran.

1. Hace mucho frío.

2. Hace calor, y está húmedo.

3. Hace mucho sol.

4. Hace viento, pero no hace frío.

5. Está lloviendo.

6. Está nevando.

Actividad 24

📝 ✦ ¿Qué tienes en tu armario?

Antes de comprar ropa para un viaje, revisa tu armario para ver qué ropa tienes. Organiza todo lo que tienes en estas categorías, y da por lo menos un detalle para cada prenda (color, material, uso, etc.).

ropa de invierno	ropa de verano	ropa deportiva	ropa elegante	otras cosas

Modelo

En mi ropa de invierno, tengo tres abrigos, cuatro suéteres (uno azul, dos café, uno negro) y tres bufandas (una roja, una azul y una negra).

Mi progreso comunicativo

I can describe clothing that is appropriate for different weather conditions.

Además se dice: Prendas y accesorios

el bolso	*purse, handbag*
la falda	*skirt*
el traje	*suit*
el vestido	*dress*

Mi progreso comunicativo

I can make recommendations for clothing appropriate for different conditions and situations.

Expresiones útiles: Recomendaciones

Es importante + infinitivo

Es importante usar crema de protección solar cuando hace mucho sol.

Es mejor + infinitivo

Es mejor usar botas cuando llueve.

Hay que + infinitivo

Hay que usar repelente de insectos en la selva tropical.

Tienes que + infinitivo

Tienes que llevar una bufanda cuando hace frío.

Actividad 25

 ⊕ **Preparamos una excursión**

Basándote en la lista de ropa en la **Actividad 23**, ¿qué ropa o accesorios tienes que comprar para estas excursiones o eventos?

1. Quieres hacer senderismo.

2. Te gustaría navegar en kayak en el lago.

3. Vas a participar en una carrera de 5K.

4. Te interesa ver todos los museos de la ciudad.

5. Un amigo te invita a cenar con su familia.

Actividad 26

Excursiones en nuestra región

Paso 1: ¿Qué lugares son interesantes?

Trabajando con un/a compañero/a, escojan cuatro lugares diferentes en su región que son de interés para turistas. ¿Qué tiempo hace típicamente en estos lugares?

Paso 2: ¿Cómo preparamos las excursiones?

Preparen una infografía con la información básica sobre el clima y la ropa adecuada para una excursión a los lugares escogidos.

Paso 3: Nuestras infografías

Presenten la información en la infografía a la clase.

Mi progreso comunicativo

I can describe points of interest to visitors to my community in an oral presentation.

Los parques nacionales protegen los entornos naturales de Colombia.

Cartagena de Indias tiene zonas históricas y modernas.

Observa 3

Mi pasaporte en 2030

¿Cómo va a ser tu pasaporte en 2030? ¿Qué lugares vas a visitar? ¿Qué quieres aprender?

Tengo que sacar mi pasaporte para viajar al extranjero.

Quiero conocer todos los países de Latinoamérica.

Me gustaría saber más de las diferentes culturas de mi país.

Voy a estudiar un semestre en Puerto Rico, con National Student Exchange.

Sueño con ir a Australia algún día.

Me interesa aprender más lenguas. *Quiero ser* multilingüe.

¿Qué observas?

Observe the two verbs in the bold expressions. Which one is conjugated to show who is doing the action? What form is the second verb? Does any other word connect the two verbs? Discuss your observations with a **compañero/compañera de clase,** view the **Observa 3** resources online in Explorer, and check the **Síntesis de gramática** at the end of this section of the unit.

Actividad 27

  ¿Cómo lograr estos sueños?

Lee los sueños o metas (*goals*) a la izquierda, y empareja cada uno con una recomendación posible a la derecha.

Sueños o metas	Recomendaciones
1. Quiero ser arquitecto.	a. Tienes que buscar oportunidades con organizaciones locales.
2. Me gustaría perfeccionar mi español.	b. Tienes que practicar tu deporte mucho.
3. Sueño con trabajar en el extranjero.	c. Tienes que conversar con hispanohablantes y leer mucho en español.
4. Me interesa trabajar con niños bilingües.	d. Tienes que sacar buenas notas y participar en muchas actividades.
5. Me gustaría ser músico.	e. Tienes que crear un plan y trabajar con un mentor.
6. Quiero ayudar a mi comunidad.	f. Tienes que estudiar educación.
7. Me gustaría tener más amigos.	g. Tienes que hacer una pasantía (*internship*) en una compañía internacional.
8. Me gustaría estudiar en una buena universidad.	h. Tienes que participar en más actividades que te gustan.
9. Quiero ser atleta profesional.	i. Tienes que practicar tu instrumento y estudiar con un experto.
10. Sueño con tener mi propio negocio.	j. Tienes que visitar muchos edificios y monumentos.

Expresiones útiles: *To know*

The English verb "to know" has two different translations into Spanish; they are not interchangeable.

saber = know a fact
¿Sabes el nombre de ese estudiante colombiano?
Do you know the name of that Colombian student?

conocer = be familiar with (a person, a custom, a work of art, etc.)
¿Conoces a ese estudiante colombiano?
Do you know that Colombian student?

The **yo** form of both verbs is irregular:

Yo **sé** la respuesta. *I know the answer.*
No lo **sé**. *I don't know.*

Conozco a muchos colombianos.
I know lots of Colombians.

No **conozco** a nadie aquí.
I don't know anybody here.

El aeropuerto El Dorado de Bogotá es el punto de inicio para muchos visitantes a Colombia.

Saber leer los paneles de información es fundamental para un viaje exitoso.

Mi progreso comunicativo

I can talk about future plans for how I will interact with other cultures.

Actividad 28

✏️ ✳️ ¿Qué quieres saber? ¿A quién quieres conocer?

Aprender es una actividad de por vida. ¿Qué cosas y personas pueden enriquecer tu vida? Apunta ideas para tus futuras pasiones y metas.

Actividad 29

✏️ ¿Retos o excusas?

¿Qué retos reales no te permiten lograr *(achieve)* tus sueños? Muchas veces inventamos excusas para no hacer las cosas que queremos. Sé honesto/a contigo mismo/a, y escribe los retos y excusas ahora ¡para vencerlos *(conquer them)* para siempre!

Modelo

No puedo _____.

Tengo que _____ en vez de *(instead of)* _____.

Actividad 30

Mi vida "EntreCulturas"

✏️ ✳️ Paso 1: ¿Qué voy a hacer?

¿Qué aventuras interculturales vas a tener para el año 2030? Imagina que no existen obstáculos, y escribe por lo menos seis cosas que vas a hacer para el año 2030.

Modelo

Voy a ir a México en 2022, y voy a estudiar español por seis meses.

🎤 ✳️ Paso 2: PechaKucha

Prepara fotos o imágenes para representar las actividades del **Paso 1**. Presenta tus aventuras a la clase en formato de PechaKucha.

Reflexión intercultural

Mi progreso intercultural

I can outline plans for intercultural experiences now and in my future.

How can international travel and intercultural experiences contribute to your life now and into the future? Will you travel for work, study, or enjoyment? Share when, where and for what purpose you would like to travel. How can life in your own community today be an intercultural experience?

¿Qué lugares quieres conocer?

Even if you don't travel to Colombia soon, you can use your Spanish beyond the classroom! Here are some tips to get you started!

Estrategias

Discover Ways to Use Spanish Outside Class

In your community and online, you can find many ways to enjoy using—and increasing—your Spanish skills.

Look for brochures in Spanish in museums, libraries, stores, and offices. Read them in Spanish, then check your understanding by looking at the English version.

Visit restaurants and attend festivals with foods from Spanish-speaking countries. Converse with the servers about their favorite foods, or ask questions about the ingredientes and preparation.

Read a translation of a favorite book, or watch a movie you know well, but set the language to Spanish. If your local library has a children's story hour in Spanish, volunteer to help out.

Go to a music site online and check out the top 10 song playlist in a Spanish-speaking country. Listen to the songs, find one you like, and search for the lyrics. Listen to the song again and follow with the lyrics.

If you have a hobby, explore websites in Spanish relating to your passion. If you like to cook, watch cooking videos in Spanish. If you love fashion, check out the latest styles of Spanish-speaking designers on their websites.

For more ideas, view the video "Discover Ways to use Spanish Outside the Classroom" online in your Explorer course!

Síntesis de gramática

A. Cómo hablar del tiempo y las temperaturas

To talk about weather and temperatures, English uses almost exclusively the verb *be: it is hot, it is cloudy, it is raining,* etc. Spanish, in contrast, uses a wide range of grammatical structures:

Hace + noun: hace calor, hace frío, hace sol, hace viento, hace buen tiempo
Estar + adjective: está nublado, está seco, está húmedo
Estar + -ndo form: está lloviendo, está nevando

Remember that if you are talking about the temperature of your body (and other things that you feel or experience), use **tener** + noun:

Tengo frío.	*I'm cold.*
Tengo calor.	*I'm hot.*
Tengo hambre.	*I'm hungry.*

To modify these expressions, nouns take **mucho/a**, and adjectives take **muy**:

Hace **mucho** calor.	*It's very hot.*
Tengo **mucha** hambre.	*I'm really hungry.*
Hoy está **muy** nublado.	*It's very cloudy.*
Este verano está **muy** seco.	*This summer is very dry.*

B. El presente progresivo: estar + -ndo

The simple present tense in Spanish can refer to habitual, future, or ongoing actions:

(habitual)   **Trabajo** en la playa todos los veranos.
   I work at the beach every summer.

(future)   **Trabajo** en la playa la próxima semana.
   I'll work at the beach next week.

(ongoing)   **Trabajo** en la playa ahora; no puedo hablar contigo.
   I'm working at the beach now; I can't talk to you.

If you want to emphasize that the action is ongoing at the moment you are speaking, use **estar** + the **-ndo** form of the verb:

Estoy trabajando en la playa ahora; no puedo hablar contigo.
I'm working at the beach right now; I can't talk to you.

Está lloviendo mucho, y no quiero salir de casa.
It's raining hard; I don't want to go outside.

Estamos planeando un viaje a España. ¿Quieres participar?
We're planning a trip to Spain. Do you want to join us?

To make the **-ndo** form (present participle), remove the **-ar, -er,** or **-ir** of the infinitive and add **-ando** (for **-ar**) or **-iendo** (for **-er** and **-ir**):

tomar ⟶ tom**ando**
correr ⟶ corr**iendo**
escribir ⟶ escrib**iendo**

Some verbs have spelling changes:

dormir ⟶ d**u**rm**iendo**
pedir ⟶ p**i**d**iendo**
ir ⟶ **yendo**
leer ⟶ le**yendo**

C. Combinaciones de verbos

The most basic type of sentence usually has just one verb, which is conjugated in Spanish to show who is doing the action. But more sophisticated ideas may require two or more verbs. To combine them in one sentence, Spanish has three possibilities:

1. Conjugate one verb; add an infinitive:
   Me **gusta** viajar mucho.
   Me **gustaría** conocer las culturas de Centroamérica.
   Quiero ir a Europa en el futuro.

2. Conjugate the first verb; add a present participle (**-ndo** form):
   Estoy estudiando español ahora.
   Aprendo mejor practicando la conversación con mis amigos.

3. Conjugate the first verb; add a linking word (preposition or **que**) before the infinitive:
   Voy a viajar a Colombia el año que viene.
   Aprendí a hablar español en México.
   Trato de estudiar un poco todos los días.
   Sueño con ir a Chile en el futuro.
   Tengo que estudiar más.

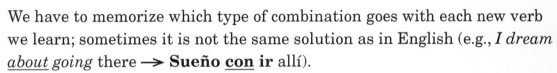

We have to memorize which type of combination goes with each new verb we learn; sometimes it is not the same solution as in English (e.g., *I dream about going* there ⟶ **Sueño con ir** allí).

If the different actions are independent or sequential, each verb is conjugated to show who carries them out:

Vamos a Perú todos los años y **pasamos** el verano con mis primos allí.
We go to Peru every year and spend the summer with my cousins there.

Vocabulario

I can identify geographical features and weather conditions. (Así se dice 1)

aquí	here
allí	there
la altitud	altitude
bajar	go down; lower
bonito/a	pretty; beautiful
el calor	heat
el centro	center; middle
el clima	climate
la costa	coast; shore
el desierto	desert
la estación	season
el este	east
feo/a	ugly
el frío	cold
el llano	plain
la lluvia	rain
el mar	sea
la montaña	mountain
el norte	north
la nieve	snow
el oeste	west
la playa	beach
el río	river
seco/a	dry
la selva tropical	tropical forest
subir	go up; rise
el sur	south
la temperatura	temperature
el tiempo	weather; time
el valle	valley

Cómo hablar del tiempo (Así se dice 1)

está nublado	it's cloudy
hace buen tiempo	it's nice weather
hace calor	it's hot
hace frío	it's cold
hace sol	it's sunny
hace viento	it's windy
llover (u ⟶ ue)	rain
mucho/a	a lot; very
muchísimo/a	really a lot; very, very
nevar (e ⟶ ie)	snow
poco/a	a little; not much

Expresiones útiles: Hablando de fenómenos generales

a veces	sometimes
en general	in general
típicamente	typically
frecuentemente	frequently; often

El Carnaval de Cartagena, Colombia, refleja las raíces caribeñas de la región.

I can share information about activities for visitors (Así se dice 2)

colaborar	to collaborate; to work together
conocer (zc)	to be familiar with; to know
cubrir	to cover
el cuerpo	body
cuidar	to take care of
el espíritu	spirit; soul
esquiar	to ski
la gastronomía	food culture; cooking
hacer senderismo	to go hiking
el mercado de artesanía	arts and crafts market
montar a caballo	to ride a horse
el museo	museum
nadar	to swim
navegar en canoa	to go canoeing
el peregrinaje	pilgrimage
probar (o ⟶ ue)	to try (a food, a drink, etc,)
tomar el sol	to sunbathe; lay out
visitar	to visit
la zona urbana	urban area

I can identify appropriate clothing for different activities and weather conditions (Así se dice 3)

el abrigo	coat
los bluejeans	jeans
la blusa	blouse
el bolso	purse; handbag
las botas	boots
la bufanda	scarf
los calcetines	socks
la camisa	shirt
la camiseta	t-shirt
la chaqueta	jacket
corto/a	short
la falda	skirt
las gafas de sol	sunglasses
la gorra	cap
el impermeable	raincoat
largo/a	long
ligero/a	light (weight)
la mochila	backpack
los pantalones	pants
el paraguas	umbrella
la ropa	clothing
la ropa interior	underwear
las sandalias	sandals
el sombrero	hat
la sudadera	sweatshirt
el suéter	sweater
el traje	suit
el traje de baño	swimming suit
el vestido	dress
los zapatos	shoes
saber (yo sé)	to know (a fact)
viajar al extranjero	to travel abroad

Expresiones útiles: Recomendaciones

es importante + infinitivo	it's important to + verb
es mejor + infinitivo	it's better to + verb
hay que + infinitivo	one must + verb
tener que + infinitivo	have to + verb

En camino

Actividad 31

🎙 ⊕ El informe del tiempo

Your school's online newspaper wants to publish a bilingual version (Spanish and English). Prepare a podcast with information about the weather, including the conditions for today and tomorrow.

Modelo

Hoy es el [fecha]. Aquí en _____ hace _____.

La temperatura alta está a _____, y la baja está a _____.

Mañana va a hacer _____, con temperaturas entre _____ y _____ grados.

Actividad 32

✏ ⊕ Preparando la excursión

The parents of some bilingual students at your school want to know how to prepare their children for a field trip. Write some recommendations including the following information:

- a point of interest in your community
- tomorrow's weather
- appropriate clothing for the children.

Actividad 33

💬 ⊕ Planes en común

Working in groups of four, interview your classmates to learn their dreams and plans for the future. Who are compatible? Who have ideas that are completely incompatible?

Actividad 34

Recomendaciones de Melissa

◈ Paso 1: Anticipación/visualización

Melissa, our video blogger from Colombia, explains what she likes to wear in her climate. Before listening to her blog entry, review the information you have learned in this unit about the climate of Bogotá, and answer the following questions.

1. ¿En qué zona climática de Colombia está Bogotá?

2. ¿Cuántas estaciones hay en el año en esta zona?

3. ¿Qué tiempo hace en Bogotá típicamente?

4. ¿Qué ropa es, probablemente, más apropiada para este clima?

🎧 ◈ Paso 2: Lo que lleva Melissa

Now listen as Melissa explains her clothing preferences. Write down all the clothing items that she mentions. When you are finished, how would you sum up Melissa's style—formal or informal?

Colombia tiene una rica tradición musical; los géneros más conocidos son la cumbia y el vallenato.

Mi progreso comunicativo

I can understand information in a short video presentation about climate and clothing.

El clima de Bogotá, Colombia, es variable.

Explora

Essential Questions: What makes a place unique?
How do my surroundings shape my identity?

Overview

Local transportation systems and global trade routes shape our
interactions and help define the places we live. Explore how the
historical and present-day connections between Colombia and Florida
have shaped these places.

Ideas de hoy para el futuro

Increase your awareness and civic pride in your community by
documenting what makes it unique, as well as aspects that could
improve in the future.

**El Castillo de San Felipe de Barajas,
una antigua fortificación colonial
en Cartagena de Indias, Colombia.**

El transporte nos conecta

Actividad 35

🗨️ ⊕ Tu perfil como viajero urbano

Entrevista a un/a compañero/a con las siguientes preguntas.

1. ¿Conoces bien tu ciudad? ¿Podrías *(could you)* ser un/a guía de tu ciudad para turistas?

2. ¿Cómo te mueves *(get around)* en el lugar donde vives? Escoge las opciones que usas, e indica con qué frecuencia:

	todos los días	de vez en cuando	rara vez	nunca
Tomo el autobús escolar				
Tomo un autobús público				
Uso el automóvil (carro/coche)				
Ando en bicicleta				
Tomo el metro (tren ligero o subterráneo)				
Tomo un tranvía *(streetcar)*				
Tomo un tren de cercanías o regional				

3. Cuando estás de vacaciones, ¿usas medios de transporte diferentes de los normales que usas en tu ciudad? ¿Cuáles?

4. ¿Te gustaría viajar en el autobús de la foto? ¿Es similar al transporte público de tu ciudad?

Actividad 36

El transporte sostenible

 ⊕ **Paso 1: Nuevos medios de transporte**

Observa las siguientes imágenes. Luego, escucha las descripciones y empareja cada una con la foto correspondiente.

1. _____ 2. _____ 3. _____ 4. _____

A. El metro

B. El carro eléctrico

C. La bicicleta pública

D. El metrocable

⑤ ⊕ **Paso 2: Características del transporte sostenible**

Lee la lista de características del transporte sostenible. ¿Cuál es la más importante en tu opinión? ¿Cuál de las opciones del **Paso 1** es más sostenible, según estos criterios?

- Es ecológico; reduce la contaminación.

- Es solidario *(just; fair)*; es accesible a todas las personas.

- Es económico; no es necesario comprar un carro.

- Reduce el estrés; puedes ver el paisaje o trabajar durante el viaje.

- Reduce el tráfico; no pierdes tiempo en atascos *(traffic jams)*.

Enfoque cultural

Práctica cultural: La Ciclovía de Bogotá

La Ciclovía es un evento regular en Bogotá. Todos los domingos y días festivos del año, de las 7:00 a.m. a las 2:00 p.m., las principales vías de la ciudad están cerradas (*closed*) a los automóviles. Se crea un circuito interconectado de más de 121 kilómetros de extensión, sólo para bicicletas y peatones (*pedestrians*), que cubre todos los sectores de la ciudad.

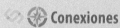 **Conexiones**

What public activities or events are important for the identity of your community?

Instituto Distrital de Recreación y Deporte de Bogotá (2016). "La Ciclovía Bogotana y su historia." Adapted from http://tinyurl.com/jf5dpw6.

Actividad 37

Las escaleras eléctricas de Medellín

Medellín, Colombia, recibió el prestigioso premio de "La ciudad más innovadora del mundo". Vas a mirar un video que presenta una de sus innovaciones en el transporte.

Paso 1: Comparaciones

Contesta a las preguntas con un/a compañero/a de clase:

1. Antes de ver el video, consideren las escaleras eléctricas en su comunidad: ¿Dónde están? ¿Están dentro o fuera de los edificios?

2. Miren y escuchen el video. ¿En qué se parecen o diferencian las escaleras eléctricas de Medellín de las de su comunidad?

Paso 2: Un tour de las escaleras eléctricas

Mira y escucha el video, y apunta por lo menos tres elementos que puedes ver o visitar durante un tour de este medio de transporte.

Desarrollo urbano en Medellín

Mi progreso comunicativo

I can infer meaning from audiovisual materials.

📖 ✤ Paso 3: La transformación

Las siguientes oraciones explican cómo este sistema de transporte ha transformado la Comuna (*neighborhood*) 13 en Medellín, Colombia. Empareja cada oración a la izquierda con la idea equivalente a la derecha.

1. Los techos (*rooftops*) están decorados con pájaros y flores.

2. Es el mejor balcón de la ciudad.

3. Aumenta la inclusión social.

4. Puedes hacer un "graffitour" de la historia del barrio.

5. Mejora la calidad de vida de la Comuna.

a. El contacto entre las personas es mejor.

b. Las paredes (*walls*) presentan la evolución de la Comuna.

c. Ofrece vistas (*views*) impresionantes.

d. Las casas son una representación de la naturaleza.

e. Transforma el barrio en un lugar mucho mejor.

🌀 Paso 4: ¿Te gustaría usar las escaleras eléctricas de Medellín?

Prioriza (*prioritize*) las respuestas siguientes según tu opinión. Evalúa cada oración de uno a cinco: 5 = Me gustaría mucho, 1 = No me importa.

_____ Sí, porque están al aire libre.

_____ Sí, porque es una manera relajada de subir (*go up*) la montaña.

_____ Sí, porque me gustan las pintadas del "graffitour".

_____ Sí, porque los jóvenes que trabajan allí son muy amables.

_____ Sí, porque la vista panorámica de Medellín es excepcional.

_____ Sí, porque es un medio de transporte muy práctico.

Actividad 38

📖 🔄 Mejoras para la ciudad

La ciudad de Medellín está implementando muchas innovaciones, además del transporte. Lee sobre las mejoras *(improvements)* en Medellín. Indica cuál de estos aspectos corresponde a cada mejora.

El centro de Medellín, Colombia

Medellín se moderniza . . .

- ✓ GOBIERNO
- ✓ ESTILO de VIDA
- ✓ ECONOMÍA
- ✓ MEDIO AMBIENTE
- ✓ MOVILIDAD
- ✓ TIC*

*tecnologías de la información y la comunicación

Actividad comercial debajo de las vías del tren en Medellín, Colombia

1. El metro transporta a personas de barrios distantes a sus lugares de trabajo.

2. El metrocable llega a barrios que no han tenido *(haven't had)* transporte público.

3. Los nuevos autobuses producen menos contaminación.

4. Hay muchas zonas de wifi gratis en espacios públicos de la ciudad de Medellín.

5. La variedad de transportes son una atracción turística de la ciudad.

6. Los diferentes modos de transporte reducen los atascos *(traffic jams)* porque hay menos carros en las calles.

7. El uso de transporte público transforma la mentalidad de los ciudadanos y aumenta el orgullo *(pride)* cívico.

8. Las estaciones de transporte son espacios públicos con arte y cultura.

La historia nos conecta y define

Actividad 39

Fortificaciones españolas en el Caribe

🔍 💭 **Paso 1: ¿Dónde están?**

Observa las fotos e identifica dónde están las fortificaciones españolas en el mapa. ¿Qué tienen en común los lugares en los que están?

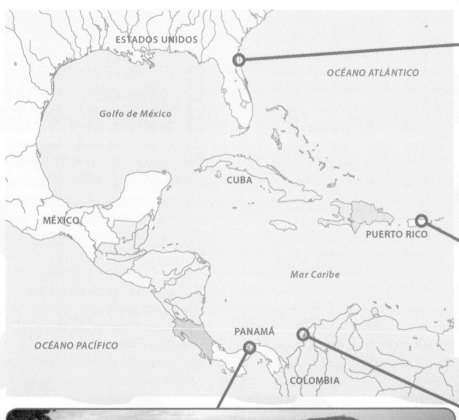

Adapted from National Parks Service, www.nps.gov.

📖 ↩ **Paso 2: Los países actuales**

¿En qué países actuales se ubican estas fortificaciones?
¿Cuáles son las capitales modernas de estos países?

Galeón español en San
Agustín, Florida

Actividad 40

↩ Un impacto moderno de las rutas históricas

¿Puede el comercio del pasado afectar la lengua del presente?
Compara las pronunciaciones de la pregunta **¿Cómo estás?**
en diferentes lugares, y contesta a las preguntas. ([h] es el
sonido inicial de "happy" en inglés.)

La Ciudad de México	[ko mo es tás]
Veracruz, México	[ko mo eh táh]
Bogotá, Colombia	[ko mo es tás]
Cartagena, Colombia	[ko mo eh táh]
La Habana, Cuba	[ko mo eh táh]
San Juan, Puerto Rico	[ko mo eh táh]
Madrid, España	[ko mo es tás]
Sevilla, España	[ko mo eh táh]

Castillo de los Tres Reyes del
Morro, La Habana, Cuba

1. ¿Qué lugares tienen la misma pronunciación?

2. ¿Qué tienen en común geográficamente los lugares con la misma pronunciación?

3. ¿Cuál es la conexión probable entre estos lugares? Estudia el mapa y consulta **Enfoque cultural** en la página 348 para encontrar la respuesta.

Puerto de Sevilla,
España, siglo XVI

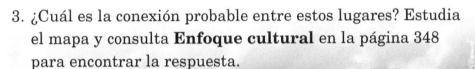

Enfoque cultural

Perspectiva cultural: La globalización—ayer y hoy

La globalización no es un fenómeno reciente. En el siglo XVI, los exploradores europeos empiezan a cruzar el Atlántico y el Pacífico, conectando los continentes. Personas y productos de Asia, América, Europa y África entran en contacto, iniciando el comercio global. Especias, seda *(silk)* y porcelana cruzan el Pacífico desde China, y los galeones españoles llevan oro, plata, vainilla, chocolate y tabaco de América a Sevilla, España.

En esta época, los piratas aterrorizan a todo el Caribe, y, junto con los huracanes y los arrecifes *(reefs)*, causan pérdidas *(losses)* al comercio. Las fortificaciones españolas en el Caribe son un elemento fundamental para la protección del comercio global.

🔄 🧭 Conexiones

What products are important in global trade today? What products that you use every day come from other countries? What countries are important in world trade today?

Este sello colombiano representa un galeón español y su tesoro *(treasure)*.

Miami, Florida

Actividad 41

📖 🧭 Defiende las ideas

Por supuesto, cada país tiene su capital política, pero Miami, Florida (EE. UU.), puede considerarse la capital de América Latina. Busca dos detalles de las infografías de la página 349 que justifican cada designación.

Idea	Evidencia de la infografía (1)	Evidencia de la infografía (2)
A. Miami: Capital comercial de América Latina		
B. Miami: Capital intercultural		
C. Miami: Ciudad conectada globalmente		

Miami: ¿La capital de América Latina?

Rutas aéreas

Vuelos domésticos (negro) y vuelos internacionales (en rojo) desde Miami, Florida (EE. UU.)

Miami

Población

El condado de Miami-Dade

La población latina o hispana es un **66.2%**

Nació en otro país un **51.4%**

Habla una lengua que no sea el inglés un **70%**

Source: US Census Bureau, 2010-2014

Comercio internacional

Importaciones y exportaciones, Miami-Dade (2014)

■ Importaciones ■ Exportaciones

Zona: América del Sur, Centroam./Caribe, Asia*, Europa, Norteamérica, África

0 5 10 15 20 25 30 35 40

Mil millones de US$

Source: www.miamidade.gov

Reflexión intercultural

How do transportation systems in our communities, and trade routes between distant places impact our lives? Compare what you have learned about Colombia and Miami to your community.

Mi progreso intercultural

I can recognize the impact of local and global connections on life in different communities.

Monumento al buceador *(diver)* **de esponjas:** Este monumento conmemora la importancia histórica del mar en la vida de la comunidad griega *(Greek)*.

Negocios griegos: Tarpon Springs tiene la comunidad de griego-americanos más grande de Estados Unidos.

En mi comunidad

Ideas de hoy para el futuro

Cada comunidad tiene aspectos únicos. Pueden ser atractivos, pero también hay elementos que no son ideales. Vamos a estudiar imágenes de Tarpon Springs, Florida (EE. UU.), como ejemplo, y crear una campaña para mejorar la comunidad donde ustedes viven.

Actividad 42

Orgullo local

📖 **Paso 1: Un ejemplo de orgullo** *(pride)* **cívico**

La ubicación y la historia de Tarpon Springs, Florida, le dan una personalidad única. Estudia las fotos, lee las descripciones y asigna las etiquetas *(hashtags)* apropiadas a cada imagen.

- #bilingüismo
- #cultura
- #diversión
- #familia

- #historia
- #infraestructura
- #inmigración
- #orgullocívico

✍️ 🧭 **Paso 2: Lo mejor de mi comunidad**

¿Cuáles son los aspectos más positivos o atractivos de la comunidad donde vives? Saca fotos para ilustrar cada aspecto, y escribe una oración para describir su importancia. Añade *hashtags* también a cada foto.

Esponjas *(sponges)* **naturales:** Los griegos trajeron *(brought)* la industria de la esponja desde Grecia.

Actividad 43

¿Cómo mejorar la comunidad?

 Paso 1: Lo que no tenemos

¿Qué elementos negativos o deficiencias tiene la comunidad donde ustedes viven, en su opinión? En grupos de cuatro, apunten los elementos que no tienen.

Modelo

No tenemos muchos parques.

No tenemos transporte público.

 Paso 2: Nuestras recomendaciones

Usando las ideas del **Paso 1**, escriban una lista de recomendaciones para los líderes de la comunidad. Tienen que justificar sus ideas para convencer a los líderes.

Modelo

Nos gustaría tener más parques; los niños necesitan lugares para jugar.

Nos gustaría tener más transporte público. Es imposible llegar a muchos sitios sin *(without)* carro.

Las escaleras eléctricas en la Comuna 13 de Medellín, Colombia

 **Mi progreso comunicativo**

I can make recommendations about improvements in my community.

El autobús Transmilenio circula en Bogotá.

Vive entre culturas

¡Conoce la comunidad!

Essential Question: What makes a place unique? How do my surroundings shape my identity?

Interpretive Assessment

◉ ✦ Destino Bogotá

You are going to watch a video about Bogotá and summarize what you hear and/or see in the video.

Presentational Assessment

🎤 ✦ ¡Vengan a visitar nuestra región!

A group of high school students from Colombia wants to come to the U.S. for two weeks in May, and they are searching for a community to host them. They would like to take one hour of English classes per day and spend the rest of each day in excursions and other activities to get to know the community. You and your classmates are going to create a proposal to convince the group to choose your community and school.

Interpersonal Assessment

💬 ✦ ¿Cómo es tu comunidad?

One of the Colombian students was very impressed with the presentation you made about your community. He wants more information to share with his group, so you arrange to talk over the Internet. Listen, and answer the questions he poses.

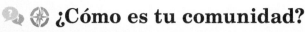

Gainesville, Florida

En la Universidad de Florida ofrecen clases de lengua.

Todos los viernes hay conciertos gratis en la Plaza Bo Diddley.

Los *Twins* de Minnesota entrenan en Ft. Myers, Florida.

El caimán es una de las atracciones de LaChua Trail, una zona natural de Gainesville.

Can-do Statements

Unidad Preliminar: ¡Hola!

Mi progreso intercultural

❏ I can identify places where Spanish is spoken around the world.*

❏ I can recognize the importance of Spanish as a language of real-world and online communication.

❏ I can recognize and use appropriate words, gestures, and body language to greet people in different cultures.

❏ I can recognize differing cultural perspectives on the seasons in areas with different climates.

Mi progreso comunicativo

❏ I can ask and answer questions to meet and greet a young person in an appropriate manner.

❏ I can understand and write out some common names in Spanish when I hear them or hear them spelled.

❏ I can spell out my first and last name using the Spanish alphabet.

❏ I can understand and say days, dates, and months in Spanish.

❏ I can read and interpret an ad in Spanish.

❏ I can understand simple written promotional material in Spanish.

❏ I can understand a short spoken presentation in which a native speaker of Spanish introduces him or herself.

❏ I can respond orally to several questions about myself.

*The Can-Do Statements are Wayside Publishing's alone and not based on the NCSSFL-ACTFL Can-Do Statements.

Unidad 1: Identidades

Mi progreso intercultural

❏ I can recognize some similarities and differences between a Paraguayan teen and myself.

❏ I can recognize some similarities and differences between young people from the Spanish - speaking world and myself.

❏ I can recognize some similarities and differences between bilingualism in Paraguay and Texas.

❏ I can understand and compare some cultural perspectives on the importance of language learning.

❏ I can recognize different perspectives on the meaning of the word *América*.

❏ I can recognize ways languages and language learning impact me and my community.

Mi progreso comunicativo

❏ I can ask and answer questions to share information about identity.

❏ I can ask and answer questions about my identity.

❏ I can write sentences to express other people's identity.

❏ I can identify key words when I read in Spanish.

❏ I can write a short note in which I introduce myself and tell what I like and dislike.

❏ I can ask and answer a few questions to get to know another person.

❏ I can talk about my identity and the identity of others.

❏ I can introduce myself and provide some details about myself.

❏ I can understand the main ideas and some details from an ad for a language program.

Unidad 2: La vida en la escuela

Mi progreso intercultural

❏ I can recognize some similarities and differences between school life in Costa Rica and in my community.

❏ I can identify some shared values between my community and a community in the Spanish-speaking world.

❏ I can compare cultural practices and perspectives reflected in the use of uniforms in my community and in Costa Rica.

❏ I can identify cultural practices from authentic digital materials.

Mi progreso comunicativo

❏ I can understand a simple written ad in Spanish.

❏ I can write a list of school supplies I need to purchase.

❏ I can express where my school activities take place.

❏ I can understand a simple written ad in Spanish.

❏ I can create a simple written promotional message.

❏ I can present information about my school day orally.

❏ I can write a simple description of my personal preferences about school.

❏ I can ask and respond to questions relating to personal preferences about school activities.

❏ I can ask and answer questions about life at school in oral conversations.

❏ I can list in writing a few of the activities I regularly do at school.

❏ I can identify and interpret familiar words when I hear students talking about their school.

❏ I can present information about my school and extracurricular activities in writing.

❏ I can interact orally to exchange information about my activities.

❏ I can identify key details from charts and graphs, and make inferences about cultural perspectives.

❏ I can identify key details and understand cultural practices when reading authentic print materials.

❏ I can create a written presentation communicating school values.

Unidad 3: Mi familia es tu familia

Mi progreso intercultural

- ❏ I can understand how family and given names reflect identity in some Spanish-speaking cultures.

- ❏ I can compare across cultures who makes up a family and how long people live together at home.

- ❏ I can compare typical family activities across different cultures.

- ❏ I can identify key details and cultural practices from authentic reading materials.

- ❏ I can identify common elements in family history across cultures.

Mi progreso comunicativo

- ❏ I can can ask and tell about family members and pets.

- ❏ I can write simple messages to compare information about my family and others.

- ❏ I can describe the members of my family.

- ❏ I can ask and answer questions about family members and where they live.

- ❏ I can talk about where I live.

- ❏ I can talk about places in the house.

- ❏ I can propose activities to do with others.

- ❏ I can understand simple texts about family activities.

- ❏ I can understand basic descriptions of families and the activities they do together.

- ❏ I can compare typical family activities across different cultures.

- ❏ I can talk about family members and pets.

- ❏ I can identify and interpret familiar words when I hear a person talk about his or her family.

- ❏ I can write phrases and simple sentences to compare and contrast family activities.

- ❏ I can identify key words, the theme, and some details in a poem about the family.

- ❏ I can identify key details from charts and graphs and make inferences about cultural perspectives.

- ❏ I can understand and identify key ideas in a Spanish blog post.

Unidad 4: La comida es cultura

Mi progreso intercultural

❏ I can recognize some similarities and differences between foods in México and in my community.

❏ I can identify some foods typically enjoyed in some Spanish-speaking communities at different meals and at different times of day.

❏ I can recognize how my food habits and preferences reflect my culture, and compare that with those of young people in Spanish-speaking countries.

❏ I can identify examples demonstrating how foods reflect interactions between cultures.

❏ I can identify opportunities to create intercultural experiences.

Mi progreso comunicativo

❏ I can identify basic foods and describe their color.

❏ I can specify the quantity of foods for purchase.

❏ I can ask and answer questions about preferences for food and drink.

❏ I can talk about what I eat at different meals, and what time I eat them.

❏ I can order street food from a vendor.

❏ I can state personal reactions to the tastes of food.

❏ I can interpret a simple menu and choose foods I would like to sample.

❏ I can talk about similarities and differences in foods across cultures.

❏ I can produce brief written descriptions of foods from the target culture.

❏ I can order foods from a basic menu or menu board.

Unidad 5: La vida es un carnaval

Mi progreso intercultural

❏ I can explain the cultural importance of activities and celebrations to the identity of my community.

❏ I can understand basic conventions for communicating in different media, like text messages.

❏ I can recognize similarities and differences between my own leisure activities and those of young people in the Spanish-speaking world.

❏ I can recognize ways sports can bridge cultural differences.

Mi progreso comunicativo

❏ I can state likes or dislikes and preferences relating to leisure activities.

❏ I can ask and answer questions in a conversation about leisure activities that I like to do everyday or during the weekends.

❏ I can describe future plans and actions.

❏ I can invite friends to social and cultural events and accept invitations.

❏ I can turn down invitations politely.

❏ I can describe social norms and rules for events and celebrations in my community.

❏ I can make simple social plans.

❏ I can describe my preferences for celebrating holidays.

❏ I can describe typical activities associated with celebrations in my community.

❏ I can talk about what I did on a recent weekend, at a party, or an event.

❏ I can understand short presentations about preferences for leisure activities.

❏ I can describe community events and celebrations.

❏ I can say a few activities that I did recently.

❏ I can exchange information about what I am going to do.

Unidad 6: El mundo en el que vivo

Mi progreso intercultural

❏ I can recognize some ways geography impacts culture.

❏ I can outline plans for intercultural experiences now and in my future.

❏ I can recognize the impact of local and global connections on life in different communities.

Mi progreso comunicativo

❏ I can identify geographical features and explain their location in relation to each other.

❏ I can describe the typical weather at different times of year in the region where I live.

❏ I can ask and answer questions in a conversation to exchange information about my activities.

❏ I can create promotional materials about activities travelers can enjoy in my community or region.

❏ I can share information about a variety of activities by describing what is happening.

❏ I can describe clothing that is appropriate for different weather conditions.

❏ I can make recommendations for clothing appropriate for different conditions and situations.

❏ I can describe points of interest to visitors to my community in an oral presentation.

❏ I can talk about future plans for how I will interact with other cultures.

❏ I can inform about weather conditions in a short oral presentation.

❏ I can make recommendations about an excursion in my community.

❏ I can exchange information in a conversation about my plans for the future.

❏ I can understand information in a short video presentation about climate and clothing.

❏ I can infer meaning from audiovisual materials.

❏ I can make recommendations about improvements in my community.

Level 1 *EntreCulturas* Analytic Growth Rubric

Interpretive Reading, Listening, Audiovisual, and Viewing

LEVEL 1 TARGET: NOVICE MID - NOVICE HIGH

DOMAINS	NOVICE LOW	NOVICE MID	NOVICE HIGH	INTERMEDIATE LOW
HOW WELL DO I UNDERSTAND? *MAIN IDEA AND/OR DETAILS*	I can recognize a few words that are very familiar to me.	I can recognize and understand some basic information with memorized words and phrases.	I can identify pieces of information and sometimes the main idea(s) without explanation when the idea is familiar, short, and simple.	I can identify the main idea(s) and some details when the idea is familiar, short, and simple.
WHAT WORDS AND STRUCTURES DO I UNDERSTAND? *VOCABULARY AND STRUCTURES IN CONTEXT*	I can recognize a few very familiar words and phrases in text or speech from well-practiced topics.	I can recognize words and phrases, including cognates, and borrowed words in text or speech from well-practiced topics.	I can understand words, phrases, simple sentences, and some structures in short, simple texts or sentence-length speech, one utterance at a time, with support, related to familiar topics of study.	I can identify words, phrases, high-frequency expressions, and some learned structures in short, simple, loosely connected texts or sentence-length speech, one utterance at a time, related to familiar topics of study.
HOW WELL CAN I UNDERSTAND UNFAMILIAR LANGUAGE? *CONTEXT CLUES*	I can understand some very basic word level meaning from short, simple authentic texts or speech on very familiar topics that include cognates and/or visual clues.	I can understand some basic meaning when authentic texts or speech on very familiar topics include cognates and/or visual clues.	I can understand basic meaning when short, non-complex authentic texts or speech include cognates and visual clues, on familiar topics.	I can understand literal meaning from authentic texts or speech on familiar topics and from highly predictable texts related to daily life.

DOMAINS	NOVICE LOW	NOVICE MID	NOVICE HIGH	INTERMEDIATE LOW
HOW WELL CAN I INFER MEANING BEYOND WHAT I READ OR HEAR? *INFERENCES*	I can make minimal inferences based on visual clues, organizational layout, inflection and/or body language.	I can make limited inferences based on visual clues, organizational layout, background knowledge, keywords, inflection and/or body language.	I can make a few inferences based on visual clues, organizational layout, background knowledge, keywords, inflection and/or body language.	I can make some inferences based on the main idea and information such as visual clues, organizational layout, background knowledge, keywords, inflection and/or body language.
HOW INTERCULTURAL AM I? *INTERCULTURALITY* *Based on classroom tasks/activities/ intercultural reflections and outside classroom experiences.*	I can recognize limited cultural products, practices, or perspectives including cultural behaviors and expressions, related to daily life.	I can identify a few cultural products, practices, perspectives including cultural behaviors and expressions related to daily life.	I can identify some cultural products, practices, perspectives, including cultural behaviors and expressions related to daily life.	I can describe cultural products, practices, perspectives, including cultural behaviors and expressions related to daily life.

Adapted from Jefferson County Public Schools World Languages: Performance Assessment Rubrics (Kentucky), Howard County Public Schools World Languages (Maryland).

Level 1 *EntreCulturas* Analytic Growth Rubric

Interpersonal Communication: Speaking and Writing

LEVEL 1 TARGET: NOVICE MID - NOVICE HIGH

DOMAINS	NOVICE LOW	NOVICE MID	NOVICE HIGH	INTERMEDIATE LOW
HOW WELL DO I MAINTAIN THE CONVERSATION? *QUALITY OF INTERACTION*	I have great difficulty maintaining a conversation. I speak with frequent hesitation, pauses, and/or repetition.	I have some difficulty maintaining simple conversations; I mainly use isolated words and memorized phrases. I speak with frequent hesitation, pauses, and/or repetition.	I can participate in short social interactions by asking and answering simple questions and relying heavily on learned phrases and short or incomplete sentences. I speak with hesitation, pauses, and/or repetition.	I can sustain the conversation by relying on phrases, simple sentences, and a few appropriate questions. I attempt to self-correct but speak with hesitation, pauses, and/or repetition.
WHAT LANGUAGE/ WORDS DO I USE? *VOCABULARY IN CONTEXT*	I can use a limited number of memorized words and expressions to identify common objects and actions.	I can use a limited number of highly practiced words and expressions to identify familiar objects and actions.	I can use learned words and phrases to interact with others in tasks and activities on familiar topics.	I can use a variety of new and previously learned words and phrases to interact with others on a range of familiar topics.
HOW DO I USE LANGUAGE? *FUNCTION AND TEXT TYPE*	I can use memorized words for functions (actions) and isolated words as structures.	I can ask and respond to highly predictable questions with words, lists, and memorized phrases. I am beginning to communicate beyond the word level, but my errors often interfere with the message.	I can use phrases, simple sentences, and questions. I am beginning to create original sentences with simple details on familiar topics, but errors sometimes interfere with the message.	I can combine words and phrases to create original sentences in present time to interact with others on familiar topics. I can sometimes vary the time frames (e.g., past, future), but errors may interfere with the message.
HOW WELL AM I UNDERSTOOD ? *COMPREHENSIBILITY*	I am understood only with great effort by someone accustomed to a language learner.	I am somewhat understood by someone accustomed to a language learner.	I am often understood by someone accustomed to a language learner.	I am usually understood by someone accustomed to a language learner.

DOMAINS	NOVICE LOW	NOVICE MID	NOVICE HIGH	INTERMEDIATE LOW
HOW WELL DO I UNDERSTAND? *COMPREHENSION*	I can understand some isolated words and expressions that I have memorized. I need continual repetition.	I can understand some familiar language, one phrase at a time. I rely on visual clues, repetition, and/or a slowed rate of speech.	I can understand pieces of information and sometimes the main idea in straightforward language that uses familiar structures. I occasionally rely on visual clues, repetition, and/or a slowed rate of speech.	I can understand the main idea in short, simple messages and conversations in sentence-length speech that uses familiar structures. I rely on restatement, paraphrasing, and/or contextual clues.
HOW INTERCULTURAL AM I? *INTERCULTURALITY* *Based on classroom tasks/activities/ intercultural reflections and outside classroom experiences.*	I can apply my knowledge of cultural products, practices, and perspectives in order to interact with respect and understanding.	I can apply my knowledge of cultural products, practices, and perspectives in order to interact with respect and understanding.	I can apply my knowledge of cultural products, practices, and perspectives in order to interact with respect and understanding.	I can apply my knowledge of cultural products, practices, and perspectives in order to interact with respect and understanding.

Adapted from Jefferson County Public Schools World Languages: Performance Assessment Rubrics (Kentucky), Howard County Public Schools World Languages (Maryland).

Level 1 *EntreCulturas* Analytic Growth Rubric

Presentational Speaking

LEVEL 1 TARGET: NOVICE MID - NOVICE HIGH

DOMAINS	NOVICE LOW	NOVICE MID	NOVICE HIGH	INTERMEDIATE LOW
WHAT LANGUAGE/ WORDS DO I USE? *VOCABULARY IN CONTEXT*	I can use a very limited number of isolated words that are repetitive.	I can use a limited number of words and expressions to identify objects and actions in familiar contexts.	I can use words and expressions that I have practiced to present familiar topics.	I can use a variety of new and previously learned words and phrases to present a range of familiar topics.
HOW DO I USE LANGUAGE? *FUNCTION AND TEXT TYPE*	I can use some isolated words.	I can use highly predictable words, lists, and memorized phrases in very familiar contexts.	I can use phrases, simple sentences, and questions. I am beginning to create original sentences with some simple details in familiar contexts.	I can use a series of simple sentences by combining words and phrases to create original sentences with some details in familiar contexts.
HOW WELL AM I UNDERSTOOD ? *COMPREHENSIBILITY*	I am understood only with great effort by someone accustomed to a language learner.	I am somewhat understood by someone accustomed to a language learner.	I am often understood by someone accustomed to a language learner.	I am usually understood by someone accustomed to a language learner.
HOW ACCURATE AM I? *STRUCTURES*	I can use a limited number of memorized words for structures.	I can use memorized words and some basic structures with frequent errors.	I can use basic structures in present time with some errors, relying on memorized phrases.	I can use basic structures with some variety in time frames (e.g., past, future) with some errors.
HOW WELL DO I DELIVER MY MESSAGE? *DELIVERY, FLUENCY, VISUALS, IMPACT ON AUDIENCE*	I can deliver my message with great difficulty, speaking with frequent hesitation, pauses, and/or repetition.	I can deliver my message using isolated words and memorized phrases, speaking with frequent hesitation, pauses, and/or repetition.	I can deliver my message by relying on learned phrases and short or incomplete sentences, speaking with hesitation, pauses, and/or repetition.	I can deliver my message by relying on phrases and simple sentences, speaking with hesitation, pauses, and/or repetition.
HOW INTERCULTURAL AM I? *INTERCULTURALITY* *Based on classroom tasks/activities/ intercultural reflections and outside classroom experiences.*	I can apply my knowledge of cultural products, practices, and perspectives in order to interact with respect and understanding.	I can apply my knowledge of cultural products, practices, and perspectives in order to interact with respect and understanding.	I can apply my knowledge of cultural products, practices, and perspectives in order to interact with respect and understanding.	I can apply my knowledge of cultural products, practices, and perspectives in order to interact with respect and understanding.

Adapted from Jefferson County Public Schools World Languages: Performance Assessment Rubrics (Kentucky), Howard County Public Schools World Languages (Maryland).

Level 1 *EntreCulturas* Analytic Growth Rubric

Presentational Writing

LEVEL 1 TARGET: NOVICE MID - NOVICE HIGH

DOMAINS	NOVICE LOW	NOVICE MID	NOVICE HIGH	INTERMEDIATE LOW
WHAT LANGUAGE/ WORDS DO I USE? *VOCABULARY IN CONTEXT*	I can use a very limited number of familiar words that are repetitive.	I can use a limited number of memorized words and phrases in a familiar context.	I can use words and expressions that I have practiced on familiar topics.	I can use a variety of new and previously learned words and phrases on a range of familiar topics.
HOW DO I USE LANGUAGE? *FUNCTION AND TEXT TYPE*	I can copy familiar words, phrases, or incomplete sentences to complete lists, forms, charts, or organizers.	I can write lists, memorized phrases, supply information in a form, chart, or organizer on familiar topics	I can use learned vocabulary and structures to create simple sentences and questions to write short messages and notes with simple details on very familiar topics.	I can write a series of simple and original sentences to describe or explain with some detail and elaboration using some connectors on familiar topics.
HOW WELL AM I UNDERSTOOD ? *COMPREHENSIBILITY*	I am understood only with great effort by someone accustomed to a language learner.	I am somewhat understood by someone accustomed to a language learner.	I am often understood by someone accustomed to a language learner.	I am usually understood by someone accustomed to a language learner.
HOW WELL DO I USE THE LANGUAGE? *LANGUAGE CONTROL*	I can use a very limited number of isolated words that are repetitive.	I am beginning to use basic structures with frequent errors.	I can use basic structures in present time with some errors and some memorized new structures in other time frames.	I can use basic structures with some variety in time frames (e.g., past, future) but more errors may occur.
HOW WELL DO I COMPLETE THE TASK? *IDEAS AND ORGANIZATION*	I can minimally complete the task with familiar content in writing.	I can complete the task with familiar content. My ideas are minimally developed and lack organization.	I can complete the task with familiar content and include some examples. My ideas are somewhat developed and organized.	I can complete the task with familiar content using some details and examples. My ideas are mostly developed and organized.
HOW INTERCULTURAL AM I? *INTERCULTURALITY* *Based on classroom tasks/activities/ intercultural reflections and outside classroom experiences.*	I can apply my knowledge of cultural products, practices, and perspectives in order to convey respect and understanding in writing.	I can apply my knowledge of cultural products, practices, and perspectives in order to convey respect and understanding in writing.	I can apply my knowledge of cultural products, practices, and perspectives in order to convey respect and understanding in writing.	I can apply my knowledge of cultural products, practices, and perspectives in order to convey respect and understanding in writing.

Adapted from Jefferson County Public Schools World Languages: Performance Assessment Rubrics (Kentucky), Howard County Public Schools World Languages (Maryland).

Level 1 *EntreCulturas* Holistic Rubric

Interpretive Reading, Listening, and Viewing: Written, Print, Audio, Visual and Audio Visual Resources

LEVEL 1 TARGET: NOVICE MID - NOVICE HIGH

Daily work, formative assessments.

1 This is still a goal.
2 Can do this with help.
3 Can do this independently.[1]

	INTERPRETIVE: READING, LISTENING, AND VIEWING	1	2	3
NL	• Recognizes and understands a few memorized words and phrases in text or speech in familiar contexts. • Makes minimal inferences from visual and/or contextual clues and cognates. • Recognizes a few cultural products, practices, or perspectives related to daily life, including cultural behaviors and expressions.			
NM	• Recognizes and understands memorized words, phrases, and basic information in text or speech in familiar contexts. • Makes limited inferences from visual and/or contextual clues and cognates or may use other interpretive strategies. • Identifies a few cultural products, practices, perspectives related to daily life, including cultural behaviors and expressions.*			
NH	• Understands and identifies words, phrases, questions, simple sentences, and sometimes the main idea in short pieces of informational text or speech in familiar contexts. • Makes a few inferences from visual and/or contextual clues, cognates and keywords or uses other interpretive strategies. • Identifies some cultural products, practices, and perspectives related to daily life, including cultural behaviors and expressions.*			
IL	• Understands and identifies the main idea and key details in short, simple, loosely connected texts or speech in familiar contexts. • Makes some inferences from visual and/or contextual clues, cognates, and keywords or uses other interpretive strategies. • Describes cultural products, practices, and perspectives related to daily life, including cultural behaviors and expressions.**			

Based on classroom tasks/activities/ intercultural reflections and outside classroom experiences.

1 LinguaFolio®, NCSSFL. (2014). Interculturality. Retrieved from http://ncssfl.org/secure/index.php?interculturality, March 6, 2016.
* Novice range: using appropriate gestures, imitating appropriate etiquette, simple interactions in stores and restaurants.
** Intermediate range: demonstrating how to be culturally respectful, forms of address, appropriate interactions in everyday life.

LEARNER SELF-REFLECTION: WHAT INTERPRETIVE STRATEGIES CAN I USE TO HELP ME UNDERSTAND WHAT I READ/HEARD/VIEWED?

SPEAKING/WRITING	LISTENING
What strategies can I use to make myself understood?	*What strategies did I use to help me understand what I heard?*
❏ I repeat words and phrases.	❏ I ask for clarification or repetition.
❏ I use facial expressions, gestures, and appropriate openings and closings.	❏ I repeat statements as questions for clarification.
❏ I self-correct when I am not understood.	❏ I listen for intonation and inflection.
❏ I imitate modeled words.	❏ I listen for cognates, familiar words, phrases, and word-order patterns.
❏ I restate and rephrase using different words.	
❏ I build upon what I've heard/read and elaborate in my response.	❏ I indicate lack of understanding.
	❏ I ask questions.
❏ I use level-appropriate vocabulary in familiar contexts.	

Adapted from Jefferson County Public Schools World Languages: Performance Assessment Rubrics (Kentucky).

Level 1 *EntreCulturas* Holistic Rubric

Interpersonal Communication: Speaking, Listening, and Writing

LEVEL 1 TARGET: NOVICE MID - NOVICE HIGH

Daily class work, participation, class discussions, pair work, group work, and formative assessments.

	1 This is still a goal.
	2 Can do this with help.
	3 Can do this independently.[1]

	INTERPERSONAL COMMUNICATION: SPEAKING, LISTENING, AND WRITING	1	2	3
NL	• Communicates with a few memorized words and expressions in familiar contexts, but needs continual repetition to understand. Frequent interference from first language. • Speaks with frequent hesitation, pauses, and/or repetition. • Makes minimal inferences from visual and/or contextual clues, cognates. • Applies knowledge of cultural products, practices, and perspectives in order to interact with respect and understanding.*			
NM	• Communicates with some memorized words and expressions in familiar contexts, but needs continual repetition. Some interference from first language. • Maintains limited simple conversations with frequent hesitation, pauses, and/or repetition. • Makes limited inferences from visual and/or contextual clues, cognates. • Applies knowledge of cultural products, practices, and perspectives in order to interact with respect and understanding.*			
NH	• Communicates and exchanges information with learned words, phrases, simple sentences, and sometimes the main idea/simple details in familiar contexts. Some interference from first language. • Participates in short social interactions by asking and answering simple questions with hesitation, pauses, and/or repetition, using a few communication strategies. • Makes a few inferences from visual and/or contextual clues, cognates, or other language features. • Applies knowledge of cultural products, practices, and perspectives in order to interact with respect and understanding.*			
IL	• Communicates and exchanges information with a variety of new and learned words, phrases, and original sentences in present tense with some details in familiar contexts. Limited interference from first language. • Participates in social interactions by asking and answering a few appropriate questions with hesitation, pauses, and/or repetition, using some communication strategies. • Makes some inferences from visual and/or contextual clues, cognates, or other language features. • Applies knowledge of cultural products, practices, and perspectives in order to interact with respect and understanding.**			

Based on classroom tasks/activities/ intercultural reflections and outside classroom experiences.

1 LinguaFolio®, NCSSFL. (2014). Interculturality. Retrieved from http://ncssfl.org/secure/index.php?interculturality, March 6, 2016.
* Novice range: using appropriate gestures, imitating appropriate etiquette, simple interactions in stores and restaurants.
** Intermediate range: demonstrating how to be culturally respectful, forms of address, appropriate interactions in everyday life.

LEARNER SELF-REFLECTION: WHAT COMMUNICATION STRATEGIES CAN I USE TO HELP ME UNDERSTAND AND MAKE MYSELF UNDERSTOOD?	
SPEAKING/WRITING *What strategies can I use to make myself understood?* ❏ I repeat words and phrases. ❏ I use facial expressions, gestures, and appropriate openings and closings. ❏ I self-correct when I am not understood. ❏ I imitate modeled words. ❏ I restate and rephrase using different words. ❏ I build upon what I've heard/read and elaborate in my response. ❏ I use level-appropriate vocabulary in familiar contexts.	**LISTENING** *What strategies did I use to help me understand what I heard?* ❏ I ask for clarification or repetition. ❏ I repeat statements as questions for clarification. ❏ I listen for intonation and inflection. ❏ I listen for cognates, familiar words, phrases, and word-order patterns. ❏ I indicate lack of understanding. ❏ I ask questions.

Adapted from Jefferson County Public Schools World Languages: Performance Assessment Rubrics (Kentucky).

Level 1 *EntreCulturas* Holistic Rubric

Presentational Speaking

LEVEL 1 TARGET: NOVICE MID - NOVICE HIGH

Daily class work, participation, share out or present to class, present to a group, formative assessments, and using Explorer audio and video recording feature.

1	This is still a goal.
2	Can do this with help.
3	Can do this independently.[1]

	PRESENTATIONAL SPEAKING	1	2	3
NL	• Uses a few memorized words and expressions in familiar contexts. Frequent interference from first language. • Delivers message with great difficulty, using isolated words as structures. Speaks with frequent hesitation, pauses, and/or repetition, • Makes minimal use of gestures, self-correction, and examples/visuals to support the message. • Applies knowledge of cultural products, practices, and perspectives in order to interact with respect and understanding.*			
NM	• Uses some memorized words and expressions in familiar contexts. Some interference from first language. • Delivers message using some highly practiced basic structures with frequent errors. Speaks with frequent hesitation, pauses, and/or repetition, • Makes limited use of gestures, self-correction, and examples/visuals to support the message. • Applies knowledge of cultural products, practices, and perspectives in order to interact with respect and understanding.*			
NH	• Uses most highly practiced/learned words, phrases, and simple sentences in familiar contexts. Some interference from first language. • Delivers message using present time frame with some errors and some memorized new structures. Speaks with hesitation, pauses, and/or repetition. • Makes some use of gestures, self-correction, and examples/visuals to support the message, or a few other communication strategies. • Applies knowledge of cultural products, practices, and perspectives in order to interact with respect and understanding.*			
IL	• Uses new and previously learned words and phrases in a series of simple sentences/questions to describe or explain with some details and elaboration in familiar contexts. Limited interference from first language. • Delivers message using basic structures with some variety in time frames (e.g., past, future) with some errors. Speaks with hesitation, pauses, and/or repetition. • Makes appropriate use of gestures, self-correction, and examples/visuals to support the message, or other communication strategies. • Applies knowledge of cultural products, practices, and perspectives in order to interact with respect and understanding.**			

Based on classroom tasks/activities/ intercultural reflections and outside classroom experiences.

1 LinguaFolio®, NCSSFL. (2014). Interculturality. Retrieved from http://ncssfl.org/secure/index.php?interculturality, March 6, 2016.
* Novice range: using appropriate gestures, imitating appropriate etiquette, simple interactions in stores and restaurants.
** Intermediate range: demonstrating how to be culturally respectful, forms of address, appropriate interactions in everyday life.

LEARNER SELF-REFLECTION: WHAT COMMUNICATION STRATEGIES DID I USE TO MAKE MYSELF UNDERSTOOD TO MY AUDIENCE?

PRESENTATIONAL SPEAKING

❏ I organize my presentation in a clear manner.

❏ I use facial expressions and gestures.

❏ I self-correct when I make mistakes.

❏ I present my own ideas.

❏ I use examples to support my message.

❏ I use visuals to support meaning.

❏ I include a hook to gain the audience's attention.

❏ I notice the reaction of the audience during the presentation.

❏ I repeat or rephrase if the audience doesn't understand.

❏ I project my voice so the audience can hear me.

❏ I practice my presentation before I present to the audience.

Adapted from Jefferson County Public Schools World Languages: Performance Assessment Rubrics (Kentucky).

Level 1 *EntreCulturas* Holistic Rubric

Presentational Writing

LEVEL 1 TARGET: NOVICE MID - NOVICE HIGH

Daily written class work, forms, organizers, charts, messages, notes, formative assessments, and using Explorer quizzes, surveys, discussion forums, and more.

| **1** This is still a goal. |
| **2** Can do this with help. |
| **3** Can do this independently.[1] |

	PRESENTATIONAL WRITING	1	2	3
NL	• Uses a few memorized words and expressions in familiar contexts. Considerable interference from first language. • Completes the task minimally, using isolated words as structures. • Makes minimal use of presentational writing strategies. • Applies knowledge of cultural products, practices, and perspectives in order to convey respect and understanding in writing.*			
NM	• Uses some memorized words, expressions, and short sentences in familiar contexts. Frequent interference from first language. • Completes the task with some highly practiced basic structures with frequent errors. Ideas lack development and organization. • Makes limited use of presentational writing strategies. • Applies knowledge of cultural products, practices, and perspectives in order to convey respect and understanding in writing.*			
NH	• Uses most highly practiced words, phrases, questions, and simple sentences to write short, simple messages with simple details in familiar contexts. Some interference from first language. • Completes the tasks using present time frame and some memorized new structures. Ideas are partially developed and somewhat organized. • Makes some use of drafting, outlining, peer review, or other presentational writing strategies. • Applies knowledge of cultural products, practices, and perspectives in order to convey respect and understanding in writing.*			
IL	• Uses a variety of new and previously learned words and phrases in a series of simple and original sentences to describe or explain in some detail with examples and elaboration. Limited interference from first language. • Completes the task using basic structures with some variety in time frames (e.g., past, future) with some errors. Ideas are mostly developed and organized. • Makes appropriate use of drafting, outlining, peer review, or other presentational writing strategies. • Applies knowledge of cultural products, practices, and perspectives in order to convey respect and understanding in writing.*			

Based on classroom tasks/activities/ intercultural reflections and outside classroom experiences.

1 LinguaFolio®, NCSSFL. (2014). Interculturality. Retrieved from http://ncssfl.org/secure/index.php?interculturality, March 6, 2016.
* Novice range: using appropriate gestures, imitating appropriate etiquette, simple interactions in stores and restaurants.
** Intermediate range: demonstrating how to be culturally respectful, forms of address, appropriate interactions in everyday life.

LEARNER SELF-REFLECTION: WHAT COMMUNICATION STRATEGIES CAN I USE TO MAKE MY MESSAGE UNDERSTOOD TO THE READER?	
PRESENTATIONAL WRITING ❏ I organize my presentation in a clear manner. ❏ I include a hook to gain the reader's attention. ❏ I present my own ideas. ❏ I write an outline before I begin to write. ❏ I cite my sources if I have done research on the topic.	❏ I write a draft of my message. ❏ I use examples to support my message. ❏ I ask someone to peer edit my draft before I submit it. ❏ I check all spelling and grammar before I submit it. ❏ I make sure my writing is clear and my handwriting is legible.

Adapted from Jefferson County Public Schools World Languages: Performance Assessment Rubrics (Kentucky).

Unidad Preliminar

Integrated Performance Assessment Rubric

Cursos de verano

DOMAINS	TASK COMPONENTS	NOVICE HIGH	NOVICE MID	NOVICE LOW
INTERPRETIVE ASSESSMENT Interpretive Reading *Paso 1*	**Identifies information and makes predictions** Student reads a banner ad, notes three details learned from the banner, and makes three predictions about what information will appear in the full text.	Accurately identifies three details and makes three reasonable predictions based on the text.	Accurately identifies at least two details and makes two reasonable predictions based on the text.	Accurately identifies one or two details and makes at least one or two reasonable predictions based on the text.
Interpretive Reading *Paso 2*	**Identifies details** Student reads the full web ad for a language school, assesses the accuracy of the predictions made in Paso 1, and identifies three additional pieces of information.	Accurately evaluates the predictions made in Paso 1 based on the information in the full text. Includes three additional pieces of information found in the full text.	Evaluates the predictions made in Paso 1 with some accuracy. Includes at least two additional pieces of information; there may be some repetition from Paso 1.	Evaluates the predictions made in Paso 1 with limited accuracy. Identifies one or two additional pieces of information; there may be repetition from Paso 1 and/or inaccurate information.
Interpretive Listening *Paso 3*	**Understands familiar words and phrases** Student listens to two students introduce themselves and completes the chart with personal information (name, origin, age and birth month).	Accurately identifies all or almost all of the required details in the chart.	Accurately identifies most of the details in the chart.	Accurately identifies some of the details in the chart.
INTERPERSONAL ASSESSMENT Interpersonal Speaking	**Responds orally to five questions requesting personal information** Student records answers to five questions, responding to a greeting, providing the following information: name and how it is spelled, origin, and birthday.	Responds appropriately to almost all of the questions using familiar words, phrases, and some short, simple sentences. The message is often understood despite errors.	Responds appropriately to most of the questions using mostly familiar words, memorized phrases and/ or questions, and may attempt simple sentences. The message is somewhat understood despite frequent errors.	Responds appropriately to some of the questions using memorized words and a few phrases. The message is understood only with great effort.

Unidad 1

Integrated Performance Assessment Rubric

Un intercambio estudiantil

DOMAINS	TASK COMPONENTS	NOVICE HIGH	NOVICE MID	NOVICE LOW
INTERPRETIVE ASSESSMENT Interpretive Audiovisual *Paso 1*	**Recognizes key words** Student checks the key words heard in student video blogs; compares with a classmate's key words.	Recognizes most of the words, phrases, and simple sentences related to the topic.	Recognizes some of the words, familiar phrases, and some simple sentences related to the topic.	Recognizes a few of the familiar words and phrases related to the topic.
Interpretive Audiovisual *Paso 2*	**Identifies information** Student completes missing information on the bloggers' enrollment forms.	Identifies most of the missing information.	Identifies some of the missing information.	Identifies a few items from the missing information.
Interpretive Reading and Audiovisual *Paso 3*	**Infers details** Student identifies key characteristics of each blogger on a checklist.	Identifies and infers most of the details of each blogger.	Identifies and infers some of the details of each blogger.	Identifies and infers a few details of each blogger.
INTERPERSONAL ASSESSMENT Interpersonal Writing	**Responds in an email** Student responds to a video blogger in an email. Greets and introduces self to the blogger, providing name, age, personal details, and similarities with blogger. Students asks two questions about likes and dislikes, remarks on student video blog, and closes email appropriately.	Message includes most of the task's components using familiar words, phrases, questions, and simple sentences. The message is often understood despite errors.	Message includes some of the task's components using some familiar words, memorized phrases, and attempts at simple questions and simple sentences. The message is somewhat understood despite frequent errors.	Message includes a few of the task's components using memorized words and phrases. The message is understood only with great effort.
INTERPERSONAL ASSESSMENT Presentational Speaking	**Creates video blog** Student prepares video blog to share with host family; includes greeting, name, age, origin, languages, two likes, and closing.	The video blog includes most of the task's components using familiar words, phrases, and some simple sentences. The delivery includes some hesitation, pauses, and/or repetition and is mostly understood by someone accustomed to a language learner.	The video blog includes some of the task's components using familiar words, memorized phrases, and attempts at a few simple sentences. The delivery includes hesitation, pauses, and/or repetition and is somewhat understood by someone accustomed to a language learner.	The video blog includes a few of the task's components using a few familiar words and memorized phrases. The delivery includes frequent hesitation, pauses, and repetition and is understood with great effort by someone accustomed to a language learner.
Cultural Comparisons	**Compares similarities** Student completes two sentences regarding two similarities with the bloggers.	Makes mostly relevant cultural comparisons.	Makes somewhat relevant cultural comparisons.	Makes limited cultural comparisons.

Unidad 2

Integrated Performance Assessment Rubric

Un programa de hermandad con una escuela en Costa Rica

DOMAINS	TASK COMPONENTS	NOVICE HIGH	NOVICE MID	NOVICE LOW
Pasos 1 and 2	**Preparation activities; not assessed.**			
INTERPRETIVE ASSESSMENT **Interpretive Audiovisual** *Paso 3*	**Recognizes key words** Student checks the key words heard in two informative videos.	Recognizes all or almost all words, phrases, and simple sentences related to the topic.	Recognizes some of the words, familiar phrases, and some simple sentences related to the topic.	Recognizes a limited number of the familiar words and phrases related to the topic.
INTERPERSONAL ASSESSMENT **Interpersonal Writing**	**Composes an email** Student greets e-pal, introduces self, tells about school (name, description, several classes, activities), states one thing he/she likes about e-pal's school, asks a question about e-pal's school, says goodbye.	Message includes all or almost all of the task's components using familiar words, phrases, questions, and simple sentences. The message is mostly understood by someone accustomed to a language learner. despite errors.	Message includes some of the task's components using familiar words, memorized phrases, a simple question, and attempts at simple sentences. The message is somewhat understood by someone accustomed to a language learner, despite frequent errors.	Message includes a few of the task's components using limited memorized words and phrases and lists. The message may be understood only with great effort by someone accustomed to a language learner.
PRESENTATIONAL ASSESSMENT **Presentational Speaking**	**PechaKucha presentation** Introduces self, states the day of week chosen for description, gives info on school start time, backpack contents, morning classes, lunch schedule, afternoon classes, favorite class, other activities, return home time; closes by asking about typical day at C.R. school.	The product includes all or almost all of the task's components using familiar words, phrases, and some simple sentences. The delivery includes some hesitation, pauses, and/or repetition, and the message is often understood despite errors.	The product includes most of the task's components using familiar words, memorized phrases, and attempts at a few simple sentences. The delivery includes frequent hesitation, pauses, and/ or repetition, and the message is somewhat understood despite frequent errors.	The product includes some of the task's components using some familiar words and memorized phrases. The delivery includes frequent hesitation, pauses, and repetition, and the message is understood only with great effort.
Comparaciones Culturales	**Cultural comparisons** Student justifies choice of partner school by comparing characteristics with home school.	States choice clearly and includes mostly relevant details in comparison.	States choice clearly and includes somewhat relevant details in comparison.	May not state a choice clearly, includes minimal details, and may lack a comparison.

Unidad 3

Integrated Performance Assessment Rubric

Familia nueva, cultura nueva

DOMAINS	TASK COMPONENTS	NOVICE HIGH	NOVICE MID	NOVICE LOW
INTERPRETIVE ASSESSMENT **Interpretive Reading** *Paso 1*	**Identifies details** Student completes a chart with personal information about the author of a post on a website facilitating international homestays.	Accurately identifies most of the details in the chart.	Identifies some details in the chart with a few inaccuracies.	Identifies a few details in the chart with some inaccuracies.
Interpretive Reading *Paso 2*	**Makes inferences** Student interprets and infers information in a blog with images to identify true and false statements about the web post.	Interprets most information accurately to identify most statements as true or false.	Interprets some information accurately to identify some statements as true or false.	Interprets limited information to identify a few of the statements as true or false.
Interpretive Reading *Paso 3*	**Identifies textual evidence and infers meaning** Student identifies textual evidence to support statements about the author of the web post.	Accurately identifies most of the textual evidence and infers meaning.	Identifies some of the textual evidence and infers with a few inaccuracies.	Identifies limited textual evidence and infers with inaccuracies.
INTERPERSONAL ASSESSMENT **Interpersonal Speaking**	**Responds to questions about family** Student hears and responds to a greeting and answers questions about his or her family, including the number of family members, their names and ages, the home, and the activities the family does together.	Understands and responds appropriately to all or almost all the questions (4-5) using memorized words, phrases, and short sentences. The message is often understood despite errors.	Understands and responds somewhat appropriately to some (3) of the questions using words and memorized phrases. The message is somewhat understood despite frequent errors.	Understands and responds with some difficulty to a few (2) questions using a few memorized words and phrases. The message is understood only with great effort.
PRESENTATIONAL ASSESSMENT **Presentational Writing**	**Creates a digital family photo album** Student prepares a digital family photo album to share with an exchange student before he/she visits. The album includes photo captions about home and family. Student includes greeting, name, age, origin, languages, two likes, and closing.	The album includes most of the task's components. Captions include familiar words, phrases, and some simple sentences. Describes with simple details. Illustrations and captions result in an adequate presentation.	The album includes some of the task's components. Captions include some familiar words, memorized phrases, and attempts at a few simple sentences. Illustrations and captions result in a basic presentation.	The album includes a few of the task's components. Captions include a few memorized words and phrases and may be repetitive. Illustrations and captions result in a presentation that is at times difficult to understand.

Unidad 4

Integrated Performance Assessment Rubric

Aquí se vende comida hispana

DOMAINS	TASK COMPONENTS	INTERMEDIATE LOW	NOVICE HIGH	NOVICE MID	NOVICE LOW
INTERPRETIVE ASSESSMENT Interpretive Reading *Paso 1*	**Identifies themes** Student identifies and matches the main ideas of (6) paragraphs in an article about a food truck in the Dominican Republic.	Accurately identifies and matches all or almost all of the main ideas of the paragraphs in the article.	Accurately identifies and matches most of the main ideas of the paragraphs in the article.	Identifies and matches some of the main ideas of the paragraphs in the article.	Recognizes some of the words in the article, which results in correctly matching one or two of the main ideas with the paragraphs.
Interpretive Reading *Paso 2*	**Makes inferences** Student infers information about the food truck and identifies true or false statements based on the article.	Infers meaning from the text and correctly identifies all or almost all statements as true or false.	Infers basic meaning from the text and correctly identifies most of the statements as true or false.	Infers some basic meaning from the text and correctly identifies some of the statements as true or false.	Infers some very basic word level meaning from the text and correctly identifies a few of the statements as true or false.
INTERPERSONAL ASSESSMENT Interpersonal Writing	**Writes a text message** Student composes a text message to a friend in which he/she responds to short prompts, including a description of the food truck, a list of the food options, and an invitation to a friend to go with him/her to get something to eat.	Responds appropriately to all or almost all of the prompts using a variety of new words, phrases, and original sentences. The message is usually understood despite some errors.	Responds appropriately to most of the prompts using learned words, phrases, and short, simple sentences. The message is mostly understood despite errors.	Responds appropriately to some of the highly predictable prompts using memorized words and phrases. The message is somewhat understood despite frequent errors.	Responds to the most predictable prompts with a few memorized words and phrases. The message may be understood with difficulty.
PRESENTATIONAL ASSESSMENT Presentational Writing	**Creates a promotional poster** Student prepares a poster promoting an international food truck to share with their school. It includes: food truck design, name, menu from two Spanish-speaking countries and prices, images, and promotional information (hours, location, specialty items).	The poster includes all or almost all of the task's components. Information is culturally accurate and includes new and familiar words, phrases, and original sentences. Illustrations and captions result in a very effective presentation.	The poster includes most of the task's components. Information, for the most part, is culturally accurate and includes familiar words, phrases, and some simple sentences. Illustrations and captions result in an effective presentation.	The poster includes some of the task's components. Captions include familiar words, memorized phrases, and attempts at a few simple sentences. Illustrations and captions result in a basic presentation.	The poster includes a few of the task's components. Captions include some familiar words and memorized phrases, and may be repetitive. Illustrations and captions result in a presentation that is at times difficult to understand.

Unidad 5

Integrated Performance Assessment Rubric

Vamos a visitar Santo Domingo

DOMAINS	TASK COMPONENTS	INTERMEDIATE LOW	NOVICE HIGH	NOVICE MID	NOVICE LOW
INTERPRETIVE ASSESSMENT Interpretive Reading *Paso 1*	**Identifies locations on a map** Student locates several cities on a map of the Dominican Republic.	Accurately identifies the cities' locations relative to Santo Domingo.	Accurately identifies most of the cities' locations relative to Santo Domingo.	Accurately identifies some of the cities' locations relative to Santo Domingo.	Accurately identifies a few of the cities' locations relative to Santo Domingo.
Interpretive Reading *Paso 2*	**Identifies details and provides textual evidence** Student reads a short informative article about Carnaval in the Dominican Republic to determine if information in the text is true or false, providing textual evidence to support the main ideas.	Demonstrates understanding of details by accurately identifying all or almost all statements as true or false and provides textual evidence for almost all of the main ideas.	Demonstrates understanding of details by accurately identifying most of the statements as true or false and provides textual evidence for most of the main ideas.	Demonstrates some understanding of details by accurately identifying some statements as true or false and provides limited textual evidence for the main ideas.	Demonstrates limited understanding of a few details by accurately identifying a few statements as true or false and may not provide textual evidence for the main ideas.
INTERPERSONAL ASSESSMENT Interpersonal Writing	**Participates in a text chat** Student participates in a simulated text chat with Paola about preparation for an upcoming visit. Questions reference preferred activities for the visit, both students' musical tastes, and their sports preferences.	Responds to all or almost all of the questions using a variety of vocabulary in a series of simple and original sentences with some detail; the message is usually understood though some errors may interfere.	Responds to most of the questions using familiar words, phrases, questions, and simple sentences; the message is mostly understood despite errors.	Responds to some questions using only familiar words, memorized phrases, and attempts at a few simple sentences; the message is somewhat understood despite frequent errors.	Responds to at least two questions using limited vocabulary and memorized phrases; the message may be understood with difficulty.
PRESENTATIONAL ASSESSMENT Presentational Speaking	**Creates an itinerary** Creates an audiovisual presentation of an itinerary for a visit to Santo Domingo including **when** the visit will take place, **where** the class will go, **with whom,** and **why.**	The presentation includes all or almost all of the task's components and uses a variety of high frequency words, phrases, and strings of original simple sentences. The itinerary description includes some details, images, and captions for an effective presentation. The delivery includes hesitation, pauses, and/or repetition; the message is usually understood despite some errors.	The presentation includes most of the task's components and uses familiar words, phrases, and some original simple sentences. The itinerary description includes simple details, images, and captions for an adequate presentation. The delivery includes hesitation, pauses, and/or repetition; the message is often understood despite errors.	The presentation includes some of the task's components and uses familiar words, memorized phrases, and attempts at a few simple sentences. The itinerary description includes minimal details, some images, and a few captions for a basic presentation. The delivery includes some hesitation, pauses, and/ or repetition; the message is somewhat understood despite frequent errors.	The presentation includes a few of the task's components and uses some memorized words and phrases. The itinerary description may include some memorized words or phrases with a few/no images and/or captions for an inadequate presentation. The delivery includes frequent hesitation, pauses, and repetition; the message is understood only with great effort.

Unidad 6

Integrated Performance Assessment Rubric

¡Conoce la comunidad!

DOMAINS	TASK COMPONENTS	INTERMEDIATE LOW	NOVICE HIGH	NOVICE MID	NOVICE LOW
INTERPRETIVE ASSESSMENT Interpretive Audiovisual	**Makes inferences** Student watches video clips of Bogotá, Colombia and makes inferences based on a list of items that may or may not be in the video.	Makes all or almost all of the correct inferences from the list provided.	Makes most of the correct inferences from the list provided.	Makes some correct inferences from the list provided.	Makes minimal correct inferences from the list provided.
PRESENTATIONAL ASSESSMENT Presentational Speaking	**Presents slideshow** Student prepares a slideshow to promote highlights of the home community: • description • climate • attractions • excursions	The presentation includes all of the task's components, using a variety of high frequency words, phrases, and strings of simple sentences. The delivery includes minimal hesitation, pauses, and/or repetition and is usually understood by a Spanish speaker.	The presentation includes almost all of the task's components, using familiar words, phrases, and some simple sentences. The delivery includes some hesitation, pauses, and/or repetition and is mostly understood despite errors.	The presentation includes most of the task's components, using familiar words, memorized phrases, and attempts at a few simple sentences. The delivery includes some hesitation, pauses, and/or repetition and is somewhat understood despite frequent errors.	The presentation includes some of the task's components, using some familiar words and memorized phrases. The delivery includes frequent hesitation, pauses, and repetition and is understood only with great effort.
INTERPERSONAL ASSESSMENT Interpersonal Speaking	**Responds to questions** Student greets and introduces self to a Colombian exchange student on an online text chat; answers the exchange student's questions about his/her home community including: • weather • clothes • activities in winter • places in the community • why he/she likes the community Student closes conversation appropriately.	Responds to all questions using a variety of vocabulary in a series of simple and original sentences with some detail; usually understood despite some errors.	Responds to most of the questions using familiar words, phrases, questions, and simple sentences; often understood despite errors.	Responds to some of the questions using only familiar words, memorized phrases, and attempts at simple sentences; may not include required questions; somewhat understood despite frequent errors.	Responds to at least two questions using limited memorized words and phrases; understood with difficulty.

EntreCulturas 1 Correlation Guide (AP®)

AP THEME	UNIT 0	UNIT 1	UNIT 2	UNIT 3	UNIT 4	UNIT 5	UNIT 6
1. LOS DESAFÍOS MUNDIALES							
Los temas económicos							
Los temas del medio ambiente							✓
El pensamiento filosófico y la religión					✓		
La población y la demografía	✓				✓	✓	✓
El bienestar social							✓
La conciencia social							✓
2. LA CIENCIA Y LA TECNOLOGÍA							
El acceso a la tecnología							
Los efectos de la tecnología en el individuo y en la sociedad							✓
El cuidado de la salud y la medicina							
Las innovaciones tecnológicas							
Los fenómenos naturales							✓
La ciencia y la ética							
3. LA VIDA CONTEMPORÁNEA							
La educación y las carreras profesionales			✓				
El entretenimiento y la diversión						✓	
Los viajes y el ocio				✓		✓	✓
Los estilos de vida				✓			
Las relaciones personales				✓			
Las tradiciones y los valores sociales	✓				✓		
El trabajo voluntario						✓	
4. LAS IDENTIDADES PERSONALES Y PÚBLICAS							
La enajenación y la asimilación							
Los héroes y los personajes históricos							
La identidad nacional y la identidad étnica		✓	✓		✓	✓	✓
Las creencias personales							
Los intereses personales		✓		✓	✓		
La autoestima							

AP THEME	UNIT 0	UNIT 1	UNIT 2	UNIT 3	UNIT 4	UNIT 5	UNIT 6
5. LAS FAMILIAS Y LAS COMUNIDADES							
Las tradiciones y los valores				✓	✓		
Las comunidades educativas			✓				
La estructura de la familia				✓			
La ciudadanía global							
La geografía humana							✓
Las redes sociales							
6. LA BELLEZA Y LA ESTÉTICA							
La arquitectura							
Definiciones de la belleza							
Definiciones de la creatividad		✓					
La moda y el diseño							

IB THEME	UNIT 0	UNIT 1	UNIT 2	UNIT 3	UNIT 4	UNIT 5	UNIT 6
1. COMUNICACIÓN Y MEDIOS	✓						
2. CUESTIONES GLOBALES							✓
3. RELACIONES SOCIALES		✓	✓	✓			
4. CIENCIA Y TECNOLOGÍA				✓			
5. COSTUMBRES Y TRADICIONES	✓			✓	✓		
6. DIVERSIDAD CULTURAL	✓	✓	✓	✓	✓	✓	✓
7. OCIO				✓		✓	✓
8. SALUD							

Glossary Spanish-English

This glossary gives the meanings of words and phrases as used in this book. The number in parentheses indicates the unit number of the first occurrence of the item in this book.

el abrigo coat (6)

abril April (0)

el/la abuelo/a grandfather/grandmother (3)

el/la actor/actriz actor (1)

la agenda escolar assignment notebook (2)

agosto August (0)

el agua water (4)

el agua fresca fruit-flavored water (4)

el aguacate avocado (4)

el ajedrez chess (5)

alegre happy (3)

alemán/alemana German (1)

el alemán German language (1)

algo something (4)

allí there (6)

almorzar (o→ue) to have lunch (2)

el almuerzo lunch (2, 4)

la altitud altitude (6)

alto/a tall (3)

amable nice, kind (3)

amarillo/a yellow (4)

anaranjado/a orange (4)

andar to walk, to go (3)

andar en bicicleta to ride a bicycle (3, 5, 6)

andar en patineta to ride a skateboard (5)

el aniversario anniversary (5)

el Año Nuevo New Year's (5)

el apartamento apartment (3)

el apellido family name (3)

apreciar to appreciate (6)

aprender to learn (2)

aquí here (6)

árabe Arabic (1)

el árabe Arabic language

el arroz rice (4)

el/la artista artist (1)

asistir to attend (3, 5)

f. - feminine

irreg. - irregular verb

m. - masculine

pl. - plural

refl. - reflexive verb

Verb conjugations:

(e → ie): like pensar (pienso, pensamos)

(e → ie/i): like preferir (prefiero, preferimos, prefirió)

(e → i): like servir (sirvo, servimos, sirvió)

(í): like variar (varío, variamos)

(o → ue): like volver (vuelvo, volvemos)

(o → ue/u): like dormir (duermo, dormimos, durmió)

Regional variations:

C.R. - Costa Rica

Esp. - España

Méx. - México

L.A. - Latinoamérica

P.R. - Puerto Rico

R.D. - República Dominicana

asistir a conciertos to go to concerts (3, 6)

asistir al Carnaval to go to Carnival (5)

el/la atleta athlete (0, 1)

el auditorio auditorium (2)

el aula classroom (2)

el autobús bus (2)

la avenida avenue, main artery (3)

ayer yesterday (5)

ayudar to help (2)

el azúcar sugar (4)

azul blue (4)

bailar to dance (1)

el/la bailarín/bailarina dancer (1)

bajar to go down, to lower (6)

el baloncesto basketball (1)

la **banda** (music) band (5)

el **baño** bathroom (3)

el **barrio** neighborhood (3)

el **batido** smoothie, shake (4)

el/la **bebé** baby (3)

beber to drink (4)

el **béisbol** baseball (5)

la **biblioteca** library (2)

la **bicicleta** bicycle (3)

bien well, fine (0)

¡Muy bien, gracias! Fine, thanks! (0)

bilingüe bilingual (1)

el/la **bisabuelo/a** great-grandfather, great-grandmother (3)

el **bistec** steak (4)

blanco/a white (2, 4)

el/la **bloguero/a** blogger (1)

los **bluejeans** jeans (6)

la **blusa** blouse (6)

la **boda** wedding (5)

el **bolígrafo** pen (2)

el **bolso** purse, handbag (6)

bonito/a pretty, beautiful (6)

el **bosque** forest, woods (6)

la **bota** boot (6)

bueno/a good, tasty (4)

Buenos días. Good morning. (0)

Buenas tardes. Good afternoon. (0)

¡Qué bueno! Great! (1)

¡Está bueno! It's delicious! (4)

el **café** coffee (4)

el **café con leche** coffee with milk (4)

los **calcetines** socks (6)

la **calculadora** calculator (2)

caliente hot (4)

callado/a quiet (3)

la **calle** street (3)

el **calor** heat (6)

caminar to walk (2)

caminar en el bosque to walk in the forest (6)

caminar por una causa to walk for a cause (3)

la **camisa** shirt (2, 6)

la **camiseta** t-shirt (6)

el **campo** field; country(side) (3)

el **campo de fútbol** soccer field (2)

la **canción** song (5)

cantar to sing (2)

la **carne** meat (4)

las **carnitas** roasted pork (4)

la **carpeta** folder (2)

la **carroza** parade float (5)

la **casa** house (3)

castaño/a brown (3)

la **catedral** cathedral (6)

catorce fourteen (0)

la **cebolla** onion (4)

la **cena** dinner (4)

cenar to eat dinner, to eat supper (3)

el **centro** center, middle (6)

el **centro comercial** shopping center (5)

la **ceremonia** ceremony (2)

la **chaqueta** jacket (6)

¡Chau! Ciao! (0)

el **chile poblano** poblano pepper (4)

el **chino** Chinese language (1)

chino/a Chinese (1)

el **chocolate** chocolate (4)

el/la **ciclista** cyclist (1)

cien/ciento one hundred (2)

la **ciencia** science (2)

cinco five (0)

cincuenta fifty (2)

el **cine** movie theater

la **ciudad** city (3)

el **clima** climate (6)

la **cocina** kitchen (3)

cocinar to cook (4)

colaborar to collaborate, to work together (6)

el **colegio** high school (2)

el **comedor** cafeteria, dining room (2, 3)

comer to eat (1)

el **cómic** comic, comic strip, comic book, graphic novel (3)

la comida food, midday meal (4)

¿Cómo? How? What? (1)

¿Cómo está usted? How are you? (formal) (0)

¿Cómo estás? How are you? (informal) (0)

¿Cómo llegamos? How will we get there? (5)

¿Cómo te llamas? What's your name? (0, 1)

el/la compañero/a de clase classmate (1, 2)

comprar to buy (4)

la computadora computer (2)

con with (5)

conmigo with me (5)

conocer (zc) to get to know, be familiar with, meet (6)

conocer a amigos nuevos to make, meet new friends (6)

contigo with you (5)

correr to run (3)

corto/a short (6)

la costa coast, shore (6)

el cuaderno notebook (2)

¿Cuál? Which one?, What? (1)

¿Cuál es tu deporte favorito? What is your favorite sport? (1)

¿Cuándo? When? (1)

¿Cuándo es tu cumpleaños? When is your birthday? (1)

¿Cuánto/a? How much? (1)

¿Cuánto cuesta(n)? How much does it/do they cost? (2)

¿Cuántos/as? How many? (1)

¿Cuántos años tienes? How old are you? (1)

cuarenta forty (2)

cuatro four (0)

cuatrocientos/as four hundred (2)

cubrir to cover (6)

el cuerpo body (6)

cuidar to take care of (6)

cuidar a los niños to babysit, watch the kids (3)

el cumpleaños birthday (0, 5)

dar (irreg.) to give (3)

dar de comer a las mascotas to feed the pets (3)

dar un paseo to go for a walk/ride (3)

dar un paseo en el campo to go for a walk/ride in the country (6)

decorar to decorate (5)

delgado/a thin (3)

delicioso/a delicious (4)

el deporte sport(s) (1)

derecho/a right(-side) (3)

a la derecha (de) to the right (of) (3)

el desayuno breakfast (4)

descubrir to discover, to explore (6)

el desfile parade (5)

detrás (de) behind (3)

el día day (0)

Día de Acción de Gracias Thanksgiving (5)

Día de Independencia Independence Day (5)

el diccionario dictionary (2)

diciembre December (0)

diecinueve nineteen (0)

dieciocho eighteen (0)

dieciséis sixteen (0)

diecisiete seventeen (0)

diez ten (0)

diez mil ten thousand (2)

el/la director/a principal (2)

el disfraz costume (5)

divertido/a fun (3)

doce twelve (0)

domingo Sunday (0)

el domingo on Sunday (0)

los domingos on Sundays (0)

el dominó dominoes (5)

¿Dónde? Where? (1)

¿De dónde eres? Where are you from? (1)

dormir (o→ue) to sleep (5)

dormir una siesta to take a nap (5)

el dormitorio bedroom (3)

dos two (0)

doscientos/as two hundred (2)

dulce sweet (4)

el **edificio** building (2)

educado/a polite (3)

empezar (e→ie) to begin (2)

en in, on (4)

enero January (0)

la **ensalada** salad (4)

enseñar to teach (2)

entre between (2)

el/la **entrenador/a** trainer, coach (1)

el **equipo** team (2, 5)

escalar montañas to climb mountains (6)

escribir to write (1)

escuchar to listen to (1)

el **escudo** logo, crest, emblem (2)

la **escuela** school (2)

los **espaguetis** spaghetti (4)

español/a Spanish (1)

el **español** Spanish language (1)

las **espinacas** spinach (4)

el/la **esposo/a** husband/wife (3)

esquiar to ski (6)

la **estación** season (6)

estar (irreg.) to be (2, 3, 4, 5, 6)

Estoy bien. ¿Y tú? I'm fine. And you? (0)

el **este** east (6)

este/esta this (4)

estos/estas these (4)

el/la **estudiante** student (1)

estudiar to study (1, 2)

los **estudios sociales** social studies (2)

explorar to explore (3)

la **falda** skirt (2, 6)

febrero February (0)

feo/a ugly (6)

la **fiesta** party (5)

la fiesta de disfraces costume party (5)

la fiesta de graduación graduation party (5)

la fiesta sorpresa surprise party (5)

el **flan** egg custard (4)

la **flor** flower (5)

al fondo (de) in the back (of) (3)

la **foto** photo, picture (5)

el/la **fotógrafo/a** photographer (1)

el **francés** French language (1)

francés/francesa French (1)

frecuentemente frequently, often (3)

la **fresa** strawberry (4)

fresco/a fresh (4)

los **frijoles** beans (4)

el **frío** cold (weather) (6)

frío/a cold (4)

los **fuegos artificiales** fireworks (5)

fuerte strong (4)

el/la **futbolista** soccer player (1)

las **gafas de sol** sunglasses (6)

el **garaje** garage (3)

la **gastronomía** food culture, cooking (6)

el **gato** cat (3)

la **geografía** geography (2)

el **gimnasio** gym(nasium) (2)

el/la **gimnasta** gymnast (1)

el **glaciar** glacier (6)

el **globo** balloon (6)

gordo/a fat (3)

la **gorra** cap (6)

gracioso/a funny, comical (3)

grande big (3)

la **guagua** (Cuba, P.R., R.D.) bus (5)

guaraní Guaraní (1)

el **guaraní** Guaraní language (1)

el/la **guitarrista** guitarist (1)

gustar to be pleasing, to like (3, 4)

Me gusta la pizza. I like pizza. (4)

No me gustan las espinacas. I don't like spinach. (4)

No me gusta(n) para nada. I don't like it/them at all. (4)

hablar to speak, talk (1)

hacer (irreg.) to do, make (3, 5, 6)

hace buen tiempo it's nice weather (6)

hace calor it's hot (6)

hace frío it's cold (6)

hace sol it's sunny (6)

hace viento it's windy (6)

hacer camping to go camping (3)

hacer ejercicio to get exercise, to work out (3)

hacer esquí acuático to water ski (5)

hacer la cama to make the bed (3)

hacer manualidades to do arts and crafts (3)

hacer senderismo to go hiking (6)

hacer tareas domésticas to do chores (3)

hacer un tour con guía to take a guided tour (6)

la hamburguesa hamburger (4)

hasta until (0, 5)

Hasta el sábado. See you on Saturday. (5)

Hasta la próxima. See you next time. (5)

Hasta luego. See you later. (0)

hay there is/there are (2)

helado/a iced (4)

el helado (de vainilla, chocolate) vanilla, chocolate ice cream (4)

el/la hermano/a brother/sister (3)

el hielo ice (6)

el/la hijo/a son/daughter (3)

el himno nacional national anthem (2)

la historia history (2)

la hoja leaf, sheet (2)

hoja de papel sheet of paper (2)

¡Hola! Hello!, Hi! (0)

honesto/a honest (3)

la hora hour, time of day

¿A qué hora? (At) what time? (2, 5)

el horario schedule (2)

el huevo egg (4)

los huevos fritos/rancheros fried/ranchero-style eggs (4)

la iglesia church (5)

impaciente impatient (3)

el impermeable raincoat (6)

la informática computer science (2)

inglés/inglesa English (1)

el inglés English language (1)

el intercambio exchange (2)

interesante interesting (1)

¡Qué interesante! (How) interesting! (1)

el invierno winter (0)

ir (irreg.) to go (3, 5)

ir al cine to go to the movies (3, 5)

ir a pie to go on foot (5)

ir de compras to go shopping (3)

la isla island (6)

italiano/a Italian (1)

el italiano Italian language (1)

izquierdo/a left(-side) (3)

a la izquierda (de) to the left (of) (3)

el jamón ham (4)

el jardín garden; yard (3)

joven (pl. jóvenes) young (3)

jueves Thursday (0)

jugar (u→ue) to play (a game, sport) (5)

jugar al baloncesto to play basketball (1)

jugar al ajedrez to play chess (5)

jugar deportes to play sports (3)

jugar al dominó to play dominoes (5)

el jugo juice (4)

julio July (0)

junio June (0)

juntos/as together (5)

el laboratorio laboratory (2)

el lado side (3)

al lado (de) beside (3)

el lápiz (pl. lápices) pencil (2)

largo/a long (6)

la lechuga lettuce (4)

leer to read (3)

el libro (de texto) (text)book (2)

ligero/a light (weight) (6)

light low-calorie (4)

limpiar to clean (3)

llamarse to be called, to be named (0)

¿Cómo te llamas? What is your name?

Me llamo ___. My name is ___. (0)

el llano plain (6)

llegar to arrive (5)

llevar to wear, to bring (2, 4)

llover (u→ue) to rain (6)

la lluvia rain (6)

Lo siento. I'm sorry. (3, 5)

lunes Monday (0)

la madre mother (3)

el/la maestro/a (elementary school) teacher (2)

el maíz corn (4)

mal bad, not well (0)

las manualidades arts and crafts (3)

la manzana apple (4)

el mar sea (6)

martes Tuesday (0)

marzo March (0)

más o menos so-so, just O.K. (0)

la máscara mask (5)

la mascota pet (3)

las matemáticas math (2)

mayo May (0)

mayor (que) older (than) (3)

el medio middle (3)

en medio (de) in the middle (of) (3)

el mediodía noon (2)

al mediodía at noon (2)

encantar to love (something)

Me encanta la pizza. I love pizza. (4)

Me encantan los espaguetis. I love spaghetti. (4)

¡Me encantaría! I would love to! (5)

el melón melon (4)

menor (que) younger (than) (3)

merendar (e→ie) to have a snack (3)

el metro metro, subway (5)

la mezquita mosque (5)

miércoles Wednesday (0)

mil one thousand (2)

cinco mil five thousand (2)

diez mil ten thousand (2)

mirar to watch, look at (1)

mirar una película to watch a movie (1)

la mochila backpack (2, 6)

la montaña mountain (6)

montar a caballo to ride horseback (6)

morado/a purple (4)

muchísimo/a really a lot (of), very (6)

mucho/a a lot (of) (6)

muchos/as many (2)

el museo museum (3, 5)

la música music (1)

muy very (0)

¡Muy bien, gracias! Great, thanks! (0)

nadar to swim (3, 6)

la naranja orange (4)

navegar to navigate (1, 6)

navegar en canoa to paddle a canoe (6)

navegar en/por internet to surf the web (1)

necesitar to need (2)

negro/a black (2, 4)

nevar (e→ie) to snow (6)

el/la nieto/a grandson/granddaughter (3)

la nieve snow (6)

el nombre (given, first) name (3)

el norte north (6)

¡Nos vemos! See you later! (0)

novecientos/as nine hundred (2)

noventa ninety (2)

noviembre November (0)

nublado/a cloudy (6)

está nublado it's cloudy (6)

nueve nine (0)

nunca never (3)

ochenta eighty (2)

ocho eight (0)

ochocientos/as eight hundred (2)

octubre October (0)

el oeste west (6)

la oficina office (2)

once eleven (0)

ordenado/a organized (3)

el otoño fall (0)

el padre father (3)

los padres parents (3)

pagar to pay (4)

pagar en efectivo to pay cash (4)

pagar con tarjeta de crédito to pay by credit card (4)

el pan bread (4)

el **pan dulce** sweet bread (4)

los **pantalones (cortos/largos)** (short/long) pants (2, 5, 6)

la **papa** potato (4)

las **papas fritas** French fries (4)

el **papel** paper (2)

el **paquete** packet, package (2)

el **paraguas** umbrella (6)

el **parque** park (5)

el **parque nacional** national park (6)

participar to participate (2)

pasear al perro to walk the dog (3)

el **pasillo** hallway (2)

el **pastel** cake, pastry (4)

la **patineta** skateboard

el **patio** patio, courtyard (3)

el **pay de manzana** apple pie (4)

pedir (e→i) to ask for, to order (4)

la **película** film, movie (1, 3, 5)

la **pelota** ball, baseball (P.R., R.D.) (5)

la **pena** pain, pity (1)

¡Qué pena! That's too bad! What a shame! (1)

el **pepino** cucumber (4)

pequeño/a small (3)

el **perro** dog (3)

el **pescado** fish (4)

pescar to fish (6)

picante spicy (4)

la **piña** pineapple (4)

pintar to paint (1)

la **piscina** swimming pool (2, 5)

el **piso** floor, flat, apartment (Esp.) (3)

el **plan** plan (5)

Ya tengo planes. I already have plans. (5)

el **plátano** banana (Méx., Esp.), plantain (L.A.) (4)

la **playa** beach (5, 6)

poco/a a little, not much (6)

poder (o→ue) to be able to, can (4)

No puedo. I can't. (3, 5)

el **poema** poem (3, 4)

el/la **poeta** poet (1)

polaco/a Polish (1)

el **polaco** Polish language (1)

el **pollo** chicken (4)

el **pollo con mole** chicken with mole sauce (4)

poner (g) to put, to place (3)

poner la mesa to set the table (3)

por by, through, for (1, 2, 5)

por la mañana in the morning (2)

por la tarde in the afternoon (2)

¿Por qué? Why? (1, 5)

¿Por qué estudias español? Why are you studying Spanish? (1)

porque because (2)

portugués/portuguesa Portuguese (1)

el **portugués** Portuguese language (1)

el **postre** dessert (4)

practicar to practice (1)

preferir (e→ie) to prefer (4)

preparar to prepare (4)

prestar atención to pay attention (2)

la **primavera** spring (0)

primero/a first (0)

el **primero de mayo** the first of May (0)

el/la **primo/a** cousin (3)

probar (o→ue) to try (4)

el/la **profesor/a** teacher, professor (secondary, university) (2)

el **programa** (m.) program

el **programa deportivo** sports show (5)

próximo/a next (5)

la **próxima vez** next time (5)

el **pueblo** town (3)

el **puesto** stand (4)

¿Qué? What? (1)

¿Qué necesitas? What do you need? (2)

¿Qué pasa? What's going on? (5)

¿Qué te gusta hacer? What do you like to do? (1)

¿Qué te gustaría hacer? What would you like to do? (3)

¡Qué + adjective! How + adjective! (1)

¡Qué asco! How disgusting!, Gross! (4)

¡Qué rico! Yum! How delicious! (4)

querer (e→ie) to want (4)

la **quesadilla** quesadilla (4)

la **química** chemistry (2)

quince fifteen (0)

quinientos/as five hundred (2)

recomendar (i→ie) to recommend (4)

el **recreo** break (between classes) (2)

el **refresco** soft drink (4)

el **regalo** gift, present (5)

regresar to go back home, to return (2)

regular O.K., not good (Esp.) (0)

relajarse to relax (6)

el **receso** break (between classes) (2)

rico/a delicious (4)

el **río** river (6)

rojo/a red (4)

la **ropa** clothing (6)

la **ropa formal/informal** formal/informal clothes (5)

la **ropa interior** underwear (6)

rosado/a pink (4)

ruso/a Russian (1)

el **ruso** Russian language (1)

sábado Saturday (0)

sabroso/a tasty, delicious (4)

sacar fotos to take pictures (6)

la **sal** salt (4)

la **sala** living room (3)

salado/a salty, savory (4)

salir to go out, leave (3)

el **salón de clase** classroom (1)

la **salsa** salsa, sauce (4)

la **sandalia** sandal (5, 6)

la **sandía** watermelon (4)

el **sándwich (de queso)** (cheese) sandwich (4)

sé I know (a fact, first person present of **saber**) (6)

seco/a dry (6)

el/la **secretario/a** secretary (2)

seis six (0)

seiscientos/as 600 (2)

la **selva tropical** tropical forest (6)

la **semana** week (0)

una vez por semana once a week (3)

septiembre September (0)

ser (irreg.) to be

serio/a serious (3)

servir (e→i) to serve (4)

sesenta sixty (2)

setecientos/as seven hundred (2)

setenta seventy (2)

siempre always (3)

siete seven (0)

simpático/a nice, friendly (3)

sin without (4)

sin gluten gluten-free (4)

el/la **sobrino/a** nephew/niece (3)

la **soda** cafeteria (C.R.) (1)

soltero/a unmarried, single (3)

el **sombrero** hat (6)

la **sopa** soup (4)

la **sopa azteca/de tomate** tortilla/tomato soup (4)

subir to go up, rise (6)

la **sudadera** sweatshirt (6)

el **suéter** sweater (6)

el **sur** south (6)

la **táblet** tablet computer (2)

el **taco** taco (4)

los **tacos de carne asada** beef tacos (4)

los **tacos de carnitas** pork tacos (4)

los **tacos de pescado** fish tacos (4)

el **tagalo** Tagalog language (1)

talentoso/a talented (3)

también also (1)

la **taquería** taco stand, restaurant (4)

tarde late (5)

el **taxi** taxi (5)

el **té** tea (4)

el **té helado** iced tea (4)

la **televisión** television, TV (3)

la **temperatura** temperature (6)

el **templo** temple, church (5)

tener (irreg.) to have (4, 5, 6)

tener ganas de + inf. to feel like + -ing (4)
tener hambre to be hungry (4)
tener que + infinitivo I have to + verb (3)
tener sed to be thirsty (4)
terminar to end (2)
la **terraza** terrace (3)
el **tiempo** weather, time (6)
las **tijeras** scissors (2)
el/la **tío/a** uncle/aunt (3)
tocar to play (music), to touch (5)
tocar en una banda to play in a band (5)
tocar un instrumento to play an instrument (1)
todo/a all, every (3)
todos los días every day (3)
tomar to take (2)
tomar el sol to sunbathe, lay out (6)
la **tortilla** tortilla (flat corn cake, Méx.), omelette (L.A., Esp.) (4)
la **tortilla de harina** flour tortilla (4)
la **tortilla de maíz** corn tortilla (4)
la **tostada** toast (4)
trabajar to work (1)
trabajar en equipo to work in teams (2)
traer (g) to bring (5)
el **traje** suit (5, 6)
tranquilo/a quiet, peaceful (3)
trece thirteen (0)
treinta thirty (0, 2)
treinta y dos thirty-two (2)
treinta y uno thirty-one (0, 2)
tres three (0)
trescientos/as three hundred (2)
el **uniforme (escolar)** (school) uniform (2)
un/uno/una one (0, 2)
unos/unas some (2)
usar to use, wear (2)
la **uva** grape (4)
la **vainilla** vanilla (4)
vegetariano/a vegetarian (1)
veinte twenty (0)
veinticinco twenty-five (0)
veinticuatro twenty-four (0)

veintidós twenty-two (0)
veintinueve twenty-nine (0)
veintiocho twenty-eight (0)
veintiséis twenty-six (0)
veintisiete twenty-seven (0)
veintitrés twenty-three (0)
veintiuno twenty-one (0)
vender to sell (4)
ver to see, watch (5)
ver la televisión/una película to watch television/a movie (3)
ver los programas deportivos to watch sports on TV (5)
el **verano** summer (0)
verde green (2, 4)
el **vestido** dress (5, 6)
la **vez** time (in a series) (3)
a veces sometimes (3)
una vez once (3)
dos veces twice (3)
viajar to travel (6)
viejo/a old (3)
viernes Friday (0)
vietnamita Vietnamese (1)
el **vietnamita** Vietnamese language (1)
visitar to visit (3, 6)
vivir to live (1)
el/la **voluntario/a** volunteer (1)
¡Yo también! Me too!, So do/am I! (1)
el **yogur con frutas** yogurt with fruit (4)
el **zapato** shoe (2, 6)
el **zoo** zoo (6)

Expresiones útiles

¿A qué hora empieza la fiesta? What time does the party start? (5)

¿A qué hora? At what time? (3)

a veces sometimes (6)

al mediodía at noon (2)

alegre happy (5)

Aquí lo tiene. Here you go., Here it is. (4)

azul blue (3)

el/la bebé baby (3)

el/la bisabuelo/a great-grandfather/great-grandmother (3)

callado/a quiet (3)

castaño/a brown (3)

el centro the center, middle (5)

cien gramos 100 grams (4)

¿Cómo estuvo el evento? How was the event? (5)

¿Cómo llegamos a la fiesta? How do we get to the party? (5)

¿Con qué frecuencia? How often? (3)

¿Con qué salsa? With which salsa? (4)

¿Con quién? With whom? (3)

conocer (zc) to be familiar with (a person, a custom, a work of art, etc.) (6)

¿Conoces a ese estudiante colombiano? Do you know that Colombian student? (6)

Conozco a muchos colombianos. I know lots of Colombians. (6)

¿Cuándo voy a recibir la invitación? When will I receive the invitation? (5)

¿Cuánto es? How much is it? (4)

¿Cuánto tiempo va a durar? How long will it last? (5)

un cuarto de kilo (de) fourth of a kilo (of) (4)

De acuerdo. Agreed. (3)

de color café brown (3)

divertido/a fun (3)

el/la doble double (5)

¿Dónde es la fiesta? Where is the party? (5)

¿Dónde estás? Where are you? (2)

¿Dónde? Where? (3)

educado/a polite (3)

el domingo on Sunday (5)

el lunes on Monday (5)

en general in general (6)

entre semana during the (work) week (5)

Es diferente. It's different. (4)

Es guapo/a. He is handsome. She is pretty. (3)

es importante + infinitivo it's important to + verb (6)

es más grande que It's bigger than (4)

es más nutritivo que It's more nutritious than (4)

es mejor + infinitivo it's better to + verb (6)

Es moreno/a. He/she is dark complected. (3)

Es pelirrojo/a. He/she is a red-head. (3)

Es rubio/a. He/she is blond(e). (3)

Es similar. It's similar. (4)

el/la esposo/a husband/wife (3)

estar aburrido/a to be bored (5)

estar alegre/feliz/contento/a to be happy (5)

estar cansado/a to be tired (5)

estar emocionado/a to be excited (5)

estar enojado/a to be angry (5)

estar genial to be great, super (5)

estar interesado/a to be interested (5)

estar nervioso/a to be nervous (5)

estar ocupado/a to be busy (5)

estar preocupado/a to be worried (5)

estar triste to be sad (5)

Estoy en ____. I'm in ____. (2)

Estuvo aburrido. It was boring. (5)

¡Estuvo chévere! It was great! (5)

¡Estuvo fantástico! It was fantastic! (5)

¡Estuvo genial! It was great! (5)

Estuvo horrible. It was horrible. (5)

los **extremos** the edges, sides (5)

la **ficha** domino tile (5)

frecuentemente frequently, often (6)

gracioso/a funny, comical (3)

hay que + infinitivo one must + infinitive (6)

honesto/a honest (3)

impaciente impatient (3)

los/las **jugadores** players (5)

jugar en pareja to play in pairs (5)

¡La pasé bomba! I had an awesome time! (5)

Lo siento. I'm sorry. (3)

los domingos on Sundays (2, 5)

los fines de semana on the weekends (5)

los lunes on Mondays (5)

los sábados on Saturdays (2)

mayor (que) older (than) (3)

¡Me divertí mucho! I had lots of fun! (5)

Me gustaría I would like (3)

¡Me gustó mucho! I liked it a lot! (5)

medio kilo (de) half a kilo (of) (4)

menor (que) younger (than) (3)

mi propia habitación my own room (3)

negro/a black (2, 3, 4)

No conozco a nadie aquí. I don't know anybody here. (6)

No es para tanto. It's no big deal. It doesn't matter. (5)

No hice nada especial/interesante/ divertido. I didn't do anything special/ interesting/fun. (5)

No lo sé. I don't know. (6)

No me gustó nada. I didn't like it at all. (5)

No puedo. I can't. (3)

¡No seas tonto/a! Don't be silly! (3)

ordenado/a organized (3)

¿Para aquí o para llevar? For here or to go? (4)

Para mí es importante... For me...is important. (3)

Para mí/ Para nosotros/as ____ es/son importante/s ____ . For me/for us ____ is/are important. (2)

Póngame por favor... Give me... (4)

Por eso prefiero ____. That's why I prefer ____. (2)

por la mañana in the morning (2)

por la noche in the evening (2)

por la tarde in the afternoon (2)

¿Por qué empieza tan tarde? Why does it start so late? (5)

porque el/la profesor/a es dinámico/a because the teacher is dynamic (2)

porque estoy cansado/a because I'm tired (2)

porque estoy descansado/a because I'm rested (2)

porque la clase es aburrida because the class is boring (2)

porque me duermo because I fall asleep (2)

porque tengo muchos amigos en la clase because I have a lot of friends in the class (2)

los **puntos** points (5)

¡Qué bueno! Great! (1)

¿Qué factores son importantes para ti/para Uds.? Which factors are important for you/all of you? (2)

¡Qué interesante! Interesting! (1)

¿Qué le pongo? What can I serve you? (4)

¿Qué más? What else? (3)

¡Qué pena! Too bad! (1)

¿Qué tal si tenemos...? What if we have...? (3)

¿Qué va a llevar? What can I get for you? (4)

¿Qué vamos a comer en la fiesta? What are we going to eat at the party? (5)

¿Quién va a ir a la fiesta? Who is going to go to the party? (5)

Quiero tres tacos de pescado, por favor. I want three fish tacos, please. (4)

Quiero... I'd like... (4)

repartir to deal (cards) (5)

saber to know a fact (6)

¿Sabes el nombre de ese estudiante colombiano? Do you know the name of that Colombian student? (6)

serio/a serious (3)

¿Sirven aguas frescas? Do you serve aguas frescas? (4)

el/la **sobrino/a** nephew/niece (3)

soltero/a unmarried, single (3)

Son 30 pesos. It'll be 30 pesos. (4)

Susana tiene razón. Susana is right. (3)

el **tapete de dominó** domino mat (5)

¿Te gustaría ir con nosotros? Would you like to go with us? (3)

tener que + infinitivo to have to + verb (6)

Tengo calor. I'm hot. (5)

Tengo ganas de comer unos tacos de camarón. I feel like eating some shrimp tacos. (4)

Tengo hambre. I'm hungry (4)

Tengo que ayudar en la casa. I have to help around the house. (3)

Tengo que cuidar a mi hermano menor. I have to watch my little brother. (3)

Tengo que estudiar. I have to study. (3)

Tengo sed. I'm thirsty. (4,5)

Tiene el pelo oscuro. He/she has dark hair. (3)

Tiene el pelo rubio. He/she has blond hair. (3)

Tiene los ojos... He/she has...eyes. (3)

¿Tienes frío? Are you cold? (5)

¿Tienes hambre? Are you hungry? (5)

típicamente typically (6)

un kilo (de) a kilo (of) (4)

una docena (de) a dozen (4)

el/la **vencedor/a** winner (5)

verde green (3)

Yo prefiero... I prefer... (3)

Yo sé la respuesta I know the answer. (6)

¡Yo también! Me too! (1)

Glossary English-Spanish

This glossary gives the meanings of words and phrases as used in this book.

actor el/la actor/actriz (1)

afternoon la tarde (2)

all todo/a

also también (1)

altitude la altitud (6)

always siempre (3)

anniversary el aniversario (5)

apartment el apartamento, el piso (3)

apple la manzana (4)

apple pie el pay de manzana (4)

to **appreciate** apreciar (6)

April abril (0)

Arabic language el árabe (1)

Arabic árabe (1)

to **arrive** llegar (5)

to **arrive late** llegar tarde (5)

artist el/la artista (1)

arts and crafts las manualidades (3)

to **ask for** pedir (e→i) (4)

assignment notebook la agenda escolar (2)

at noon al mediodía (2)

athlete el/la atleta (1)

to **attend** asistir (3, 5)

auditorium el auditorio (2)

August agosto (0)

aunt la tía (3)

avenue la avenida

avocado el aguacate (4)

baby el/la bebé (3)

to **babysit** cuidar a los niños (3)

back: in the back al fondo (3)

backpack la mochila (2)

bad, not well mal (0)

ball la pelota (5)

balloon el globo (5)

banana el plátano (4)

band (music group) la banda (5)

baseball el béisbol; la pelota (P.R., R.D.) (5)

basketball el baloncesto (1)

f. - feminine

irreg. - irregular verb

m. - masculine

pl. - plural

refl. - reflexive verb

Verb conjugations:

(e → ie): like pensar (pienso, pensamos)

(e → ie/i): like preferir (prefiero, preferimos, prefirió)

(e → i): like servir (sirvo, servimos, sirvió)

(í): like variar (varío, variamos)

(o → ue): like volver (vuelvo, volvemos)

(o → ue/u): like dormir (duermo, dormimos, durmió)

Regional variations:

C.R. - Costa Rica

Esp. - España

Méx. - México

L.A. - Latinoamérica

P.R. - Puerto Rico

R.D. - República Dominicana

bathroom el baño (3)

to **be** estar (irreg.), ser (irreg.) (1)

to **be angry** estar enojado/a (5)

to **be bored** estar aburrido/a (5)

to **be busy** estar ocupado/a (5)

to **be cold** tener frío (5)

to **be excited** estar emocionado/a (5)

to **be great; to be super** estar genial (5)

to **be happy** estar alegre (5)

to **be hot** tener calor (5)

to **be interested** estar interesado/a (5)

to **be nervous** estar nervioso/a (5)

to **be sad** estar triste (5)

to **be tired** estar cansado/a (5)

to **be worried** estar preocupado/a (5)

to **be able to, can** poder (o→ue) (4)

to be familiar with, to know conocer (zc) (6)

to be hungry tener hambre (4)

to be named llamarse (0)

to be thirsty tener sed (4)

beach la playa (5)

beans los frijoles (4)

beautiful bonito/a (6)

because porque (2)

bedroom el dormitorio (3)

beef tacos los tacos de carne asada (4)

to begin empezar (e→ie) (2)

behind detrás (de) (3)

beside al lado (de) (3)

between entre (2)

bicycle la bicicleta

big grande (3)

bilingual bilingüe (1)

birthday el cumpleaños (0)

black negro/a (2)

blogger el/la bloguero/a (1)

blouse la blusa (6)

blue azul (3)

body el cuerpo (6)

book el libro (2)

boot la bota (6)

bread el pan (4)

break (between classes) el recreo, receso (2)

breakfast el desayuno (4)

to bring traer (g) (5)

brother el hermano (3)

building el edificio (2)

bus el autobús, la guagua (Cuba, P.R., R.D.) (5)

to buy comprar (4)

by por

cafeteria el comedor, la soda (C.R.) (2)

cake el pastel (4)

calculator la calculadora (2)

can (be able to) poder (o→ue)

cap la gorra (6)

care: I don't care. Me da igual., No me importa.

cash: to pay in cash pagar en efectivo (4)

cat el gato (3)

cathedral la catedral

center el centro (6)

ceremony la ceremonia (2)

cheese el queso (4)

chemistry la química (2)

chess el ajedrez (5)

chicken el pollo (4)

Chinese language el chino (1)

Chinese chino/a (1)

chocolate el chocolate

chores las tareas domésticas (3)

church la iglesia (5)

Ciao! ¡Chau! (0)

city la ciudad (3)

class la clase (2)

The class begins at... La clase empieza a... (2)

The class ends at... La clase termina a... (2)

classmate el/la compañero/a de clase (1)

classroom el aula (f.), salón de clase (2)

to clean limpiar (3)

climate el clima (6)

to climb mountains escalar montañas (5)

clothes la ropa (6)

clothing la ropa (6)

cloudy nublado/a; **it's cloudy** está nublado (6)

coach el/la entrenador/a (1)

coast la costa (6)

coat el abrigo (6)

coffee (with milk) el café (con leche) (4)

cold frío/a; **it's cold** hace frío (6)

cold (weather) el frío (6)

to collaborate colaborar (6)

comic, comic book, comic strip el cómic (3)

computer la computadora (2)

computer science la informática (2)

to cook cocinar (4)

corn el maíz (4)

costume el disfraz (5)

costume party la fiesta de disfraces (5)

courtyard el patio (3)

cousin el/la primo/a (3)

to cover cubrir (6)

cover el cubierto (6)

credit card la tarjeta de crédito (4)

crest el escudo (2)

cucumber el pepino (4)

cyclist el/la ciclista (1)

to dance bailar (1)

dancer el bailarín/la bailarina (1)

daughter la hija (3)

day el día (0)

December diciembre (0)

to decorate decorar (5)

delicious rico/a, delicioso/a (4)

desert el desierto (6)

dessert el postre (4)

dictionary el diccionario (2)

dining room el comedor (3)

dinner la cena (4)

to discover descubrir (6)

to do hacer (irreg.) (3, 5, 6)

to do arts and crafts hacer manualidades (3)

to do chores hacer tareas domésticas (3)

dog el perro (3)

dominoes el dominó (5)

dress el vestido (6)

to drink beber (4)

dry seco/a (6)

during the (work) week entre semana (5)

east el este (6)

to eat comer (1)

to eat dinner/supper cenar (3)

egg el huevo (4)

egg custard el flan (4)

eight ocho (0)

eight hundred ochocientos/as (2)

eight thousand ocho mil (2)

eighteen dieciocho (0)

eighty ochenta (2)

eleven once (0)

emblem el escudo (2)

to end terminar (2)

English language el inglés (1)

English inglés/a (1)

every todos/as (3)

everybody todo el mundo (5)

every day todos los días (3)

everything todo (5)

exchange el intercambio

to explore explorar (3)

fall (season) el otoño (0)

fat gordo/a (3)

father el padre (3)

February febrero (0)

to feed the pets dar de comer a las mascotas (3)

to feel like + -ing tener ganas de + infinitivo (4)

field el campo (3)

fifteen quince (0)

fifty cincuenta (2)

film la película (1, 3, 5)

fine bien (0)

Fine, thanks! ¡Muy bien, gracias! (0)

fireworks los fuegos artificiales (5)

first primero/a (0)

fish el pescado (4)

to fish pescar (6)

fish tacos los tacos de pescado (4)

five cinco (0)

five hundred quinientos/as (2)

floor el piso (3)

flour tortilla la tortilla de harina (4)

flower la flor (5)

folder la carpeta (2)

food la comida (4)

food culture la gastronomía (6)

for por, para

forest el bosque (6)

forty cuarenta (0)

four cuatro (0)

four hundred cuatrocientos/as (2)

fourteen catorce (0)

fourth of a kilo (of) un cuarto de kilo (de) (4)

French language el francés (1)
French francés/francesa (1)
French fries papas fritas (4)
frequently frecuentemente (3)
fresh fresco/a (4)
Friday viernes (0)
fried/ranchero-style eggs huevos fritos/
  rancheros (4)
friendly simpático/a (3)
fruit-flavored water el agua fresca (f.) (4)
fun divertido/a (3)
  to **have fun** pasarla bien, divertirse
funny gracioso/a, cómico/a (3)
garage el garaje (3)
garden el jardín (3)
geography la geografía (2)
German language el alemán (1)
German alemán/alemana (1)
to **get exercise** hacer ejercicio (3)
to **get to know** conocer (zc) (6)
  gift el regalo (5)
to **give** dar (irreg.) (3)
  glacier el glaciar (6)
  gluten-free sin gluten (4)
to **go** ir (irreg.) (3, 5)
to **go back** regresar (2)
to **go camping** hacer camping (3)
to **go canoeing** navegar en canoa (6)
to **go down, lower** bajar (6)
to **go for a walk, ride** dar un paseo (3)
to **go for a walk, ride in the country** dar un
    paseo en el campo (3)
to **go hiking** hacer senderismo (6)
to **go on foot** ir a pie (5)
to **go out with friends** salir con amigos (3)
to **go shopping** ir de compras (3)
to **go to Carnival** asistir al Carnaval (5)
to **go to concerts** asistir a conciertos (3)
to **go to the movies** ir al cine (3)
to **go up, rise** subir (6)
  good bueno/a (4)
  Goodbye! ¡Adiós! (0)
  Good afternoon. Buenas tardes. (0)

Good morning. Buenos días. (0)
graduation party la fiesta de graduación (5)
granddaughter la nieta (3)
grandfather el abuelo (3)
grandmother la abuela (3)
grandson el nieto (3)
grape la uva (4)
great-grandfather el bisabuelo (3)
great-grandmother la bisabuela (3)
Great, thanks! ¡Muy bien, gracias! (0)
Great! ¡Qué bueno! (1)
green verde (2)
Guaraní guaraní (1)
guitarist el/la guitarrista (1)
gym(nasium) el gimnasio (2)
gymnast el/la gimnasta (1)
hallway el pasillo (2)
ham el jamón (4)
hamburger la hamburguesa (4)
happy alegre (3)
hat el sombrero (6)
to **have** tener (irreg.) (4, 5, 6)
to **have a snack** merendar (e→ie) (3)
to **have lunch** almorzar (o→ue) (2)
  heat el calor (6)
  Hello! ¡Hola! (0)
to **help** ayudar (2)
  here aquí (6)
  high alto/a (3)
  high school el colegio (2)
  history la historia (2)
  honest honesto/a (3)
  hot caliente (6)
  hour la hora
  house la casa (3)
  How? ¿Cómo? (1)
  How + adjective! ¡Qué + adjetivo! (4)
  How are you? (formal) ¿Cómo está usted? (0)
  How are you? (informal) ¿Cómo estás? (0)
  How disgusting! ¡Qué asco! (4)
  How many? ¿Cuántos/as? (1)
  How much does it/do they cost? ¿Cuánto
    cuesta(n)? (2)

How much? ¿Cuánto/a? (1)

How old are you? ¿Cuántos años tienes? (1)

How will we get there? ¿Cómo llegamos? (5)

hundred cien/ciento (2)

husband el esposo (3)

in the afternoon por la tarde (2)

I already have plans. Ya tengo planes. (5)

I don't like it/them at all. No me gusta(n) para nada. (4)

I have Tengo (2)

I need Necesito (2)

I would love to! ¡Me encantaría! (5)

I'm fine. And you? Estoy bien. ¿Y tú? (0)

I'm from Soy de (0)

I'm sorry Lo siento (5)

ice el hielo (6)

ice cream el helado (4)

iced helado/a (4)

iced tea el té helado

impatient impaciente (3)

in en (3)

in the back (of) al fondo (de) (3)

in the city en el ciudad (3)

in the country en el campo (3)

in the middle (of) en medio (de) (3)

in the neighborhood en el barrio (3)

in the town en el pueblo (3)

Independence Day el Día de Independencia (5)

interesting interesante

in the middle of en medio de (3)

in the morning por la mañana (2)

island la isla

Italian language el italiano (1)

Italian italiano/a

It's hot hace calor (6)

It's no big deal. No es para tanto. (5)

It's sunny hace sol (6)

It's windy hace viento (6)

jacket la chaqueta (6)

January enero (0)

jeans los bluejeans (6)

juice el jugo (4)

July julio (0)

June junio (0)

kitchen la cocina (3)

to know conocer (zc) (6)

to know (a fact) saber (yo sé) (6)

laboratory el laboratorio (2)

late tarde (5)

leaf la hoja (2)

to learn aprender (2)

left (side) izquierdo/a (3)

to the left of a la izquierda de (3)

lettuce la lechuga (4)

library la biblioteca (2)

light (weight) ligero/a (6)

to like gustar (3, 4)

I like pizza. Me gusta la pizza. (4)

to listen to escuchar (1)

little (small) pequeño/a (3)

to live vivir (1)

living room la sala (3)

logo el escudo (2)

long largo/a (6)

lot: a lot of mucho/a (6)

really a lot muchísimo/a (6)

to love (something) encantar (4)

I love pizza. Me encanta la pizza. (4)

low-calorie light (4)

lunch el almuerzo (2)

to make haver (irreg.) (3, 5, 6)

to make the bed hacer la cama (3)

to make, meet new friends conocer a amigos nuevos (6)

many muchos/as (2)

March marzo (0)

market (arts and crafts) el mercado (de artesanías) (6)

mask la máscara (5)

math las matemáticas (2)

May mayo (0)

Me too! ¡Yo también! (1)

meal la comida (4)

meat la carne (4)

melon el melón (4)

metro (subway) el metro (5)
middle el medio (3)
Monday lunes (0)
morning la mañana (2)
mosque la mezquita (5)
mother la madre (3)
mountain la montaña (6)
movie la película
movie theater el cine (5)
much mucho/a (6)
museum el museo (6)
music la música (1)
my mi(s)
My birthday is ___. Mi cumpleaños es ___. (0)
my little sister mi hermana menor
My name is ___. Me llamo ___., Mi nombre es (0)
name el nombre (3)
national anthem el himno nacional (2)
national park el parque nacional (6)
to **navigate** navegar (1, 6)
to **need** necesitar (2)
neighborhood el barrio (3)
nephew el sobrino (3)
never nunca (3)
New Year's el Año Nuevo (5)
next próximo/a (5)
next time la próxima vez (5)
nice (friendly) simpático/a (3)
nice (good, acceptable) bueno/a (4)
nice (kind) amable (3)
nice (weather) hace buen tiempo (6)
niece la sobrina (3)
nine nueve (0)
nine hundred novecientos/as (2)
nineteen diecinueve (0)
ninety noventa (2)
no one nadie (5)
noon el mediodía (2)
north el norte (6)
not much poco/a (6)
notebook el cuaderno (2)

nothing nada (5)
November noviembre (0)
O.K. está bien (2, 5)
October octubre (0)
office la oficina (2)
often frecuentemente (3)
old viejo/a (3)
older (than) mayor (que) (3)
omelette la tortilla (Spain), omelet (Méx.)
on en, **(with days of the week)** el, los (5)
on a main street en una avenida (3)
on a quiet street en una calle tranquila (3)
on Sunday el domingo (5)
on Sundays los domingos (5)
once una vez (3)
once a week una vez por semana
one un/uno/una (2)
onion la cebolla (4)
orange la naranja (4)
orange (color) anaranjado/a (4)
to **order** pedir (e→i) (4)
organized ordenado/a (3)
packet, package el paquete (2)
to **paddle a canoe** navegar en canoa (6)
to **paint** pintar (1)
pants los pantalones (2)
paper el papel (2)
parade el desfile (5)
parade float la carroza (5)
parents los padres (3)
park el parque (5)
to **participate** participar (2)
party la fiesta (5)
pastry el pastel (4)
patio el patio (3)
to **pay** pagar (4)
to **pay attention** prestar atención (2)
pen el bolígrafo (2)
pencil el lápiz (pl. lápices) (2)
pet la mascota (3)
photo, picture la foto (5)
photographer el/la fotógrafo/a (1)

pilgrimage el peregrinaje (6)

pineapple la piña (4)

pink rosado/a (4)

pity: What a pity! ¡Qué pena! (1)

place el lugar (2)

to **place** poner (irreg.) (3)

plain (geographical feature) el llano (6)

plan el plan (5)

plantain el plátano (4)

to **play (a game, sport)** jugar (u→ue) (1)

to **play (music, an instrument)** tocar (1, 5)

to **play basketball** jugar al baloncesto (1)

to **play chess** jugar al ajedrez (5)

to **play dominoes** jugar al dominó (5)

to **play in a band** tocar en una banda (5)

to **play sports** jugar deportes (1)

poblano pepper el chile poblano (4)

poem el poema (3, 4)

poet el/la poeta (1)

Polish language el polaco (1)

Polish polaco/a (1)

polite educado/a (3)

pool la piscina (5)

pork tacos los tacos de carnitas (4)

Portuguese language el portugués (1)

Portuguese portugués/portuguesa (1)

potato la papa, la patata (Esp.) (4)

to **practice** practicar (1)

to **practice sports** practicar deportes (1)

to **prefer** preferir (e→ie) (4)

to **prepare** preparar (4)

pretty bonito/a (6)

principal el/la director/a (2)

program el programa (m.)

purple morado/a (4)

purse el bolso (6)

to **put** poner (irreg.) (3)

quesadilla la quesadilla (4)

quiet (peaceful) tranquilo/a (3)

quiet (shy, silent) callado/a (3)

to **rain** llover (u→ue) (6)

rain la lluvia (6)

raincoat el impermeable (6)

to **read** leer (3)

to **recommend** recomendar (i→ie) (4)

red rojo/a (4)

to **relax** relajarse (6)

rice el arroz (4)

to **ride a bicycle** andar en bicicleta (3)

to **ride a skateboard** andar en patineta (5)

to **ride horseback** montar a caballo (6)

right (side) derecho/a (3)

river el río (6)

roasted pork las carnitas (4)

to **run** correr (3)

Russian language el ruso (1)

Russian ruso/a (1)

salad la ensalada (4)

salsa la salsa (4)

salt la sal (4)

salty salado/a (4)

sandal la sandalia (5)

sandwich el sándwich (4)

Saturday sábado/a (0)

sauce la salsa (4)

schedule el horario (2)

school la escuela (2)

science la ciencia (2)

scissors las tijeras (2)

sea el mar (6)

season la estación (6)

secretary el/la secretario/a (2)

See you later! ¡Nos vemos!, ¡Hasta luego! (0)

See you next time. Hasta la próxima. (5)

See you on Saturday. Hasta el sábado. (5)

to **see** ver (5)

to **sell** vender (4)

September septiembre (0)

serious serio/a (3)

to **serve** servir (e→i) (4)

to **set the table** poner la mesa (3)

seven siete (0)

seven hundred setecientos/as (2)

seventeen diecisiete (0)

seventy setenta (2)

shame: What a shame! ¡Qué pena!

sheet (of paper) la hoja (de papel) (2)

shirt la camisa (2)

shoe el zapato (2)

shopping center el centro comercial (5)

shore la costa (6)

short corto/a (5)

side el lado

to sing cantar (2)

single (unmarried) soltero/a (3)

sister la hermana (3)

six seis (0)

six hundred seiscientos/as (2)

sixteen dieciséis (0)

sixty sesenta (2)

skateboard la patineta (5)

to ski esquiar (6)

skirt la falda (2)

to sleep dormir (o→ue) (5)

small pequeño/a (3)

smoothie el batido (4)

to snow nevar (e→ie) (6)

snow la nieve (6)

so-so más o menos (0)

soccer field el campo de fútbol (2)

soccer player el/la futbolista (1)

social studies los estudios sociales (2)

socks los calcetines (6)

soft drink el refresco (4)

some unos/unas (2)

someone alguien (5)

something algo (5)

sometimes a veces (3)

son el hijo (3)

song la canción (5)

sorry: I'm sorry. Lo siento. (3)

soup la sopa (4)

south el sur (6)

spaghetti los espaguetis (4)

Spanish language el español (1)

Spanish español/a (1)

to speak hablar (1)

spicy picante (4)

spinach las espinacas (4)

spirit el espíritu (6)

sport el deporte (1)

sports show el programa deportivo (5)

spring la primavera (0)

stand el puesto (4)

steak el bistec (4)

strawberry la fresa (4)

street la calle (3)

strong fuerte (4)

student el/la estudiante (1)

to study estudiar (1)

subway el metro (5)

sugar el azúcar (4)

suit el traje (6)

summer el verano (0)

sun el sol (6)

to sunbathe tomar el sol (6)

Sunday domingo (0)

sunglasses las gafas de sol (6)

to surf the web navegar en/por internet (1)

surname el apellido (3)

surprise party la fiesta sorpresa (5)

sweater el suéter (6)

sweatshirt la sudadera (6)

sweet dulce (4)

sweet bread el pan dulce (4)

to swim nadar (6)

swimming pool la piscina (2)

swimsuit el traje de baño (5)

t-shirt la camiseta (6)

tablet computer la táblet (2)

taco el taco (4)

taco stand, restaurant la taquería (4)

Tagalog language tagalo (1)

to take tomar (2)

to take a guided tour hacer un tour con guía (6)

to take a nap dormir una siesta (5)

to take care of cuidar (6)

to take out llevar (4)

to **take pictures** sacar fotos (6)

talented talentoso/a (3)

to **talk** hablar (1)

tall alto/a (3)

tasty rico/a, sabroso/a (4)

taxi el taxi (5)

tea el té (4)

to **teach** enseñar (2)

teacher el/la maestro/a (elementary school); profesor/a (secondary, university) (2)

team el equipo (2, 5)

television la televisión (3)

temperature la temperatura (6)

temple el templo (5)

ten diez (0)

ten thousand diez mil (2)

terrace la terraza (3)

textbook el libro de texto (2)

Thanksgiving el Día de Acción de Gracias (5)

the ___ of ___ (month) el ___ de (mes) (0)

the first of (month) el primero de (mes) (0)

there allí (6)

there is/there are hay (2)

these estos/estas (4)

thin delgado/a (3)

thirteen trece (0)

thirty treinta (0)

thirty-one treinta y uno (0)

thirty-two treinta y dos (2)

this este/esta (4)

thousand mil (2)

three tres (0)

three hundred trescientos/as (2)

through por (6)

Thursday jueves (0)

time (in a series) la vez (pl. veces) (3)

time (in general) el tiempo (6)

time (of day) la hora (5)

toast la tostada (4)

together juntos/as (3)

tomato soup la sopa de tomate (4)

tortilla (flat corn cake, Méx.) la tortilla (4)

tortilla soup la sopa azteca (4)

to **the right of** a la derecha (de) (3)

to **touch** tocar (5)

town el pueblo (3)

trainer el/la entrenador/a (1)

to **travel** viajar (6)

tropical forest la selva tropical (6)

to **try** probar (o→ue) (4, 6)

Tuesday martes (0)

twelve doce (0)

twenty veinte (0)

twenty-eight veintiocho (0)

twenty-five veinticinco (0)

twenty-four veinticuatro (0)

twenty-nine veintinueve (0)

twenty-one veintiuno (0)

twenty-seven veintisiete (0)

twenty-six veintiséis (0)

twenty-three veintitrés (0)

twenty-two veintidós (0)

twice dos veces (3)

two dos (0)

two hundred doscientos/as (2)

ugly feo/a (6)

umbrella el paraguas (6)

uncle el tío (3)

underwear la ropa interior (6)

uniform el uniforme (2)

unmarried soltero/a (3)

until hasta (0, 5)

to **use** usar (2)

urban area la zona urbana (6)

valley el valle (6)

vanilla la vainilla (4)

vegetarian vegetariano/a (1)

very muy (0)

Vietnamese language el vietnamita (1)

Vietnamese vietnamita (1)

to **visit** visitar (6)

volunteer el/la voluntario/a (1)

to **walk** caminar, andar (2)

to **walk for a cause** caminar por una causa (3)

to **walk in the forest** caminar en el bosque (6)

to **walk the dog** pasear al perro (3)

to **want** querer (e→ie) (4)

to **watch a movie** mirar, ver una película (1)

to **watch sports on TV** mirar, ver los programas deportivos (5)

to **watch television** mirar, ver la televisión (3)

to **watch, look at** mirar (1)

water el agua (4)

to **water ski** hacer esquí acuático (5)

watermelon la sandía (4)

to **wear** llevar (2)

weather el tiempo (6)

wedding la boda (5)

Wednesday miércoles (0)

week la semana

weekend el fin de semana (5)

well bien (0)

west el oeste (6)

What? ¿Qué? ¿Cómo? (1)

What do you like to do? ¿Qué te gusta hacer? (1)

What do you need? ¿Qué necesitas? (2)

What is your favorite sport? ¿Cuál es tu deporte favorito? (1)

(At) what time? ¿A qué hora?

What would you like to do? ¿Qué te gustaría hacer? (3)

What's going on? ¿Qué pasa? (5)

What's your name? ¿Cómo te llamas? (0)

When? ¿Cuándo? (1)

When is your birthday? ¿Cuándo es tu cumpleaños? (0,1)

Where? ¿Dónde? (1)

Where are you from? ¿De dónde eres? (0)

Which one? What? ¿Cuál? (1)

white blanco/a (2)

Why? ¿Por qué? (1)

Why are you studying Spanish? ¿Por qué estudias español? (1)

wife la esposa (3)

wind el viento (6)

it's windy hace viento (6)

winter el invierno (0)

with con

with me conmigo (5)

with you contigo (5)

without sin (4)

woods el bosque (6)

to **work** trabajar (1)

to **work in teams** trabajar en equipo (2)

to **work out** hacer ejercicio (3)

to **work together** colaborar, trabajar juntos/as (6)

to **write** escribir (1)

yard el jardín, la yarda (EE. UU.) (3)

yellow amarillo/a (4)

yesterday ayer (5)

yogurt with fruit el yogur con frutas (4)

young joven (pl. jóvenes) (3)

younger (than) menor (que) (3)

Yum! ¡Qué rico! (4)

zoo el zoo (6)

Expresiones útiles

100 grams cien gramos (4)

a dozen una docena (de) (4)

a kilo (of) un kilo (de) (4)

Agreed. De acuerdo. (3)

angry estar enojado/a (5)

Are you cold? ¿Tienes frío? (5)

Are you hungry? ¿Tienes hambre? (5)

at noon al mediodía (2)

At what time? ¿A qué hora? (2)

baby el/la bebé (3)

because I fall asleep porque me duermo (2)

because I have a lot of friends in the class porque tengo muchos amigos en la clase (2)

because I'm rested porque estoy descansado/a (2)

because I'm tired porque estoy cansado/a (2)

because the class is boring porque la clase es aburrida (2)

because the teacher is dynamic porque el/la profesor/a es dinámico/a (2)

black negro/a (2, 3, 4)

blue azul (3)

bored estar aburrido/a (5)

brown castaño/a (3)

brown de color café (3)

busy estar ocupado/a (5)

center, middle el centro (5)

Do you know that Colombian student? ¿Conoces a ese estudiante colombiano? (6)

Do you know the name of that Colombian student? ¿Sabes el nombre de ese estudiante colombiano? (6)

Do you serve aguas frescas? ¿Sirven aguas frescas? (4)

domino mat el tapete de dominó (5)

domino tile la ficha (5)

Don't be silly! ¡No seas tonto/a! (3)

double el/la doble (5)

during the (work) week entre semana (5)

edges, sides los extremos (5)

excited estar emocionado/a (5)

For here or to go? ¿Para aquí o para llevar? (4)

For me...is important. Para mí es importante... (3)

For me/for us ____ is/are important. Para mí/ Para nosotros/as ____ es/ son importante/s ____. (2)

fourth of a kilo (of) un cuarto de kilo (de) (4)

frequently, often frecuentemente (6)

fun divertido/a (3)

funny, comical gracioso/a (3)

Give me... Póngame por favor... (4)

great-grandfather/great-grandmother el/la bisabuelo/a (3)

great, super estar genial (5)

Great! ¡Qué bueno! (1)

green verde (3)

half a kilo (of) medio kilo (de) (4)

happy alegre (5)

happy estar alegre/feliz/contento/a (5)

have to + verb tener que + infinitivo (6)

He is handsome. She is pretty. Es guapo/a. (3)

He/she has blond hair. Tiene el pelo rubio. (3)

He/she has dark hair. Tiene el pelo oscuro. (3)

He/she has...eyes. Tiene los ojos... (3)

He/she is a red-head. Es pelirrojo/a. (3)

He/she is blond(e). Es rubio/a. (3)

He/she is dark complected. Es moreno/a. (3)

Here you go., Here it is. Aquí lo tiene. (4)

honest honesto/a (3)

How do we get to the party? ¿Cómo llegamos a la fiesta? (5)

How long will it last? ¿Cuánto tiempo va a durar? (5)

How much is it? ¿Cuánto es? (4)

How often? ¿Con qué frecuencia? (3)

How was the event? ¿Cómo estuvo el evento? (5)

husband/wife el/la esposo/a (3)

I can't. No puedo. (3)

I didn't do anything special/interesting/ fun. No hice nada especial/interesante/ divertido. (5)

I didn't like it at all. No me gustó nada. (5)

I don't know anybody here. No conozco a nadie aquí. (6)

I don't know. No lo sé. (6)

I feel like eating some shrimp tacos. Tengo ganas de comer unos tacos de camarón. (4)

I had an awesome time! ¡La pasé bomba! (5)

I had lots of fun! ¡Me divertí mucho! (5)

I have to help around the house. Tengo que ayudar en la casa. (3)

I have to study. Tengo que estudiar. (3)

I have to watch my little brother. Tengo que cuidar a mi hermano menor. (3)

I know lots of Colombians. Conozco a muchos colombianos. (6)

I know the answer. Yo sé la respuesta (6)

I liked it a lot! ¡Me gustó mucho! (5)

I prefer... Yo prefiero... (3)

I want three fish tacos, please. Quiero tres tacos de pescado, por favor. (4)

I would like Me gustaría (3)

I'd like... Quiero... (4)

I'm hot. Tengo calor. (5)

I'm hungry Tengo hambre. (4)

I'm in ____. Estoy en ____. (2)

I'm sorry. Lo siento. (3)

I'm thirsty. Tengo sed. (4,5)

impatient impaciente (3)

in general en general (6)

in the afternoon por la tarde (2)

in the evening por la noche (2)

in the morning por la mañana (2)

interested estar interesado/a (5)

Interesting! ¡Qué interesante! (1)

It was boring. Estuvo aburrido. (5)

It was fantastic! ¡Estuvo fantástico! (5)

It was great! ¡Estuvo chévere! (5)

It was great! ¡Estuvo genial! (5)

It was horrible. Estuvo horrible. (5)

It'll be 30 pesos. Son 30 pesos. (4)

it's better to + verb es mejor + infinitivo (6)

It's bigger than Es más grande que (4)

It's cold. Es frío. (4)

It's different. Es diferente. (4)

It's hot. Es caliente. (4)

it's important to + verb es importante + infinitivo (6)

It's no big deal, it doesn't matter. No es para tanto. (5)

It's more nutritious than Es más nutritivo que (4)

It's similar. Es similar. (4)

Me too! ¡Yo también! (1)

my own room mi propia habitación (3)

nephew/niece el/la sobrino/a (3)

nervous estar nervioso/a (5)

older (than) mayor (que) (3)

on Monday el lunes (5)

on Mondays los lunes (5)

on Saturdays los sábados (2)

on Sunday el domingo (5)

on Sundays los domingos (2,5)

on the weekends los fines de semana (5)

one must + infinitivo hay que + infinitivo (6)

organized ordenado/a (3)

players los/las jugadores (5)

points los puntos (5)

polite educado/a (3)

quiet callado/a (3)

sad estar triste (5)

serious serio/a (3)

sometimes a veces (6)

Susana is right. Susana tiene razón. (3)

That's why I prefer ____. Por eso prefiero ____. (2)

tired estar cansado/a (5)

to be familiar with (a person, a custom, a work of art, etc.) conocer (6)

to deal (cards) repartir (5)

to know a fact saber (6)

to play in pairs jugar en pareja (5)

Too bad! ¡Qué pena! (1)

typically típicamente (6)

unmarried, single soltero/a (3)

What are we going to eat at the party? ¿Qué vamos a comer en la fiesta? (5)

What can I get for you? ¿Qué va a llevar? (4)

What can I serve you? ¿Qué le pongo? (4)

What else? ¿Qué más? (3)

What if we have...? ¿Qué tal si tenemos...? (3)

What time does the party start? ¿A qué hora empieza la fiesta? (5)

When will I receive the invitation? ¿Cuándo voy a recibir la invitación? (5)

Where are you? ¿Dónde estás? (2)

Where is the party? ¿Dónde es la fiesta? (5)

Where? ¿Dónde? (3)

Which factors are important for you/all of you? ¿Qué factores son importantes para ti/ para Uds.? (2)

Who is going to the party? ¿Quién va a ir a la fiesta? (5)

Why does it start so late? ¿Por qué empieza tan tarde? (5)

winner el/la vencedor/a (5)

With which salsa? ¿Con qué salsa? (4)

With whom? ¿Con quién? (3)

worried estar preocupado/a (5)

Would you like to go with us? ¿Te gustaría ir con nosotros? (3)

younger (than) menor (que) (3)

Credits

Every effort has been made to determine the copyright owners. In case of any omissions, the publisher will be happy to make suitable acknowledgements in future editions. All credits are listed in the order of appearance.

All images are © Shutterstock and © Thinkstock, except as noted below.

* To protect the privacy of these generous Spanish speakers we have changed or omitted their last names.

Unidad Preliminar

© Edición Culturizando, "10 idiomas más usados en Internet", Retrieved from www.culturizando.com.

© Alberto Martinez, "Ranking de países por número de hablantes y de nativos del español", Retrieved from http://www.spanishintour.com/blog/es/spanish-in-tour-es/ranking-de-paises-por-numero-de-hablantes-y-de-nativos-del-espanol.html/. 15 June 2014.

© Maria Reina Eskola, "Abecedario", Adapted from http://aulasptmariareinaeskola.es/segundo/lenguaje/abecedario/.

© Calendario 365, "Calendario 2017", Adapted from http://www.calendario-365.es/calendario-2017.html. 2016.

Unidad Preliminar Images

12 © Laurence Mouton/AltoPress/Maxppp

16 (letter ñ) © Gerardo Posada, "Se habla español", Retrieved from http://gerar2.deviantart.com/art/Se-habla-espaniol-108992873

21 (Península Nicoya, Costa Rica) © G. Watson-López

22 (Sor Juana Inés de la Cruz) © Miguel Cabrera - http://es.wikipedia.org/wiki/, Public Domain, Retrieved from https://commons.wikimedia.org/w/index.php?curid=11050491

22 (Isabel Allende) © Mutari, "Isabel Allende", Own work, Public Domain, https://commons.wikimedia.org/w/index.php?curid=4075178

22 (Simón Bolivar) © M.N. Bate - Public Domain, Retrieved from https://commons.wikimedia.org/w/index.php?curid=3505823

22 (Eva Perón) © Archivo gráfico de la Nación, "Eva Perón (1919-1952)", Public Domain, Retrieved from https://commons.wikimedia.org/w/index.php?curid=5710246

22 (Felipe de Borbón) © Rubén Ortega, "Felipe de Borbón", CC-BY-SA 4.0: https://creativecommons.org/licenses/by-sa/4.0/legalcode, Retrieved from https://commons.wikimedia.org/wiki/File:King_of_Spain_2015_%28cropped%29.JPG

23 (poster) © Ayuntamiento de Pamplona (Autor: Pedro-Martín Balda), "San Fermín 1960", Retrieved from http://www.pamplona.es/

26 (Carlos Vives) © «CarlosVives». CC BY 2.0: https://creativecommons.org/licenses/by/2.0/legalcode, Retrieved from - https://commons.wikimedia.org/wiki/File:CarlosVives.jpg#/media/File:CarlosVives.jpg

29 (poster) © Equip Media Camp, "Media Camp 2014", Retrieved from www.mediacamp.es, 2014.

31 (advertisement) Best efforts made © Centro de estudios metodo, "Curso intensivo de inglés, alemán, francés verano 2014", Adapted from http://alcala-de-henares.anundos.com, 2014.

Unidad 1

© AMERICA Written by ENRIQUE FRANCO, Publisher: TN EDICIONES MUSICALES, Copyright Secured. Used By Permission, All Rights Reserved

© Centro Virtual Cervantes, Information for graphs retrieved from http://cvc.cervantes.es/lengua/anuario/anuario_05/melia/p05.htm.

© United States Census, American Fact Finder, Community Facts, Retrieved from http://factfinder.census.gov/faces/nav/jsf/pages/index.xhtml. 2015.

© Instituto Superior de Estudios Humanísticos y Filosóficos (ISEHF), "Aprende Guaraní", Adapted from http://www.isehf.edu.py/?p=1648. 21 July 2014.

Unidad 1 Images

35 (María Laura) © María Laura*

36 (Asunción) © Felipe Antonio, «Capital de Paraguay», CC BY-SA 3.0: https://creativecommons.org/licenses/by-sa/3.0/legalcode, Retrieved from https://commons.wikimedia.org/wiki/File:CAPITAL_DE_PARAGUAY.jpg [Edited]

36 (Cabeza de Vaca) © Public Domain, Retrieved from https://commons.wikimedia.org/wiki/File:Cabeza_de_Vaca_Portrait.jpg

37 (Houston) © RJN, CC BY-SA 2.0: https://creativecommons.org/licenses/by-sa/2.0/legalcode. Retrieved from https://commons.wikimedia.org/wiki/File:DowntownHouston.jpg

37 (Alfredo Stroessner) © Public Domain, Retrieved from https://commons.wikimedia.org/wiki/File:Alfredo_Stroessner2.jpg

Unidad 2

Unidad 2 Images

Unidad 3

© Institute of International Education, "Open Doors Data", Information retrieved from http://www.iie.org/en/Research-and-Publications/Open-Doors/Data/US-Study-Abroad/Leading-Destinations#.V8TMjLVCSRt and http://www.iie.org/Research-and-Publications/Open-Doors/Data/US-Study-Abroad/Leading-Destinations/2002-04.

© Visit Denver, "Visit Denver" advertisement, Colorado Guía Turística, Recreated from http://content.yudu.com/A1ilj6/Colorado2010Spanish/resources/index.htm. 2010.

© Ana Serna Vara, "Manuela Mi Abuela", Poesia de ayer y de hoy para chicos y grandes (Madrid: Susaeta, 1993).

© "Baile En El Jardín" from IN MY FAMILY by Carmen Lomas Garza. Text & Illustration Copyright © 2000 Carmen Lomas Garza. Permission arranged with © Children's Book Press, an Imprint of LEE & LOW BOOKS, Inc., New York, NY 10016. All rights not specifically granted herein are reserved.

© Institute of International Education, "Top 25 Destinations of U.S. Study Abroad Students, 2012/13 -2013/14", Open Doors Report on International Educational Exchange, Retrieved from http://www.iie.org/opendoors, 2015.

© José Antonio, Intercambio, Retrieved from http://www.quieroaprenderidiomas.com/vivir-en-el-extranjero/intercambio-familia-de-acogida/.

Unidad 3 Images

137 (Marina) © Marina*

138 (Helen Robinson) © Bain News Service, Photographer unknown - Library of Congress, Prints & Photographs Division, "Helen Ring Robinson", Public Domain. Retrieved from https://commons.wikimedia.org/w/index.php?curid=6561517.

139 (Clara Campoamor) © Luis García, CC BY-SA 2.0: https://creativecommons.org/licenses/by-sa/2.0/legalcode, Retrieved from https://commons.wikimedia.org/w/index.php?curid=1503778

139 (Felipe VI) © Rubén Ortega, "Felipe de Borbón, cropped", CC-BY-SA 4.0: https://creativecommons.org/licenses/by/4.0/legalcode, Retrieved from https://commons.wikimedia.org/wiki/File:King_of_Spain_2015_%28cropped%29.JPG.

142 (Marina family pictures) © Marina*

144, 148, 150 (all family pictures) © Lourdes*

146 (Paola) © Paola*

153 Spanish Royal Family) zixia / Alamy Stock Photo.

154 (una calle tranquila, una avenida) © Robert Davis.

157 (Paola) © Paola*

171 (Christian) © Christian*

171 (María Laura) © María Laura*

171 (Isaac) © Isaac*

185 (painting) "Baile En El Jardín" from IN MY FAMILY by Carmen Lomas Garza. Text & Illustration Copyright © 2000

Carmen Lomas Garza. Permission arranged with Children's Book Press, an Imprint of LEE & LOW BOOKS, Inc., New York, NY 10016. All rights not specifically granted herein are reserved.

190 (Jose Antonio) © Jose Antonio

193 (Marina family picture) © Marina*

Unidad 4

© United States Census Bureau, "North Carolina Becomes Ninth State With 10 Million or More People, Census Bureau Reports", Information retrieved from https://www.census.gov/newsroom/press-releases/2015/cb15-215.html, 22 Dec 2015.

© La Parilla Missión, Menú de desayuno, 2016.

© Iowa State University, Iowa Community Indicators Program, "Urban Percentage of the Population for States, Historical", Information Retrieved from http://www.icip.iastate.edu/tables/population/urban-pct-states.

"Los latinos en los Estados Unidos" map, Information retrieved from www.pewhispanic.org and www.csg.org.

"Población Latina en Carolina del Norte", Information retrieved from the United States Census Bureau.

© Best efforts made: GestionRestaurantes.com, "EE. UU.-Una cadena de comida rapida Mexicana en Carolina del Norte expande sus operaciones", Retrieved from http://www.gestionrestaurantes.com/eeuu-una-cadena-de-comida-rapida-mexicana-en-carolina-del-norte-expande-sus-operaciones/, 29 July 2009.

© DELEGACIÓN COYOACÁN 2012-2015 · JEFE DELEGACIONAL MAURICIO TOLEDO GUTIÉRREZ, "3ra feria internacional del tamal" poster, Retrieved from http://www.dondehayferia.com/3ra-feria-internacional-del-tamal-coyoacan-2015.

© Barbecue Festival, "Poster for 32nd Annual Barbecue Festival Lexington, North Carolina", 2015.

© EFE, www.efeamerica.com, "México bate récord con línea de tacos de cochinata pibil más grande del mundo", Retrieved from http://elestimulo.com/bienmesabe/mexico-bate-record-con-linea-tacos-cochinita-pibil-mas-grande-mundo/, 15 Feb 2015.

© Mauricio Arias, Don Camaron Food Truck, "Don Camarón Menu", Text retrieved from https://www.facebook.com/DonCamaronFoodTruck/photos/a.959667337435211.1073741829.880487605353185/973725526029392/?type=3&theater.

Unidad 4 Images

197, 202 (Christian) © Christian*

198 (Hernando de Soto) © SEWilco - "Florida's Centennial", Library of Congress, March 3, 1945, Public Domain, Retrieved from https://commons.wikimedia.org/w/index.php?curid=1400960

198 (Aztec art) © Juan de Tovar, Public Domain, Retrieved from https://commons.wikimedia.org/wiki/File:The_Eagle,_the_Snake,_and_the_Cactus_in_the_Founding_of_

Unidad 5

Unidad 5 Images

Unidad 6

Unidad 6 Images